3 - 70

FREEDOM IN MODERN THEOLOGY

FREEDOM
IN
MODERN THEOLOGY

by

ROBERT T. OSBORN

THE WESTMINSTER PRESS
Philadelphia

Scripture quotations from the Revised Standard Ver-
sion of the Bible are copyright, 1946 and 1952, by the
Division of Christian Education of the National Coun-
cil of Churches, and are used by permission.

Acknowledgment for permission to use quotations is made to the following publishers:

Charles Scribner's Sons, for *Freedom and the Spirit,* by Nicolas
Berdyaev, tr. by Oliver Fielding Clarke. 1935.

The World Publishing Company, for *Existence and Faith: Shorter
Writings of Rudolf Bultmann,* selected, translated, and introduced
by Schubert M. Ogden. An Original Living Age Book, first published by Meridian Books, Inc., May, 1960, and copyright © 1960
by Meridian Books, Inc.

The University of Chicago Press for *Systematic Theology,* Vol. II,
by Paul Tillich. Copyright © 1957, The University of Chicago
Press.

Yale University Press, for *The Courage to Be,* by Paul Tillich.
Copyright 1952 by Yale University Press.

YMCA Press, Paris, for *The Meaning of the Creative Act,* by
Nicolas Berdyaev, tr. by Donald A. Lowrie. Copyright by YMCA
Press. Harper & Brothers and Victor Gollancz, London, 1954.

LIBRARY OF CONGRESS CATALOG CARD NO. 67–11862

Published by The Westminster Press ®
PRINTED IN THE UNITED STATES OF AMERICA

CONTENTS

ACKNOWLEDGMENTS

I WOULD NOT want this book to go to print without expressing my appreciation and affection for two distinguished teachers who, more than others, made this writing possible — Professor David C. Shipley, formerly of Garrett Theological Seminary and now of the Methodist Seminary in Ohio, who introduced me to theology; and the late Professor Carl Michalson, of Drew Theological Seminary, who taught me about freedom. Also, I offer most happily a special word of gratitude to Mrs. Alfreda Kaplan, of Durham, North Carolina, who not only typed a flawless final draft but read and corrected, with care and concern, a not so flawless copy. Finally, and foremost, I thank my wife for unmerited patience and faithful encouragement.

R. T. O.

1

INTRODUCTION

MOST RECENT STUDIES in contemporary theology have placed a special stress upon the idea of freedom — both as a Christological and as an ethical category.[1] However, the notion of freedom has been a fundamental motif of the mainstream of twentieth-century theology. This book is a study of the idea of freedom in this mainstream, specifically in the theologies of Rudolf Bultmann, Paul Tillich, Karl Barth, and Nicolas Berdyaev. I have chosen to concentrate on these four because of their obvious historical importance, because they represent significant and distinct ways of doing theology, and because the idea of freedom is crucial to each. For Bultmann, freedom is synonymous with salvation. He states that "the Word of God addresses man in his personal existence and thereby gives him freedom."[2] Paul Tillich says that "man is man because he has freedom."[3] Indeed, "man is finite freedom," for it is finite freedom which gives rise to existence itself.[4] As regards Barth, a quick perusal of the table of contents of the *Church Dog-*

1 See Paul M. van Buren, *The Secular Meaning of the Gospel* (The Macmillan Company, 1963), pp. 121–126; and Harvey Cox, *The Secular City* (The Macmillan Company, 1965), pp. 40, 60–84, 109, 129.

2 Rudolf Bultmann, *Jesus Christ and Mythology* (Charles Scribner's Sons, 1958), p. 40.

3 Paul Tillich, *Systematic Theology* (3 vols., The University of Chicago Press, 1951, 1957, and 1963), I, 182.

4 Tillich, *Systematic Theology*, II, 31.

matics will make it evident that his theology could well be called a theology of freedom. The twelfth chapter of the *Church Dogmatics* (Vol. III, Part 4), entitled "The Law of God the Creator," might have been just as appropriately entitled "The Freedom of the Creature," since each of its four sections deals with man's freedom — "freedom before God," "freedom in fellowship," "freedom to live," and "freedom within limits." In Vol. I, Part 2, on the Word of God, Barth devotes fifty pages to "the freedom of man for God" and ninety pages to "freedom in the Church." The importance of freedom for Berdyaev is just as obvious when one considers such titles as *Freedom and the Spirit* and *Slavery and Freedom.* To the bishop who said that Berdyaev was a captive of freedom Berdyaev responded: "I do indeed love freedom above all else. Man came forth out of freedom and issues into freedom. . . . I have put Freedom, rather than Being, at the basis of my philosophy." [5]

Just as evident as the importance of freedom for modern theology is the need for clarification of its meaning, for in theologies as different from one another as these the notion of freedom must surely receive different interpretations. This study aims at a clarification and evaluation of these interpretations and finally at some conclusions regarding the nature of freedom and a proper theology of freedom.

New Testament and Hellenistic Views

Since the question of freedom is broad indeed, this investigation is of necessity limited — primarily to a study of the freedom of the Christian man, the "freedom for which Christ has set us free." This means also that it is not concerned, except secondarily, with the question of "free will." Broadly speaking, its focus is not the psychology of the self as such, but rather the self in its relationship to Christ. This distinction points to two basic approaches to the question of freedom —

---

[5] Nicolas Berdyaev, *Dream and Reality,* tr. by Katherine Lampert (The Macmillan Company, 1950), p. 46.

the Hellenistic and the Christian. In the Hellenistic tradition freedom refers generally to the situation of man when he is integrated and self-determining. Salvation or liberation thus means a return to one's self and the recovery of self-control. Originally, freedom designated the freedom from slavery and freedom for the self-determination that was the blessing of citizenship in the Greek polis. With the decline of the polis this political view of freedom was exchanged for the rationalistic — the view of freedom as liberation through reason from the tyranny of the affections and fate. Finally, with the emergence of a radical dualism and pessimism freedom falls beyond the reach of ordinary, empirical man, and can be had only as he escapes to his heavenly origin through a gift of gnosis. Ernst Fuchs comments on this threefold development in the Greek view of freedom: " If at first it concerned a *who* [the free in contrast to the barbarian], then later it concerned a *how* [thinking in contrast to the futility of error], and so finally a *where* [heaven instead of earth] because the world as a whole had become questionable." [6] Freedom is at first a personal position in the world provided by citizenship; then it is a way to overcome the world through reason; and finally, a place beyond the world to which one escapes through gnosis. But whether it be through citizenship, reason, or gnosis, freedom in the Greek tradition means a coming to the true self and the gaining of self-control. Differences in views of freedom within this tradition reflect materially different concepts of the controlling self. In all expressions a basic and common presupposition is what might be designated " nature " — the concept of an original, immanent, and authentic self which is there to take control. The problem of freedom is therefore not a problem *of* the self but a problem *for* the self; it involves a relation of the self to itself and to the world.

The New Testament approach to freedom is quite different. Freedom is not understood as a coming to the self or a return

6 Ernst Fuchs, " Freiheit," *Die Religion in Geschichte und Gegenwart*, 3d ed., II, 1102.

to " nature," because the New Testament charges that the self itself is problematic, fallen, and unfree. It is not a matter of a reduction of all things to the truth of the inner self, but of the commitment or surrender of the self to another, to a redemptive and creative power. Therefore, " man achieves self-control only as he lets go of himself." [7] Freedom is not a function of the self, but a function of a relationship — a relationship to God. Freedom, says Paul, rests in a heavenly and not an earthly citizenship.[8] Yet even here and now, through the Spirit, or rather in the Spirit, the Christian has freedom: " For the law of the Spirit of life in Christ Jesus has set me free from the law of sin and death." [9] Indeed, it is "for freedom" that " Christ has set us free." [10] Ernst Fuchs summarizes the New Testament position: " What occurs [with the gift of freedom] is not a new means to a formerly unsuccessful attempt at self-determination, but rather a new determination of the self. Freedom now means no longer that I do what I will, but rather that I do what God does." [11]

Since freedom in the New Testament is not a self-determination but a determination of the self, Christian theology begins not with existence as such but with existence in the church — the realm of Christ and his Spirit. " It is therefore a mistake," says Fuchs, " simply to carry over into the theology of the New Testament the problem of the will that has come into focus in the history of freedom." [12] The issue is not a faculty of the self — whether it be will, reason, or whatever — but rather the will of God and the renewal of self. Freedom is not in man; rather, man is in freedom.

The Christian view of freedom never stands alone, however,

[7] Heinrich Schleier, " Eleutheros," *Theologisches Wörterbuch zum Neuen Testament,* ed. by Gerhard Kittel, II (1935), 492.

[8] Gal. 4:26-28.

[9] Rom. 8:2.

[10] Gal. 5:1.

[11] This brief review of Hellenistic and Biblical views of freedom is obviously in debt to the very lucid discussion of freedom by Ernst Fuchs. See " Freiheit," pp. 1102–1104.

[12] *Ibid.,* p. 1103.

and in the development of the history of dogma the New Testament concept is immediately combined with the Hellenistic. Indeed, as Fuchs indicates, the appearance of this very word " freedom " in the New Testament is to be explained by the Hellenistic understanding of authentic life as freedom. By New Testament times the Hellenistic world was less and less inclined to expect freedom or salvation from men, a fact that was becoming evident in the development of Gnosticism. Thus, when the Christian message of salvation was proclaimed, Hellenistic Christianity quite readily and understandably interpreted it as a gift of freedom.[13] This development is anticipated in the Old Testament itself as it progresses from an emphasis upon the people of God to the prophetic concern for the purity of heart (similar to personal freedom) , and finally to apocalyptic visions of salvation.[14] Fuchs's claim that Christianity did not offer a concept of freedom, but only freedom itself, is another matter, and a concern of this study will be to discover whether the gift of freedom does not mean also a new definition of freedom. In any event, the use of a word that was fraught with meaning in the Hellenistic world to describe the content of Christian salvation contributed to the Hellenizing of the New Testament understanding in the history of dogma. The result is that freedom came to signify not only a penitent surrender of the self to God, but also an active return of the self to itself. In this latter respect freedom entails a denial of a false dimension of the self and an affirmation of the essential self. The asceticism of early Christianity is to be understood in terms of this dialectic of self-denial and self-affirmation wherein freedom in God becomes also a freedom from the flesh for the spirit, and the freedom of heavenly citizenship is had only at the price of freedom from responsible citizenship in Rome. It becomes increasingly difficult to render unto God what is God's and also unto Caesar what is his.

This confusion of the New Testament and Hellenism is the issue of the decisive debate between Augustine and Pelagius

---

[13] *Ibid.,* p. 1102.   [14] *Ibid.*

which gave to the two viewpoints the labels of Augustinianism
and Pelagianism. Augustine's spiritual pilgrimage is in a sense
a recapitulation of the history of the Greek view of freedom,
in which his search for freedom by return to the self or nature,
no matter how many self-understandings he ventures, is finally
frustrated and issues in a cry for salvation. His despair is answered by God, by grace, and by the gift of freedom. " And
this was the result, that I willed not to do what I willed, and
willed to do what thou willedst." [15] Freedom now means for
Augustine not a return to his self or nature, but the liberation
of nature itself by God and grace. " Neither the knowledge of
God's law nor nature, nor the mere remission of sins is the
grace which is given to us through our Lord Jesus Christ; but
it is this very grace which accomplished the fulfilment of the
law, and the liberation of nature, and the removal and dominion of sin." [16]

Pelagius, on the other hand, viewed freedom as a return to
and an exercise of nature. The gospel sharpens the law and
invokes the responsibility and freedom of man's natural or
created self. Those who argue otherwise are guilty of a " blind
madness," for they " accuse God of a twofold ignorance, — that
He does not seem to know what He has made, nor what He
has commanded, — as if forgetting the human weaknesses of
which He himself is the Author, He has imposed laws on man
which he cannot endure." [17] God has not endowed man with
human weakness, says Pelagius, and " man is able to be without sin." [18] Augustine quotes him as contending that " all men
are ruled by their own will." [19] More specifically, Pelagius
spoke of three faculties — " capacity," " volition," and " ac-

[15] *Confessions*, Book 7, ch. 1.

[16] " On Grace and Free Will," ch. xxvii, *The Basic Writings of St. Augustine*, 2 vols., ed., by Whitney J. Oates (Random House, Inc. 1948) , I,
755.

[17] Benjamin Warfield, " Introduction to Anti-Pelagian Writings of Augustine," *The Nicene and Post-Nicene Fathers*, ed. by Philip Schaff
(Charles Scribner's Sons, 1902) , V, xiv.

[18] *Ibid.*, p. xv.

[19] " A Work on the Proceedings of Pelagius," Schaff, p. 185.

tion." "The 'ability' [capacity] we place in our nature, the 'volition' in our will, and the 'actuality' in the effect."[20] The ability is thanks to nature; the willing and actuality are thanks to man (except insofar as God originally endows man with will by nature, although it is man who exercises it). Grace does not therefore mean a new nature, but rather a return to and unity with nature. God is the one "who evermore, by the help of His grace, assists this very [natural] capacity."[21] Thus the position of Pelagius reflects rather clearly the classical Greek-Hellenistic tradition. Augustine objects on behalf of the Biblical tradition that freedom is not a faculty of human nature, but rather a relationship to divine grace. Man's nature is so "frail and corrupt" that the assistance rendered to it by grace is all that matters.[22] As Paul wrote, "It is God which worketh in you both to will and to perform."[23] The faculties of freedom are of God and not man, of grace and not nature.

About this chapter in the story of freedom little more need be said. The story continues down through the history of the church, as in the debate between Luther and Erasmus, and in the debate between Barth and Harnack. In the theologies to be investigated by this study the attempt of each of the theologians is to remain within the Augustinian tradition, but just as Paul employed a Hellenistic concept to speak of the life of faith, so do Bultmann, Tillich, Barth, and Berdyaev. And just like the fathers, each employs the language of philosophy to translate and interpret the language of faith. The question that we ask is to what extent this translation effects, as it did originally, a synthesis of the New Testament and Hellenistic notions — a new accommodation of Pelagius.

20 "On the Grace of Christ," Schaff, p. 219.
21 *Ibid.*, p. 220.
22 "On the Proceedings of Pelagius," Schaff, p. 192.
23 "On the Grace of Christ," Schaff, p. 219.

MODERN HELLENISTIC VIEWS

As Fuchs indicated, the material content of freedom as conceived from the Hellenistic viewpoint varies according to the
many possible understandings of human nature. Of course,
from the Biblical perspective these differences are relative, for
the issue is not nature but grace. Thus Barth, for instance,
prefers to designate such "natural" definitions of man and
freedom as "phenomenal," whereas a noumenal or essential
definition begins with God and grace.[24] Berdyaev makes a
similar point when he suggests that to get at the reality of
freedom Kant needed a new critique, a critique of the spirit,
without which man in his essence — the thing-in-itself — could
not appear. Nevertheless, the noumenal becomes phenomenal;
it finds symbolic expression in man's nature, with which it
can readily be confused. It is in order then that we briefly
identify some of the modern forms of a Greek or "natural"
view of freedom. I follow here the categorization suggested by
Barth. He identifies four — the naturalistic, idealistic, existentialist, and theistic.[25] Each of these philosophical views understands man as a whole from the standpoint of a certain phenomenon of the true self which appears only in grace. The
materialist, or the naturalist of the most primitive variety,
views man from the perspective of his continuity with nature.
Freedom at this level of man's existence means essentially
"doing what comes naturally." The free man is the man who
does not fight his biology — the man who lets nature take its
course. Certainly a man who acts as if he did not have a body
that is subject to the natural processes, the so-called "laws of

[24] *Die Kirchliche Dogmatik* (Vols. I–IV, Zollikon-Zürich: Evangelischer
Verlag, 1932–1955), Vol. III, Part 2, pp. 82 ff. (71 ff.). All references are
made to the German original, henceforth in this form: IV, 3; II, 2, etc.
Translations of *K. Dogmatik* are my own. In parentheses is the pagination
of the authorized English translation, *Church Dogmatics*, ed. and tr. by
G. W. Bromiley and T. F. Torrance; Vol. I, Part 1, tr. by G. T. Thomson
(Charles Scribner's Sons, 1936–1962), Vol. I, Part 1, through Vol. IV,
Part 3.

[25] *Kirchliche Dogmatik*, III, Part 2, 82–157 (71–132).

nature," is not free. On the other hand, it is rather foolish to
think that to be free in this sense constitutes the substance of
humanity; after all, the animals have this freedom in abundance.

Modern idealism and Kantian thought protest against natu-
ralism, insisting that man's humanity is more truly realized
as he transcends nature. Man's true realm of existence is the
realm of ideas, and freedom means subjection to the dictates
of a clear idea. The concept " freedom " is applicable here to
the extent that this subjection to the realm of ideas means a
certain liberation from the realm of nature, or " concupiscence," as Plato denotes it. Plato held that when reason is
allowed to function it " will rule over the concupiscence which
in each of us is the largest part." [26] It will, in other words,
liberate us. Descartes expresses the same idea when he says
that liberty involves the ability to withhold assent from
" what is not in every respect certain and undoubted." [27] Positively, it is the freedom of reason or freedom for reason. This
can be termed freedom, however, only under the hypothesis
that this part (reason) " constitutes our true self " [28] and that
" it has the care of the whole soul." [29] In this event, freedom
means to return to the rule of reason — the ability of a clear
idea to demand assent and to determine the end of man's existence. Reason is the good which to know is to obey. We
" never err," says Descartes, "unless when we judge of something which we do not sufficiently apprehend." We are de-
ceived because " we judge without possessing an exact knowledge of what we judge." [30] When we *know* — when we understand — we *do* of necessity. This is the freedom of reason — so
to direct and compel action.

To act of necessity is, however, a dubious freedom. As long
as man's " largest part " is his bodily existence the absolute

26 Plato, *Republic*, IV, 442.
27 Descartes, *Principles*, XXXIX.
28 Aristotle, *Nicomachean Ethics*, Book I, 10.
29 Plato, *Republic*, IV, 441.
30 Descartes, *Principles*, XXXIII.

demand of reason can be but a divisive and constraining bondage. Nevertheless, bondage to reason may be called freedom to the extent that in reason man does transcend his material existence and reason does evidence occasionally this freedom to determine man's actions.

Kant called attention to a freedom implicit in the point of view of the pure rationalists, a freedom that is not explicitly developed by them. Plato had said that *if* reason is allowed to function properly, *then* it rules. Kant saw that reason rules only if the *will* chooses it. The will is free to let reason function or not. Henry Sidgwick, commenting on Kant's idea of the freedom of the will, designated the ability of every man to choose indifferently between good and evil — between the rational and the irrational — as " neutral freedom." He pointed out, however, that Kant spoke really of another freedom which he did not consciously distinguish from the first. Sidgwick called this freedom " good " or " rational " freedom.[31] This is the freedom of rationality, which is realized when man is subject to reason. In this sense Kant is strictly idealistic. The will recognizes that it ought to respect reason, because respect for reason is respect for personality and for man as such. It is a universal obligation. Yet, for it to be one's duty, one must have the freedom to accept or not to accept it. While Kant did observe that there is a radical disease of the will, a radical evil which infects it, he maintained that as long as man " ought," he can. Kant would not reckon with the possibility of a truly bound will.

We recognize in Kant's interpretation, however, the eruption of a third level of freedom. Was not the radical evil that Kant discovered in the otherwise free will a sign of something new, something with which he could not cope? Was it not perhaps a testimony to another dimension of freedom which

[31] From an article in *Mind*, reprinted as an appendix to the sixth edition of Sidgwick's *The Methods of Ethics*, quoted by D. M. Baillie, " Philosophers and Theologians on the Freedom of the Will," *Scottish Journal of Theology*, IV (June, 1951), 117.

he could not comprehend with his categories? That "cluster of vitalisms, pragmatisms and existentialisms" [32] says yes. This new type of philosophy, which we shall consider primarily in its existentialist form, observes that while man transcends nature through his mind and mind through his will, he also transcends his will through his existence. In other words, a man's will, as well as his reason, is determined by what a man is — by man in the totality of his existence. Thus the will that in many instances serves reason finds itself with an "evil" principle as it seeks to obey reason in disobedience to its existential commitment. The will is free, says the existentialist, not as it serves reason, but as it serves the whole self. It is bound by the self.

Existentialism teaches that man becomes aware of his existence when he encounters the possibility of his nonexistence, when he confronts the limits of his existence and becomes aware that he has no grounds for being in himself. According to Jaspers, in this encounter man becomes aware of the transcendent ground of being,[33] but for the so-called early Heidegger and others of an atheistic trend, he faces nothingness. In either case, man is seen to exist in a radical freedom. He is not explained or bound ultimately by what he has — in his nature, reason, or will. Man *is free* of these. Man is freedom. He is free to make what he will of the heritage of his existence — his nature and his ideals. We are mistaken if we imagine that "our reasons for living fall from heaven ready-made: we must create them ourselves." [34] Man truly *is*, man truly exists, when he becomes aware of and accepts his freedom. One accepts freedom by using it, and one uses it as he "resolves" to be

[32] Carl Michalson, "Christian Faith and Existential Freedom," *Religion in Life*, XXI (1952), 515.

[33] Karl Jaspers, *The Perennial Scope of Philosophy* (Philosophical Library, Inc., 1949), p. 64.

[34] Quoted from Simone de Beauvoir, *Le Sang des Autres* (Paris: Librarie Gallimard, 1945), by Newton P. Stallknecht and Robert S. Brumbaugh, *The Spirit of Western Philosophy* (Longmans, Green & Co., Inc., 1952), p. 478.

what *he* plans to be or as he " leaps " into the future — into relationship with the transcendent or into an encounter with nothingness, whichever the case may be. The negative aspect of this resolution or leap is the emancipation of the self from all that it has been — all its isms, ideologies, and the like. Man's essence follows his existence; there is no precedence in the past or the present for what shall be in the future. " If existence really does precede essence, there is no explaining things away by reference to a fixed or given human nature. In other words, there is no determinism, man is free, man is freedom. . . . We are alone, with no excuses." [35] " The past," says Heidegger, " loses its unique precedence." [36] Thus, in one of Camus's novels the main character is on trial for murder, only to find that he has nothing to say in his own defense, for he exists in the moment and for the near future, whereas the trial is concerned with the past. He says: " In fact, there seemed to be a conspiracy to exclude me from the proceedings; I wasn't to have any say. . . . However, on second thoughts, I found I had nothing to say. In any case, I must admit that hearing oneself talked about loses its interest very soon. . . . I've always been far too absorbed in the present moment, or the immediate future, to think back." [37]

Freedom, then, in the language of existentialism, results from the awareness of man's lack of security, man's encounter with nothingness or transcendence. It means to accept freedom and to exercise it in resolution and faith — to leave what is for what shall be; it means to exist in order to be. Carl Michalson has summarized the meaning of freedom in existential thinking in five main points: [38] (1) " Freedom *is* the human existence." It is more basic than anything else a man is. When

[35] Jean-Paul Sartre, *Existentialism*, tr. by Bernard Frechtman (Philosophical Library, Inc., 1947) , p. 27.

[36] Martin Heidegger, *Sein und Zeit* (Tübingen: Neomarius, 1949) , p. 39.

[37] Albert Camus, *The Stranger*, tr. by Stuart Gilbert (Vintage Books, Random House, Inc., 1954) , pp. 124–127.

[38] Michalson, pp. 519 ff.

he chooses freedom, he chooses himself. (2) Freedom is nothing. That is to say, there is nothing *in* existence that explains
it. Michalson quotes Sartre's *The Reprieve:* " Inside, nothing,
not even a puff of smoke, there is no inside, there is nothing." [39]
(3) Freedom is possibility. Where there is nothing the road is
open for everything. (4) Freedom is a burden; man is " condemned " to be free. Man can relate himself or choose himself
as nothing; but one cannot exist without choosing, for nothing
is given; nothing is without choice. (5) The burden of freedom is so heavy that it becomes anxiety. One has to choose,
but he knows of nothing which is secure. This lack of knowledge makes the burden of freedom terrifying and disinclines
him to choose. Yet one must choose in order to be himself. It
is this fear of the unknown and the unwillingness to commit
oneself that paralyzes action and symbolizes the loss of freedom. To become free is to return to the self, the self as self or
freedom. Freedom is the nature of man and the ultimate
reality.

The final form of phenomenal freedom suggested by Barth
(and reminiscent of Kierkegaard's religion type A) is the freedom for God conceived by theism. While close to existentialism in that it calls man beyond the world of nature and reason, and close to the Biblical view in that it calls man unto
God, it is in reality a shadow or an echo of both views; for the
God of theism is not a God of grace who renews existence, but
a God of nature who is immanently bound up with it. He
thereby threatens both the existentialist freedom from reality
by giving to a dimension of reality the dignity and authority
of deity, and the freedom of grace by reducing it to nature so
that the relationship of God to man is one of being and
necessity.

Toward a Christian View of Freedom

The theologians investigated in this study strive for a Christian view of freedom in awareness of the danger of a reduction-

[39] *Ibid.,* p. 320.

ism in which the freedom of grace is identified with one of the aforementioned phenomenal freedoms. At the same time they are aware that the language of theology is the language of human nature whose grammar reflects one or more philosophical positions. Tillich tends to appropriate the language of post-Kantian idealism, and yet speak of Christian freedom. Bultmann prefers the language of existentialism. Barth prefers no one language and employs as many as suit his tasks. Berdyaev often combines the language of Russian Orthodoxy, mysticism, and existentialism. We may expect that in each case the language used threatens to reduce grace to nature, Christian freedom to Hellenistic types or, if not, to speak about realities that seem to bear little upon the situation of man. The purpose of this study is to see how these theologians do speak of freedom, how well they speak, and to conclude with suggestions as to how we ought to speak of freedom.

The format of the book is suggested by the words of Paul: " For freedom Christ has set us free." We are led to ask four questions of each theologian: *For* what has Christ set us free? *From* what has Christ set us free? *How* does Christ set us free? And finally, in what way may *God* be said to be free? This is the order of questioning, except in the case of Barth, who would rather answer the last question before he addresses himself to the others.

The order of treatment — Bultmann, Tillich, Barth, and Berdyaev — is in development of the thesis that Tillich speaks to problems in Bultmann's thought, that Barth overcomes objections to Tillich's method, and that Berdyaev further develops latent implications of Barth's view of freedom. In all I will conclude that in the theology of Barth and the theological philosophy of Berdyaev we are offered the material for, if not the fact of, a total and relatively satisfactory view of Christian freedom. The concluding chapter will seek to develop and make this thesis more explicit.

2

RUDOLF BULTMANN: FREEDOM AS EXISTENCE

WE STATED in the Introduction that Bultmann's theology is
an effort to interpret the Biblical faith by means of an existentialist hermeneutic. The notion of freedom is therefore ger-
mane to Bultmann's theology, just as it is to the existentialist
view of man. The basic question we will be asking is whether
he succeeds with this methodology in bringing to view the
Biblical understanding. In quest of an answer the first question
we put to Bultmann is the material one — " For what is the
Christian free? "

FREEDOM-FOR

The frequent occurrence of the imperative mood in Bultmann's writings shows that Bultmann is aware that freedom
has a goal toward which it ought to be directed and which provides a norm for its decisions. He says that the future (the
Spirit) is " the norm of practical behaviour." The divine imperative, " so far from being abrogated . . . is now grounded
on the indicative of freedom." He calls attention to " a new
servitude " and to the imperative aspect of " walking according to the Spirit." To be free means to be determined by " a
motive which transcends the present moment." [1] Bultmann's

---

[1] *Primitive Christianity in Its Contemporary Setting,* tr. by R. H. Fuller (A Living Age Original, Meridian Books, Inc., 1956), p. 205; *Theology
of the New Testament,* 2 vols., tr. by Kendrick Grobel (Charles Scribner's
Sons, 1951 and 1955), I, 332; *Jesus Christ and Mythology,* p. 40.

most characteristic designation of the normative dimension of freedom is "obedience." "Our freedom does not excuse us from the demand under which we all stand as men, for it is freedom for obedience." [2]

Biblical language pertaining to this imperative dimension is rich and varied. The Bible speaks directly or indirectly of " the law of the Spirit," " the liberating law of the cross," " the law of Christ," and " the law of love." Bultmann's task is to filter this language and remove from it those elements which are mythological, unnecessarily offensive to modern, scientific ways of thinking, and which obscure the real message. The question in this instance is what, exactly, is the imperative that freedom serves?

The language with which Bultmann interprets this dimension of the Biblical view of freedom is itself a bit confusing, and analysis suggests that he speaks in three distinctive ways about the goal or law of freedom. First, following a definite and explicitly Biblical path, he designates it as " love." Secondly, he uses what might be called negative language, which states that the goal of freedom is not of this world, but of " the future." Thirdly, he uses existential language, in which the law of freedom is the possibility of " authentic existence." Let us look at each of these languages in order.

Love

Characteristically, Bultmann understands love as the goal of freedom, as the law of freedom. The servitude which the Christian finds in his freedom is also a " serving of one another." [3] The law of Christ to which freedom is subject is " *the demand that one love*," the demand that the Christian seek not his own good but that of the neighbor.[4] " To exist from God and for God means, in practice, to exist from the

2 " New Testament and Mythology," *Kerygma and Myth: A Theological Debate*, ed. by Hans Werner Bartsch, tr. by R. H. Fuller (Harper Torchbooks, The Cloister Library, 1961), p. 21.

3 Gal. 5:13. See *Theology*, I, 332.

4 *Ibid.*, p. 344.

neighbor and for him." [5] The freedom for love is not bondage
to a principle or an ideal which one possesses in abstraction
from the neighbor himself. No, love itself "with a keen and
sure eye . . . discovers what there is to be done." [6] Consequently, Christian freedom exists only in community, and the
Christian man comes to himself only in the fellowship of the
church, within "the community of 'saints' created by God's
election and call." [7] When Bultmann speaks in this context of
"the future" as the law of freedom, the future is to be understood as the ever new encounter with the neighbor. When he
speaks of the limit situation in which man discovers his freedom, he means that situation in which man is limited by the
"thou." "Christian freedom has its limit in love for the
brother, or, better said, it does not really have its limit in love,
but rather thereby precisely manifests itself." [8] Freedom for
love is a freedom that does not know itself in abstraction from
love, for it finds in love its fulfillment rather than its limitation.[9] Love, writes Bultmann, "is a form of being together
(*Miteinandersein*) which he alone understands who understands himself as bound with another." [10] He who understands
love understands the moral as expressing "a primary connection between I and thou." It "is not true that a person first
asks how he comes to his neighbor and what he must do with
him. Much rather, my being is from the beginning a being with
another; human existence is *Miteinandersein,* and therefore, it
is historical existence in distinction from existence in na-

[5] "Meaning of Christian Faith," *Existence and Faith: Shorter Writings
of Rudolf Bultmann,* selected, translated, and introduced by Schubert M.
Ogden (An Original Living Age Book, Meridian Books, Inc., 1960) , p. 222.

[6] "The Understanding of Man and the World in the New Testament
and in the Greek World," *Essays,* tr. by James C. G. Greig (The Macmillan
Company, 1955) , p. 79.

[7] "Adam, Where Art Thou?" *Essays,* p. 126.

[8] "The Historicity of Man and Faith," *Existence,* p. 108.

[9] "Christian freedom has its limit in love for the brother, or better
said, it does not really have its limit in love, but rather precisely manifests
itself." ("Faith in God the Creator," *Existence,* p. 172.)

[10] "Das christliche Gebot der Nächstenliebe," *Glauben und Verstehen*
(Tübingen: Verlag von J. C. B. Mohr, 1933) , I, 240.

ture." [11] To be free for love is to have no freedom save in love.

Before leaving this approach to the question of the goal of freedom, we should observe parenthetically that insofar as freedom designates a dimension of human conduct, insofar as it is the freedom of man, it is not to be understood as an action directed toward *God*. When we consider the gift of freedom, the concept of salvation, and the liberation of man to freedom, we will be able to speak about a freedom from God, i.e., a freedom that proceeds from and depends upon him, but not of a freedom that directs man to God. When we speak of freedom for *God*, or Christ, or the Spirit, etc., we have to ask what we mean. We have seen that, in one instance, Bultmann means love, the law of the neighbor's need.

The Future

The concept most typical of the second type of language, negative language, is "the future." "To surrender unreservedly to the grace of God, to believe — all this is radical openness to the future," and "this radical openness to the future is the Christian's freedom." [12] The future is, at one level, a negative concept. It designates what is *not* yet, *not* now, *not* here. It is the negation of all tangible, temporal, and visible reality. When Paul speaks of freedom for the Spirit, of freedom in the Spirit, he means, says Bultmann, "the quintessence of the *non*worldly, *in*visible, *un*controllable, eternal sphere which becomes the controlling power for and in him who orients his life according to the Spirit." [13] Consequently, "the chief aim of every genuine religion is to escape from the world." [14] Since the Spirit in its normative aspect is the future — the unknown, unseen, and uncontrollable — it is nothing, no-thing, and it cannot then be a " norm " for action in the usual sense of an " objective " rule or law. " The Spirit " does not surrender

[11] *Ibid.,* pp. 320 f.
[12] *Primitive Christianity,* p. 185.
[13] *Theology,* I, 334 f.
[14] " A Reply to the Theses of J. Schniewind," *Kerygma and Myth,* p. 113.

or betray freedom into slavery under an " objective " law. For the same reason the encounter with the future is not an " objective " encounter with " God," or " Christ," or " the Spirit "; it is, rather, " an encounter with nothingness."

Freedom-as-Such

Although analysis has led to the second major dimension of freedom — freedom as freedom-from (if freedom is freedom for the future, it is also freedom from the past) — we must first give attention to the third way in which Bultmann designates positive freedom. If freedom for the future is nothing more than freedom from the past, then it is ironically subject to the past. If the future is indeed the frontier of freedom, then freedom must have some reference other than the past; it must possess its own law or structure. Bultmann has already suggested that this law might be understood as the law of the neighbor's need, the law of love. However, viewed from the standpoint of openness to the future, man appears to be a solitary individual thrust between the dead past and the unborn future, and so surrounded not by the neighbor, but by nothing except possibility. All that is left is man himself in his freedom-as-such. The " law " of the future, the " law " of freedom, appears to be the law of man's own being, the sum of his own genuine possibilities. " Freedom is obedience to a law of which the validity is recognized and accepted, which man recognizes as the law of his own being." [15] Freedom's law emerges only in freedom itself. From this perspective freedom is not to be understood in terms of the past, nor even in terms of love, but in terms of existence itself. It is in these terms that Bultmann finally talks about the law of freedom.

We have proceeded far enough to see that Bultmann poses a serious question by the fact that he can speak on the one hand as if love were the norm of freedom, and on the other hand as if freedom's norm were the future, meaning the possibilities intrinsic in freedom itself as it encounters the law. The

[15] *Jesus Christ and Mythology*, p. 57.

question is reflected in Bultmann's statement that freedom, which authorizes man to prove independently what the good is, "may demand waiving of authorization for the sake of the brother's need." [16] If love is freedom's option, can it also be its essence? If it is freedom that directs me to my neighbor, rather than my neighbor himself, is the neighbor really essential to me? Is my being (*Sein*) truly a *Miteinander-sein*? We should expect clarification of this question as we turn to our discussion of freedom as freedom-from, as we ask about that bondage which is the opposite of true freedom.

FREEDOM-FROM

If freedom is freedom for the future, it is, as we have seen, also freedom from bondage to the past. " While humanity is essentially openness for the future, the fact is that man bars his own way to the future by wanting to live unto himself. He boasts in what he has, in what he is, in what he has made out of himself, in what he can control, in what he takes to be ground for pride, in what he imagines he can offer to God. When he boasts he lays hold upon what he already is — upon his past." [17] One who is bound by the past is one who is what he is and will be what he will be by virtue of what he has been, i.e., he lives in the confidence of the past achievements of his own efforts. Such a man has no future, for his past possesses him in the present. He has no real future in the sense of something new. He is called to no real decision. He has no authentic self.[18]

[16] *Theology*, I, 342.

[17] *Jesus Christ and Mythology*, p. 41.

[18] Bultmann contrasts Christianity's view of the past with Gnosticism's view. According to Christianity, the past is a source of bondage, whereas according to Gnosticism the past is the source of life; it is out of the eternal past that man's preexistent soul and true life appear. The Gnostic man is saved as he is cognizant of and thus determined by his primordial past; in this sense he has no future. The Christian man is judged guilty for his past; his deliverance and life depend on his becoming free from the past, upon his becoming open to the possibilities of the future in which he must believe and for which he must decide. This decision is faith. The Christian is saved by faith; the Gnostic is saved by knowledge. See *Primitive Christianity*, pp. 202 f.

The Past

The past is " what [man] . . . has made out of himself." It includes nature and history (*Historie*) — nature as the realm of objective facts, the creature of man's pure reason, and history as the sequence of past events, the creature of man's practical reason. Nature and history are alike in that each is a sequence of rationally related facts, of causes and effects, so that each " new " event is already implicit in the old. History and nature are alike further in that each is " observable," knowable without any serious participation by man, without man's freedom or decision. Carl Michalson observes that history as a series of past events is in fact identical with nature, for " nature by definition is the world insofar as it is silent about the meaning of man." [19] That is, history and nature say nothing which invokes freedom, decision.

Bultmann also speaks of bondage to the past as a life lived in " subjective arbitrariness," as a sum of deeds done in immediate response to the moment, as a reply to impulses originating not from within freedom but out of the world. This is, in effect, bondage to the most immediate past, the past that is so present as to be felt without reflection, the past that possesses the present through sense and passion. Nature, history, and the immediate are " the past," that creature of man himself which the Bible designates (when one lives by it) " this world." " This world " must pass away and man must be delivered from and die to it if he is to have a future, true freedom, and genuine existence.

Sin

Bondage to the past, to history and nature, to subjective arbitrariness, is, in the language of the Bible, bondage to sin. The root and substance of sin, through which the world gains power over man, is a quality of existence itself; it is " the self-

[19] Carl Michalson, *The Hinge of History: An Existential Approach to the Christian Faith* (Charles Scribner's Sons, 1959) , p. 31.

reliant attitude of the man who puts his trust in his own strength and in that which is controllable by him." [20] In a discussion of Paul's view of "flesh and sin" Bultmann describes how man's effort at self-glorification leads to this bondage to "the past." [21] The bondage arises through the fact that the only method of self-glorification is through "control," which in turn is dependent upon that which it would control — the realm of the visible and tangible, the empirical realm, "the flesh." The will to control is the "empirical will," and the man who lives by this will lives "according to the flesh." [22] The first stage, then, in the dialectic of sin, is the effort of man to glorify himself by *control,* the effort to be by having.

The fall of man follows quickly. The effort to control leads to *desire,* desire for the possibilities in the realm subject to man's control, desire for things of the flesh. Desire, in turn, begets *care,* or anxiety, care for the self, lest it lose control and not achieve its desires, and care for the world, lest its possibilities should somehow be denied. But desire, care, and anxiety ironically betray man in his efforts to control the world, for "through his will to dispose over the world . . . [man] factually falls victim to the world," [23] and sin has succeeded in establishing the world (the realm of controllable objects) as a "*power.*" [24] Now, while man's care and anxiety born of desire create this status for the world, the world is quick to claim and effect its status through *fear* and through the power of the law. The world, of course, is not meant for the task that it is assigned by sin.[25] It cannot answer to the question of existence, and man who would find meaning by control of the world is threatened by what the poet Rilke described as "the

[20] *Theology,* I, 240.

[21] *Ibid.,* pp. 239–269.

[22] *Ibid.,* p. 239.

[23] *Ibid.,* pp. 241 f.

[24] For a further development of the concept of the world as a power, see Friedrich Gogarten's *The Reality of Faith: The Problem of Subjectivism in Theology,* tr. by Carl Michalson, *et al.* (The Westminster Press, 1959).

[25] See Gogarten, p. 45.

cracks in things." [26] These "cracks" reveal a final freedom in the world which resists man's ordering, and which gives the world a dreadful power to create fear. Michalson speaks of the "sense of panic when . . . [man] peeks into nature and senses the intangible," that which is uncontrollable.[27] Rather than flee in panic from the world as a source of life, as well he might, man is fear driven to cling all the more desperately to the tangible dimensions of the world and so avoid the intangible. Paul warns of this bondage wrought by fear when he speaks of the "slavery to fall back into fear" (Rom. 8:15).

Law

There is in man's situation, however, that which does express the divine claim upon him, but which sin and the world pervert to effect the last stage of human bondage. That agency of the divine claim is the *law* — "a fact in the existence of sinful man that . . . again and again makes audible to him the claim of God. This fact is given in the concrete demands that always encounter man." [28] The law, the sum of the concrete decisions of life, is meant to bind man to God and to true life; in sin the law binds man to itself, to the world, and to death. Paul speaks as a sinner under the law when he says: "I can will what is right, but I cannot do it" (Rom. 7:18). His willing "what is right" means that he has a "trans-subjective propensity" to seek, or to will, his authenticity, his proper determination by God, his true life.[29] This basic willing is evoked by the law, and in turn gives the law its claim and appeal, for it would appear to direct man to life. However, that I cannot "do" what is right means that the law actually misleads and misdirects. What actually proceeds from life under the law is not what man wills but its opposite — not life with God but

---

26 Michalson, *The Hinge,* pp. 65 f.
27 *Ibid.,* p. 64.
28 "Paul," *Existence,* p. 135. See also *Theology,* I, 266.
29 *Theology,* I, 151.

death in the world. Without the law, says Paul, we should not have known sin, we should not have experienced this, its deadly power. Sin effects this death by turning the law into an end in itself, into a relentless goal which man is to achieve by his own power in control of the world. So man becomes a servant of the law, and through the law also a servant of the world, since as we have seen, the only way man can control the world is by submitting to its control. The law is sin not only in the formal sense that it directs man to the wrong ends but also in the material sense that it demands the wrong means. It should bring man to the goal of life from and with God by the means of claiming the obedience of the very being of man; instead, it brings man to death in the world by demanding the works of man. (The distinction between being and works, between true and false obedience, will become clearer in the next section.)

We would misunderstand the power of the law if we thought that it had its power only in itself as an external force over man. We saw in the beginning of this discussion that man's own sinful will to self-realization creates the power of sin and the world over man. Paul is plain to say that the power of the law is the power of the sin which is *in* man, of the sin which *is* man. The law and the power of the world are able to mislead and kill because man is sick and divided, because they can appeal to the man who is sinful against the true man who wills life. " ' I ' and ' I,' self and self, are at war with each other; i.e., to be innerly divided, or not to be at one with one's self, is the essence of human existence under sin." [30] From this perspective the "fate" of being bound to the law and powers of this world is the guilt of man who is a free subject; yet, the guilt for turning to the world is the fate of man who is subject to the "power" of sin. The law awakens the sinful ego and establishes its power over the authentic, so that I would not have known sin were it not for the law; to sin is my fate. Yet the power of the law would not be effective were it not for

[30] *Ibid.*, p. 245.

the original propensity of the sinful will to self-realization; bondage to sin is my guilt.

Death

Death is the final product of the dialectic of sin. Indeed, man under sin is already dead, and this fact is merely confirmed by the grave.[31] "Because man understands himself in terms of what he accomplishes and produces, because he thus takes his god*less* being to be his authentic, his ultimate being, he is punished by death's — i.e., the death to which the whole of his present existence is subject. . . . Because he tries to cling to his provisional being he slips away from himself." [32] In sin man is fundamentally lost to himself; he is dead. This is death in its first aspect — the inner division, the separation of the empirical from the true self. This dimension of death is brought about, as we have seen, not because the good intentions which the law consciously incites go unrealized in the deed, but because the conscious intentions, good as they may be, are misdirected in the first place and lead to this separation from authenticity. The law leads man into the empirical realm where he becomes subject to death in its second aspect, death as literal, physical death. For empirical man, empirical death is death indeed. He cannot escape it. He rebels against death and knows as one who has fallen under it that he does not exist in authenticity. But he does not have the possibility through his own resources of becoming lord over it.[33] The man who would find himself in his achievements, in the world, is dead and meaningless in the presence of the fear and fact of death.

There is a third dimension to death. The sinner is dead not only in that he is separated from his authenticity and so threatened by physical death, but also in that his present existence is godless. God is the giver of life, so to be without

[31] *Ibid.*, pp. 267 f.
[32] "Revelation in the New Testament," *Existence*, p. 82.
[33] *Ibid.*, p. 72.

God is to be subject to death.

Is the law itself sinful, since it delivers man into sin and finally death? By no means! There is an irony implicit in the statements above, the irony that death which receives its power by virtue of sin actually threatens only the inauthentic self, that death destroys and brings to naught only the empirical self. From the standpoint of the true self, death is a liberator that removes the usurper and establishes the claim of authenticity. More than that, it not only puts to death the false self, but also gives rise to the true self. The law, through which death gains its power of judgment, is, from the perspective of the true self, the tutor which by bringing man to death brings him to God. Its true purpose is to bring man " into an objectively desperate situation," to lead him to death "and thereby let God appear as God, as the ' God who gives life to the dead.' " So it is in "readiness for death that faith is peculiarly fulfilled." We understand how "Paul can welcome suffering, for by bringing him to nothing it makes room, as it were, for God." [34] Should one come to understand that the self which finds itself in the past is provisional, and so be able to "surrender his provisional being, then death also could once again become something provisional for him." [35] For the man of faith " dying has . . . become . . . a ' dying as though he did not die.' " [36] The man of faith knows that the self which is subject to death is not authentic; when it dies, it is not as if man had really died at all. To encounter death as life is the gift of God in faith, the concern of our section entitled " Freedom for Freedom."

The result of our analysis so far is the understanding that the goal or norm of freedom is neither extrinsic to nor other than freedom itself. It is not to be found in the past; it is not in the future, in the sense that something is yet to be revealed. When we say that freedom is its own law, we do not mean that

[34] " Man Between the Times," *Existence*, p. 264.
[35] " Revelation in the New Testament," *Existence*, p. 82.
[36] *Ibid.*, p. 84.

it is not under the law, but that the content of the law is freedom's judgment. In this sense the law of freedom is freedom
itself, freedom-as-such. " Freedom-as-such " was the last dimension of the discussion of freedom-for, and it remains at
this point only to look back to this dimension *now* in the light
of the analysis of freedom-from, in order to view the characteristic ways in which Bultmann points to this ultimate dimension of the human spirit.

We have come to see that the true man does not live a story
told by another. He does not look back to the past to measure
the future, and he has no glimpse of the end in terms of which
he can plan the meanwhile. " Today we cannot claim to know
the end and the goal of history." [37] Man stands alone in the
present moment, unfettered by past or future; he is unlimited
save by the command to obey, and by the promise of life in
this obedience. He is free, free to obey the demand of the moment out of the law of his own being — out of his freedom.

The free man expresses himself in an *act* rather than in a
work: " In the case of works, I remain the man I am; I place
it outside myself. . . . But in the act I become. . . . I find
myself in it, live in it, and do not stand alongside it." [38] Evidently a work is akin to what is generally connoted when we
say of an undertaking that it is " hard work." In such cases we
mean most often that the task is imposed from without, that
it is fulfilled by deeds done in response to outside pressures,
that it is our part in a plan not of our own making. It is undertaken as an alien imposition that claims our efforts but not
our being. Opposed to the " work " is the " act " whose meaning lies not in the objective realm of history and nature but,
rather, in the act itself insofar as it expresses its subject; it is
an act in a play whose author is the existing individual himself. The act cannot be assessed by objective analysis but only
by subjective participation; an outside observer cannot know
whether an act is authentically mine, whether I am truly in it

[37] *Primitive Christianity*, p. 204.
[38] " Faith in God the Creator," *Essays*, p. 175.

or not. An act is an event in which the world is mine, and its
meaning is in me and from me; a work is an event in which I
am the world's, and my meaning is in the world and from the
world. To be free of myself for myself is to be myself —
not as the world knows me in my works, but as I am in my
acts.

A similar distinction is made when Bultmann states that
freedom is *subjective* and not objective. As we have seen, it
exists when man's own capacity is freed from the objective,
cosmic powers. When the world of objects ceases to be a
power and is seen as the nonbeing it really is, then my own
subjective capacity is freed and itself becomes the norm of
behavior. Then " subjective " is no longer defined by relation
to objects. I am not, for example, to be defined by the pencil
in my hand as a pencil pusher. I understand that I am the
subject of the object pencil because from the inmost depths
of true freedom and subjectivity (*Dasein*) I myself have freely
projected this particular subject-object relationship. Consistently, Bultmann insists that modern man " is undoubtedly
right in regarding . . . [his ego] in its subjective aspect as a
unity, and in refusing to allow any room for alien powers to in-
terfere in its subjective life." [39] Bultmann finds freedom's authority sanctioned by Paul, who says that " all things are law-
ful." This liberty of which Paul speaks is " the authorization,
or the right, to find oneself, by that independent ' proving,'
what the ' good ' is — and hence, is also independence from
the judgment of any other person's conscience." [40]

These same views are expressed and summarized in the conception of the free man as the *historical* (*geschichtlich*) man.
To say that man is historical (*geschichtlich*) is not to say that
he has a history, but that he writes history. He is not an object
in history, but a subject of history. *Geschichte* is what man
unfolds in his free moment-by-moment decisions; it is the sum
of man's acts, those deeds in which he freely exists and ex-

[39] " A Reply," *Kerygma and Myth*, p. 120.
[40] *Theology*, I, 342.

presses himself.[41] Freedom as history is freedom as decision; it is the awareness that the present is a moment of free decision, that the decision regarding me has not been made by the past, nor does it transcend me as some otherworldly ideal or reality; it is the decision that I myself freely make. I *am* as I in my freedom act.

Freedom is freedom from the past. It is freedom for the future — freedom for my own subjective capacities as the substance of the future, as the *law* of God. Freedom means to exist now, in the moment, not in the dead past or in the unborn *eschaton;* it is to act and not work, to be the subject of one's action and not subject to actions of the world of objects; it is to make history rather than to be made by it. It is to be in the act rather than to be acted upon.

Finally, we return to the very characteristic designation of freedom as *obedience.* Freedom is obedience because it discovers itself in response to the concrete decision of the moment when these are understood as the claim of God. Thus we have seen Bultmann designate true freedom as " freedom in obedience." [42] Freedom understood as obedience in the moment of decision is opposed to " the upward flight of . . . thoughtful contemplation," for " it is in the concrete historical event that God is to be met with, as the One who makes demands." [43] In a word, freedom as obedience is freedom as decision.

Man as act, man as subject, man as history, man as obedience — this is man as freedom.

FREEDOM FOR FREEDOM

As a Christian, Bultmann believes that free, authentic existence is not a possibility for man except as he is set free for freedom by the redemption that is in Christ.[44] Bultmann calls

---

41 See " The Understanding of Man," *Essays,* pp. 83 ff.
42 *Supra,* p. 26.
43 " The Crisis in Belief," *Essays,* p. 10.
44 " Here then is the crucial distinction between the New Testament and existentialism, between the Christian faith and the natural under-

this redemption an " event," an " act of God," an " encounter
with God," the " judgment of God," " the revelation of his
grace." With such language he intends to designate an objective encounter of the believer with a transcendent deity, an
encounter that frees the believer for and grounds him in his
true freedom. The basic question raised by the idea of a
gracious act of divine freedom that bestows human freedom is
whether human freedom, as Bultmann understands it, can
truly depend upon the freedom of another, even the freedom
of God.

Faith, Grace, and Confession

For an answer our attention focuses upon " faith " — that
event through which God's free grace is applied and in which
freedom comes to man.[45] Faith, says Bultmann, is " the attitude
of man in which he receives the gift of ' God's righteousness '
and in which the divine deed of salvation accomplishes itself." [46] Consistent with his emphasis on the priority of the
redemptive act, he insists that faith, while it is indeed an act
of man, is nevertheless wholly contingent upon and a part of
the saving event which it appropriates.[47] Faith that depends
so radically upon its object is basically an act of *trust*.

That is why faith is *"simultaneously ' confession.' "* As
confession faith points to that object in which it trusts and
upon which it depends. It includes in itself a *" knowing "* —
the realization that the object it confesses is not an illusion,
an ego projection, but an *extra nos* given to faith as an object
of genuine knowledge. Since faith and therefore freedom are
so dependent upon an *extra nos*, Bultmann can agree with

standing of Being. The New Testament speaks and faith knows of an act
of God through which man becomes capable of . . . his authentic life."
(" New Testament and Mythology," *Kerygma and Myth*, p. 33.)

[45] This discussion of faith focuses upon paragraph 35, entitled " The
Structure of Faith," in *Theology*, I, 314–324.

[46] *Ibid.*, p. 314.

[47] " Faith as response to the proclaimed word . . . like that word itself,
is a part of the salvation-occurrence. . . . The concrete realization of the
possibility of faith is itself eschatological occurrence." (*Ibid.*, p. 329.)

Paul that freedom is not original to man, but rather that it can " have its origin only in miracle." The predestinary formulations of both Paul and John bespeak the radical contingency of faith. They " mean that the decision of faith is not a choice between possibilities within this world, that arise from inner worldly impulses, and also mean that the believer in the presence of God cannot rely on his own faith. He never has his security in himself, but always only in God alone." [48] While faith receives grace, grace does not depend upon faith, for " faith does not appeal to whatever itself may be as an act or attitude but to God's prevenient deed of grace which preceded faith. . . . The attention of the believer does not turn reflectively inward upon himself, but is turned toward the object of faith." [49] These several references should serve to remove any doubt concerning Bultmann's affirmation of the radical dependence of faith upon grace. Furthermore, grace, the redeeming event, is identical with the historical fact of Jesus.[50] " The historical person of Jesus makes the preaching of Paul gospel, for Paul proclaims neither a new idea of God nor a new messianic concept, but a deed of God in history, the coming of the Messiah, who is identical with the person of Jesus." [51]

Faith, Preaching, and Obedience

There is, however, another side to Bultmann's view of faith which seems to jeopardize these affirmations. While we are aware that no statement of the relationship of faith to grace, of God's freedom to man's freedom, will be finally satisfactory, still Bultmann's statement of this problem seems especially confusing and contradictory. The other side of his thinking

[48] *Theology,* II (1955), 23.

[49] *Ibid.,* I, 319.

[50] " The gospel distinguishes itself from law not as a new epoch in the spiritual history of man, but in that it proclaims an historical fact, Jesus, as the fulfilment of the promise." (" Die Bedeutung des geschichtlichen Jesus für die Theologie des Paulus," *Glauben und Verstehen,* I, 202.)

[51] *Ibid.,* pp. 202 f.

is suggested by the fact that he conceives faith first and foremost as *obedience* and objects to the view that sees faith primarily as *trust*. It is also implicit in his constant reminder that
faith is a " free deed." When he discusses faith as confession,
maintaining that faith points beyond itself to that which it
knows and confesses, that it is committed to the dogmatic content of the kerygma, he is quick to point out that faith also
has " on the other hand, an ' undogmatic ' character insofar
as the word of proclamation is . . . no teaching about external matters which could simply be regarded as true without
any transformation of the hearer's own existence." [52] From
this perspective the important aspect of proclamation or
preaching is its kerygmatic form, its dimension as address
(*Anrede*), and not its dogmatic content. Bultmann states that
God's word is always an address to man and can only be understood as such.[53] " Not the historical Jesus, but the Jesus
Christ who is preached is the Lord." [54] Preaching is as much
the saving event as is the event of cross and resurrection.[55]
Indeed, " there is nothing in the content of Jesus' life that
needs to be taught so much as does this, that in his historical
life [the Word] had its beginning and that in the preaching
of the Church it occurs again." [56]

Carl Michalson interprets Bultmann quite correctly when in
a discussion of " the creativity of preaching " he says that
" there is more communication of the gospel in the act of
preaching than in the content of the sermon." [57] Friedrich
Gogarten, another disciple of Bultmann, makes the same
point by saying that " this word does not simply speak about

[52] *Theology*, I, 318 f.
[53] " Der Begriff des Wortes Gottes im Neuen Testament," *Glauben und
Verstehen*, I, 282.
[54] " Die Bedeutung des geschichtlichen Jesus," p. 208.
[55] *Ibid.*, p. 209.
[56] " *Es braucht also inhaltlich von Jesus nichts gelehrt zu werden als
dieses Dass, das in seinem historichen Leben seine Anfang nahm und in
der Predigt der Gemeinde weiter Ereignis wird.*" (" Der Begriff des Wortes
Gottes," p. 292.)
[57] Michalson, *The Hinge*, p. 219.

something. It immediately brings to pass what it announces." [58]

From the standpoint of preaching as address we can appreciate why Bultmann prefers " obedience " as the meaning of faith. " Trust " implies and demands an object; " obedience " implies and demands a subject. Preaching in its formal aspect as address says nothing objective; rather, it invokes the subject it addresses. Gogarten says that it " intends man himself." [59] In Bultmann's words: " The possibility of the word's being understood coincides with the possibility of man understanding himself." [60] Preaching gives man a new understanding of himself " not as a theoretical doctrine about himself, but in such a way that the event of address opens up a situation of existential self-understanding . . . which must be grasped in an act." [61] It calls man into authenticity by demanding that he step out of neutrality.[62] As man is called out of neutrality into existence as act he is constituted a true person, one who finds himself in decision and obedience rather than in works and achievements. Carl Michalson focuses the issue when he says that " the Christian Gospel is a mobilization of decision. It begins not with a series of facts, but with a call for an act of will." [63]

Preaching is so effective because as a merely formal matter, as address, it gives man no object, no worldly reality to which he can surrender himself and so forfeit his freedom and responsibility. Preaching that has no dogmatic content prescribes no work to be done by man from which he, in his very being, remains apart. Pure and authentic preaching refers to nothing or no one but the person it addresses; it calls man into being in freedom. It is " subjective " and not objective; it demands the hearer himself and not something to be heard.

One may properly object that the kerygmatic form does in-

[58] Gogarten, p. 134.
[59] *Ibid.*, p. 131.
[60] " Der Begriff des Wortes Gottes," p. 284.
[61] *Ibid.*, p. 283.
[62] *Ibid.*, p. 282.
[63] Michalson, p. 227.

deed embrace at least a minimal dogmatic content; it is, after all, a preaching about Jesus Christ. This Bultmann grants, but he also insists that when Jesus is rightly understood — as a preacher, and as the crucified — there is no conflict between the content and the form; indeed, it will be seen that the content confirms the form. According to the New Testament, Jesus himself was first of all a preacher. " His entire activity exhausts itself in the word; his works are his words." [64] Again Michalson goes to the heart of Bultmann's position in stating that " Jesus came preaching himself as the preacher." [65] To preach Jesus is to preach preaching.

But Bultmann also says of Jesus that "his words are his works," that Jesus says what he does, or that what he does is his most eloquent word.[66] The deed of Jesus that is also his word is his passion, his bearing of the cross. The cross, viewed kerygmatically, is like preaching itself — a call to freedom and obedience. The cross as a symbol of an objective sacrifice — propitiatory, vicarious, or juridical — is inadequate and inimical to freedom.[67] The Gnostic view of cosmic redemption moves the cross from the past into the eternal present — where it can be related to the present moment of decision; the Gnostic view, however, is guilty of separating the knowledge of the saving event from salvation itself, as if I could " know " my salvation

---

[64] " Der Begriff des Wortes Gottes," p. 290.

[65] Michalson, *The Hinge*, p. 218. In *Jesus and the Word* (tr. by Louise Pettibone Smith and Erminie Huntress; Charles Scribner's Sons, 1934), Bultmann shows that the Synoptics do not allow us to talk about the " fact " of Jesus' life, about the psychology of his personality. All that we can do is talk about the message of Jesus. Yet even here we are warned that " what the sources offer us first of all is the message of the early Christian community " (p. 12). But he adds, it cannot be reasonably doubted that behind it all lies a " bearer of the message." He concludes by saying: " I see then no objection to naming Jesus throughout as the speaker. Whoever prefers to put the name of Jesus always in quotation marks and let it stand as an abbreviation for the historical phenomenon of the speaker . . . is free to do so " (p. 14). In a word, we know nothing of Jesus, little of his message; we do know that he was a speaker. This suffices.

[66] *Theology*, I, 292 f.

[67] *Ibid.*, pp. 297 f.

without at once "being" saved, without participating decisively in it. Paul knows of Christ, says Bultmann, "only by knowing himself anew in the same act of recognition." [68] This existential type of knowledge occurs when the death of Christ is presented not as sacrifice or as cosmic occurrence, but as address, in preaching. The cross of Christ is recognized as the salvation event "by the fact that a crucified one is proclaimed as Lord." [69]

Bultmann is making two points: Jesus is salvation when (1) proclaimed and (2) proclaimed as "a crucified one." We have seen the power of the event of sheer proclamation. But as regards the second point, it is important to note that the anonymous "a crucified one" is not accidental. It is not the preaching of the man Jesus, but the preaching of his cross that saves. This is a dogmatic content that is purely formal; that is, a crucified one is one who is defined by his movement away from all that is material and concrete, by his movement toward death, toward nothing, toward the future. To put this picture before man is to confront man with nothing; it is to speak of nothing but the subject who is addressed. Like the form of preaching, the cross as the content of preaching is but a call to existence in freedom. Jesus as "a crucified one" is a Jesus distinguished by death. Death is not a past reality, nor is it a cosmic myth; rather, it is the original possibility of my historical existence, which can be received "as the determining power of my life." Death is the one thing that is not unique to Jesus; therefore, Jesus, conceived as "the crucified," is indeed my contemporary who offers me a genuine existential possibility. When he is proclaimed as the Messiah, as the good news, then his death (and so my death) is declared to be not simply *a* possibility, but *the* possibility, the life-giving possibility — the resurrection and the life.

Here we recall our earlier discussion of the sense in which death is the fulfillment of the law. We have seen that the law

[68] *Ibid.*, p. 301.
[69] *Ibid.*, p. 303.

brings man to the threshold of grace by destroying the inauthentic self. By the authority of the preaching of Christ crucified, faith is able to complete the step over the threshold and to see that death is not only the end of inauthenticity but also the very possibility of authenticity. Faith understands that to take up one's cross (and so to follow Christ) is to enter into true life (and so to share Christ's resurrection). If all this be so, "then . . . *the salvation occurrence is nowhere present except in the proclaiming, accosting, demanding, and promising word of preaching.*" [70] This accosting, demanding word is gospel, life-giving, because by demanding no thing it calls man into being toward death, into an encounter with the future. It delivers man from his past deed for his present doing. Preaching does this. Preaching "is itself the revelation, and does not merely speak about it," for "it addresses us; it speaks to our consciences." [71]

Faith so conceived as a responsible encounter with death is an act of original existence, an exercise of freedom that is quite understandable without reference to dogma. Since faith is an *original* possibility of existence, existence is one and unified as it moves from "the situation under the law to the situation under grace," as it moves from sin to faith. Indeed, "no break takes place; no magical or mysterious transformation of man in regard to his substance, the basis of his nature, takes place." [72] This continuity obtains because of the unity of the divine will in law and gospel, for in both law and gospel there is the fact of formal demand in which the subject is addressed. Insofar as the law while under the power of sin is filled with tangible matter, demanding now *this* thing, now *that* thing, now this work, now that work, it is a tyranny which must be and indeed is judged and destroyed by death. Thus, both gospel and law also confirm man's existence as subject to the imperative of death. Since existence is one in sin and faith, in

[70] *Ibid.*, p. 302.
[71] "Revelation in the New Testament," *Existence*, p. 78.
[72] *Theology*, I, 268 f.

nature and grace, theology can and "must" rely on "the philosophical analysis of man . . . if it at all wants to clarify existence in faith in a conceptual way." [73] The act of faith is understandable outside the Christian confession, for " the ' hearing ' of revelation [faith] is . . . ' profane ' insofar as it is perceptible as a human process . . . as a movement within man's existence." [74] In " Das Problem der natürlichen Theologie " Bultmann writes that " it is the unbelieving existence that comes to faith." [75] Philosophy " knows about faith precisely insofar as it knows about the freedom of existence, for then it knows about the questionableness that is basic and appropriate to freedom." [76] But then, mindful of the unique, dogmatic claims of Christian faith, Bultmann states, with obvious contradiction, that " faith in its genuine meaning as that which structures *Dasein,* is not perceptible; it is, insofar as it is a being grasped by God, insofar as it is *justifying faith, not a phenomenon of Dasein.*" [77]

Bultmann apparently has two views — faith as a profane reality, rooted in man's existence as freedom and history, subject to conceptual clarification by philosophical analysis, and faith as confessional, understanding itself in terms of the dogmatic content of the kerygma.

Freedom and Grace

It is possible that our analysis has falsely separated what belongs together; it is also possible that one view is quite secondary and is subsumed by the other; it is further possible that both views are correct and are to be held in paradoxical tension. As it appears, we have simple contradiction. To resolve this issue, we turn to see what happens when the two views meet. Bultmann raises the question himself when he asks

---

[73] " The Historicity of Man," *Existence,* p. 97.

[74] *Ibid.,* p. 100.

[75] " Das Problem der natürlichen Theologie," *Glauben und Verstehen,* I, 309.

[76] *Ibid.,* p. 310.

[77] *Ibid.,* p. 311.

whether it is correct to say that the Christian " ventures faith itself " or that he " ventures in faith." [78] Is faith its own end and therefore *self*-conscious, or is faith a means in which man is conscious only of that " object " toward which he ventures in faith? When faith is viewed dogmatically, confessionally, it talks about " grace," about what it knows and confesses. When it is viewed kerygmatically, it talks about itself, about knowing and confessing. Bultmann's discussion of the encounter between grace and faith, between the freedom of God and the freedom of man, as witnessed in the New Testament is instructive. Consider his interpretation of Johannine dualism, the dualism of light and darkness, life and death, etc.; this dualism means, says Bultmann, that " man is determined by his origin and in each present moment does not have himself in hand; he has only one alternative; to exist either from God (reality) or from the world (unreality). . . . And freedom is this: that by acknowledging the truth, the world opens itself to the reality from which alone it can live." [79] Bultmann seems to be saying in the first sentence that man is either a sinner or a saint, living either from the world and knowing not reality, or from reality and knowing not the world, and having, in either instance, no freedom for the other. The only alternative, and this is the one Bultmann pursues, is to understand that man lives from himself in a freedom to judge over both reality and unreality. A freedom of this sort would belong only to him who is determined neither by God nor by the world, but is *a se,* with his own spirit his only law.[80] So, after all, man is not determined by God or the world; the determination, the decision is with man. Dualism does not mean, then, that man is lost in darkness, that he belongs to the world, that he is under the judgment of God, that he has no freedom save through a miraculous rebirth. No, it means only that man has an original freedom of choice between two principles —

[78] " Faith as Venture," *Existence,* p. 55.
[79] *Theology,* II, 20.
[80] *Ibid.*

the law of self (God) and not-self (Satan).[81] Freedom is intrinsic to existence; it is prior to grace and grace depends upon it.

By the same token, Bultmann cannot accommodate the determinism of the Fourth Gospel which makes sense only on the premise of a radical indisposition of man's freedom toward grace. So it is with desperation that he wrests his confidence in the freedom of man from a Johannine passage which much more evidently gives praise to God's freedom. He writes: " Inasmuch as the assertion that no one can come to Jesus whom the Father does not ' draw ' (6:44) is followed by the statement, ' Everyone who has heard and learned from the Father comes to me,' the *pas* by itself (' everyone ') indicates that everyone has the possibility of letting himself be drawn by the Father (and also the possibility of resisting) ." The objective students of this passage would most likely read that only those to whom God has spoken and who are taught by him have the possibility of being drawn by him. The words that follow present even more difficulties: " The Father's ' drawing ' does not precede the believer's ' coming ' to Jesus — in other words, does not take place before the decision of faith — but, as the surrendering of one's certainty and self-assertion, occurs in that coming, in that decision of faith." [82] This is a confusing passage which demands clarification. Bultmann identifies the Father's " drawing " with the believer's " surrendering of [his] own capacity and self-assertion." And " coming to Jesus " is identical with " faith." Faith, as we have seen, is also equivalent to the surrender of " one's own capacity and self-assertion." The believer's " faith," his " coming to Jesus," and the Father's " drawing " are equivalent and mean " the surrendering of

[81] See Hermann Diem's discussion of Bultmann's exegesis of the Fourth Gospel in *Dogmatics* (Edinburgh: Oliver & Boyd, Ltd., 1959), pp. 244 f. Diem writes, commenting on Bultmann's view of the man of faith: " It is now the believing hearer himself who has to authorize and verify the fact of revelation and the whole Gospel message by means of his own personal history " (p. 249).

[82] *Theology*, II, 23.

one's own certainty and self-assertion." Bultmann in one sentence sets out to make a statement about God, but in fact paraphrases in a gross tautology " the surrendering of one's own certainty and self-assertion." Where John asserts that " the Father's drawing " (grace) is the possibility of " the believer's coming " (faith), Bultmann asserts the opposite, " that faith is the paradoxical act of renunciation of every work in the view that grace is received only in such renunciation." [83] Indeed, " the relationship of so many beings with God is wrecked just here. . . . For it is only for such surrender [of self] that God's grace becomes effective." [84] We have seen that the self that is surrendered in faith is the inauthentic self and that in the act of surrendering the free, authentic self appears.

It then appears that grace is redundant, for the authentic, free man — man as act, as freedom from the past — emerges in faith prior to grace. Kerygmatic faith is identical with authentic humanity. Faith that was understood as miracle, as an act of God through which God in his grace bestows freedom, is now understood as an exercise of that freedom itself. Faith is identical with the deed it would mediate. For Bultmann, grace not only presupposes faith, but it is also replaced by faith.[85]

---

[83] " Grace and Freedom," *Essays*, p. 176.

[84] *Ibid.*, p. 175. Italics mine.

[85] Roy Harrisville, in a discussion of " Bultmann's Concept of the Transition from Inauthentic to Authentic Existence " (*Kerygma and History*, ed. by Carl E. Braaten and Roy A. Harrisville; Abingdon Press, 1962), speaks to the conflict between faith as a response to grace and faith as an original ontological possibility. He argues that according to existentialist ontology " prior to the choice of concrete possibilities there occurs a ' choosing of choice,' before any concrete decision there is a ' choosing of choice to be a self ' " (p. 221). This means that according to Heidegger the decision for authenticity is ontological. Faith, therefore, " as a purely ontical possibility is at least without the philosophical support he assumed for it " (" Bultmann's Concept," pp. 221 f.) . Faith cannot, therefore, " constitute the basic condition of the *Dasein* anew " (Bultmann, " Das Problem," *Glauben und Verstehen*, I, 310) . Furthermore, if faith were a genuine ontological possibility, then, since " according to the existential analytic, for which knowledge and being are identical, it is inconceivable that man could be aware of a possibility without at the same time being

The difficulty with Bultmann's view of redemption and faith, the problem he has in maintaining that freedom is a gift, is that he conceives of a freedom that by definition cannot be granted as a gift, certainly not in the radical way in which Christianity, by Bultmann's own confession, claims. Freedom as freedom from the past, as openness to the future, understood as the call to fill the future with the law of its own spirit, cannot be granted by another. Freedom that is fundamentally man's aseity cannot be seriously related to an *extra nos*. At best, something *extra nos*, like a crucified Jesus, serves as reminder to man of the possibility he already possesses, the possibility of turning from the past to the future. But a faith that subjects man to dogma, to the *content* of the kerygma, is a faith that cannot bestow freedom, freedom to fill life with its own creative content, its own dogma.[86] A view of faith that conceives man as a solitary individual, cut off from past and future, from the world and nature, and subject only to the law of his own spirit, cannot find a radical place for the neighbor, not even for the divine neighbor, Jesus.[87] Our contention here becomes very clear as we turn to the last section, the doctrine of the freedom of God.

---

able to seize it. Bultmann, knowing full well that a concession to this axiom would eliminate the necessity of the grace event, stubbornly differentiates a knowledge of from a mastery of authenticity, a ' theoretical from an actual possibility' " (*Kerygma and History*, p. 224).

[86] We see why Schubert Ogden protests against Macquarrie's insistence that the existentialist interpretation also needs to be " supplemented " by reference to "a minimum core of factuality" (John Macquarrie, *The Scope of Demythologizing*, pp. 176 f.; London: SCM Press, Ltd., 1960). Ogden asks: " Is not the demand for such a supplement an implicit denial of man's radical freedom and responsibility? " (*Christ Without Myth: A Study Based on the Theology of Rudolf Bultmann*, p. 181; Harper & Brothers, 1961).

[87] Malavez speaks for a host of critics of Bultmann when he writes, concerning Jesus in Bultmann's theology, that " he is, we do not know why, the human organ of the Word of God; that is all, his person lacks mystery, and has no peculiar relation to the God who sends him " (L. Malavez, *The Christian Message and Myth*, tr. by Olive Wyon, p. 117; London: SCM Press, Ltd., 1958).

THE FREEDOM OF GOD

This section of our discussion poses some difficulty. Macquarrie states that Father Malavez " may be exaggerating, but he has some grounds for saying that Bultmann's theology is ' absolutely silent about the God whom it urges us to worship; there is nothing about his nature or attributes.' " [88] Bultmann himself poses the problem when he asks: " What meaning is there in talk about God? " The question is real if one understands God as " the almighty, the all-determining," for such a God is not present in talk " about " (*über*) him in which he becomes an object determined by canons of knowledge.[89] Then one would not understand " what determination by the existence of God means, for it means that God claims us in such a way that every stance outside God [as when he is an object of my knowledge] is a denial of his claim upon us, is Godlessness, sin." [90] To talk about the determining God is also to talk as one determined, is to talk about oneself. But then, do I not do just that and talk about myself rather than about God? " Do we not thus stand between two prohibitions, between which resignation and silence seem the only alternatives? " [91]

Talk About God

Let it be granted for the moment that we can talk about God only by talking about our own existence. What then do we gain, since we have seen that we cannot talk *about* our own existence? Existence is a project, an ongoing act of freedom. We cannot speak about it because it is found only in the future. The existence about which one can speak — achieved, objectified existence — is the past from which authentic existence is ever free. Existence that can be talked about is no

---

[88] Malavez, p. 156, cited by Macquarrie, p. 127.
[89] " Welches Sinn ist es von Gott zu reden," *Glauben und Verstehen*, I, 26–37.
[90] *Ibid.*, p. 28.
[91] *Ibid.*, p. 29.

more authentic than is the talked-about God. What man usually conceives of when he talks about God or self is, on the one hand, a world view — a cosmic order objective to and apart from existence and, on the other hand, existence as a particular instance within this order, " a case of the general rule." [92] He sees the world as the whole, himself as a part.

The question then remains as to how one may *speak* about God. The first point in answer is to understand that " if we take seriously the thought of God as the almighty and the totally other . . . then obviously a self-oriented question and decision grounded in reflection as to whether we should speak or be silent, act or rest, is entirely inappropriate. For the decision in this case is God's; to us it remains whether we *must* act or not act." [93] Granted, however, that we can and must speak only when spoken to, how can we *speak* without objectifying and thus falsifying? Bultmann answers that " when our existence is grounded in God and is not present outside God, then the comprehending of our existence is also a comprehending of God." [94] But since we comprehend our existence only as we *act* it rather than as we objectively study it, it follows that God appears only as man *does*. Since man does not appear in *what* is done, but in the *doing,* so also does God appear. Our question remains: What, then, can be *said* about God? Is any *concept* implicit in this thinking?

" Totally Other "

Yes, indeed! When Bultmann raises the question about the reasonableness of talk about God, it is apparent that he has in mind a very definite conception of God — God as the " almighty and totally other." [95] This concept of God is implicit in the existential analysis; he is the God implicit in the understanding of man as historical. One of the most vivid, and least

92 *Ibid.,* p. 31.
93 *Ibid.,* p. 34.
94 *Ibid.,* p. 36.
95 *Ibid.,* p. 34.

sophisticated, statements of this position is found in an early sermon of Bultmann's, " The Hidden and Revealed God," [96] where he states that " God must be a hidden and mysterious God, full of contradictions and riddles. Otherwise our inner life would become static, and we would lose the power to obtain experience from life's fullness." [97] If the world were replete with answers, we would not have the burden of freedom and responsibility. The contradiction and riddle which manifest the hiddenness of God and mystery of life and which make room for man and freedom are the harsh realities of life. In 1917, when this sermon was preached, these were the misery and despair of a war-weary world. He then declared: " But has the war not also revealed all of the dark, demonic forces of the human heart . . . ? Do we dare say here also that we gaze into the depths of God? Yes. . . . For this sight is a powerful reflection on ourselves and a perception of the miraculous riches of all the opposed forces and passions . . . in the soul of man . . . for the human soul is still *one* great unity. . . . What a mysterious wisdom of God is revealed here. . . . What a hidden wisdom of God that uses all the wild, unleashed passions only in order to put man's dignity to the supreme test, to give him the highest nobility of being." [98] Thus: " Indeed, what is God, if not the infinite fullness of all the powers of life that rage around us." [99] Through " the picture of promise and redemption in the crucified Christ " as " the embodiment of the hidden and revealed wisdom of God " we are given to know " that the powers really are faces of life and God." [100] God is the hidden source (or reality?) of the powers that face us, the apparent nothingness that summons us to freedom and responsibility. Because God is totally other, he is the God of human freedom.

Another characteristic way in which Bultmann designates

[96] " The Hidden and Revealed God," *Existence*, pp. 23 f.
[97] *Ibid.*, p. 27.
[98] *Ibid.*, pp. 32 f.
[99] *Ibid.*, p. 26.
[100] *Ibid.*, p. 33.

God is as " the one who limits man and who brings him to his authenticity in this limitation." [101] This understanding, given in faith, establishes the preunderstanding that man already possesses. One is free from the past, from the world and nature, because God is not found there, because this realm is subject to death. The God who is the " totally other " sets radical limits to the efforts of man to find himself and his God in the world. He is a God who demands that man not rest in the world but go on in freedom toward the future, toward the hidden presence of God.

Bultmann has been a consistent advocate of natural theology. The fact that man can understand the sentences of faith, the phenomenon of religion and general talk about " God," and the fact of the humanity common to the believer and the unbeliever point to the natural knowledge of God.[102] Man knows " about his historicity and to that extent about God." [103] In the generic concept " God " there is revealed a self-knowledge in which a true, but limited, knowledge of God is implicit: " Knowledge about God is in the first instance a knowledge which man has about himself and his finitude, and God is reckoned to be the power which breaks through this finitude and thereby raises him up to his real nature." [104] When man calls God " omnipotent," he means only that man is subject to unknown powers. When he calls God " holy," man means that he is guilty, that his past is not self-justifying, that he is not yet what he ought to be. When he calls God " eternal," he means that his life is transitory, hidden to both past and present, and that he must move into the future. In short, man has a natural awareness that he is radically questioned by limiting powers. Natural theology cannot identify these limiting powers; it " has only reached the stage of inquiry about God." [105] Such preliminary knowledge is sin insofar as it presumes to an-

[101] " Revelation in the New Testament," *Existence*, p. 88.
[102] See "Das Problem der natürlichen Theologie," p. 295.
[103] *Ibid.*, p. 304.
[104] " The Question of Natural Revelation," *Essays*, p. 98.
[105] *Ibid.*, p. 94.

swer the question it naturally raises. There is nothing "in individual persons, in the sway of history, in history as source of
present decision" that allows man to do more than question;
to answer the question himself and arbitrarily designate as
"God" that for which he seeks is sin. This designation can
be made only by God himself through faith in Christ. Where
faith appears man is able to surrender premature answers,
worldly answers, for answers which are beyond the world and
which appear in this world only as questions. In a word, faith
allows the question to be the answer. The man of faith finds
"his real nature . . . in what is *not* in the sense of being
within the world — it is eschatological and transcendent." [106]
To allow the question to be the answer means to allow man's
act toward the future to speak for God.

With these several references we are brought back to our
initial thought: God is the ground of freedom, the hidden
source and reality of the mysterious powers that challenge
man, the limiting and determining powers that prevent man
from resting and force him into existence as history, as question. This questioning is natural, a natural preunderstanding
of God which in faith becomes the divine answer, the ultimate
understanding.

What may we say, then, about the freedom of God? It is, in
the first place, his *hiddenness,* his transcendence of and freedom from man. This, his freedom from man, is, paradoxically,
his freedom for man; for it is because God is distant from man,
present only in his hiddenness, that man has room and is called
into freedom.

In the second place, God's freedom is his freedom to reveal
himself as *God* in his hiddenness. This is the freedom of God's
immanence in the powers that limit and put man in question.
While the divine freedom in its first dimension calls man into
freedom, the freedom of God in his revelation is the grace that
gives man the courage of freedom. The hiddenness of God calls
forth freedom; the revelation in the hiddenness encourages
freedom. "Thus there is law and order in God's working. If we

[106] *Ibid.,* p. 111.

have once acquired an ear for the divine melody, then it is always the same old theme endlessly proceeding in ever new ways, always blending itself into new harmonies, always more tempestuous, always more powerful. And if we kneel at first humbly and reverently before the hidden God of the riddle, we then kneel humbly and reverently before the revealed God of grace. And thus we are permitted to see ' what no eye has seen, nor ear heard, nor the heart of man conceived, what God has prepared for those who love him.' " [107]

We cannot leave Bultmann's doctrine of God at this point. There appears in his writings another set of statements in different language. We have seen that the preceding understanding of God is based largely upon the implications of the understanding of existence as freedom or history. This other type of language proceeds more directly from the Biblical witness to Christ. He writes: " Yes, there is a mediator between God and the world who brings God near to us, in whom God becomes evident to us, and through whom the world becomes God's creation for us. If we know him, we know God; and if we do not know him, we do not know God. But how does he bring God near to us? How does God become evident to us in him? Is he a personification of all the world's laws and vital forces? By no means! He is an individual man like us in whose action God acts, in whose destiny God is at work, in whose word God speaks. He has died on the cross for us; and he now lives in eternity — for us! And only when we understand this do we understand that God is the creator; and so it is through him that the world becomes God's creation — for us! " [108]

In the light of the Bible, Bultmann speaks of the " Word of forgiving grace " in which God " exercises a power which nothing in the world possesses." [109] This new power is the power which " judges me as a sinner and forgives me my sin," and which " directs my attention to the ' thou ' and commands me to hear the claims of the ' moment ' in love." It understands

[107] " The Hidden and Revealed God," *Existence*, pp. 33 f.
[108] " Faith in God the Creator," *Existence*, pp. 179 f.
[109] " The Question of Natural Revelation," p. 109.

" the claims of the ' moment ' to be those of the ' thou ' and of the demand to *love*." [110] It is not that in Christ one gains an *idea* of God, of " thou," and love. No, in Christ man meets God himself. " That is what Christianity means by *God's becoming man:* the reality of God is not that of the idea but of the concrete happening; and the reality of his forgiveness is met with only in the concrete *Word* authenticated by him." [111]

God is a thou — a reality who meets us concretely through the word addressed to us in Christ. But he meets us not as just any thou, but as the one who speaks the word of forgiving grace, who establishes man in his love. In a word, God is revealed as the personal God of love. " Belief in love is only possible as belief in a love . . . which is infinite, i.e., *the love of God*. . . . I may believe in the love of God only when it is real in the history in which I stand, when it confronts me there. . . . That, however, is the meaning of the Christian Gospel, that God's forgiving love is already there, having come through Christ." [112]

Who is God? He is the personal God of love who confronts us in Christ with the Word of his love; he is the one who confronts us in our neighbor with the call of love. What is the freedom of God? First, it is the freedom that he possesses to be present to us in forgiving and renewing love in Christ. It is his freedom *for us* in Christ, his freedom to be so radically for us that we find ourselves in him, rooted and grounded in love. It is this creative freedom which makes the Christ event the eschatological event in which man is led back to " *the original creation*, to that lost, meaningless possibility." [113] It is the freedom of God so to bind himself to me that I become bound to him and to my fellowman, and love becomes the " power which determines my life." [114]

The freedom of God is also his transcendence in his love, his freedom *from us* in Christ. " Love is above all no property,

110 " The Crisis in Belief," *Essays*, pp. 14 f.
111 *Ibid.*, p. 16.
112 " Das christliche Gebot der Nächstenliebe," p. 242.
113 " Das Problem der natürlichen Theologie," p. 311.
114 " Das christliche Gebot der Nächstenliebe," p. 241.

no some-thing *in* man, but a manner of his being with another." [115] Love is given, therefore, only by another. This means that Christ as the love of God is not found as a result of human effort. We have already seen, in our earlier discussion of the gift of freedom, that Christ confronts us as the Word of God only as a result of divine freedom and gracious decision. This freedom is implicit in love, in the fact that God is one who forgives, who does not regard us for what we are, who is motivated not externally but inwardly by the freedom of his own love.

Can it be said that these two views are different ways of looking at the same reality? In each instance there is an emphasis on the existential significance of Christ; in each instance God is not known as God or met as God without the agency of Christ. In each instance Christ is the saving word. In the first instance his word frees the believer to accept the limiting powers of existence as the power of God. In the second instance his word frees the believer to accept the love of Christ as the personal love of God. In both instances his freedom is the charter of man's freedom.

The differences are, however, more noteworthy. Viewed from the standpoint of Christ, God's freedom is for the sake of love — it has its end in the event of Christ's love and the Christian's love of neighbor. From the standpoint of the existential analysis, the love of God is unto the end of freedom. This is very clear from our earlier sections. In the first instance, God's free, forgiving grace grounds man in Christ and becomes the power that determines man's life as togetherness with and love for the neighbor. Love is the very essence of freedom. In the second instance, God's forgiving grace establishes man's existence as a question, as existence in freedom and history, open to the future. Love is but a possibility of freedom.

Who Is God?

Bultmann's famous essay " The Historicity of Man and Faith " is perhaps his most express effort to bring together

[115] *Ibid.*, p. 287.

these views [116] represented here by Heidegger and Gogarten.

The first view, we have seen, proceeds from the requirements of existence understood as freedom. Heidegger is largely responsible for this concept of existence. He makes a distinction between the ontological and the ontic — between the fundamental structures and possibilities of existence on the one hand and the concrete, historical realization of these possibilities on the other. Ontologically, existence is determined by its movement toward death. " Because he knows that he will die, *Dasein* (existence) takes possession, like no other thing does, of the course of his personal destiny, even before it is in fact realized. Consequently, when Heidegger speaks of *Dasein* as Being-toward-death *(Sein-zum-Tode)* he signals the finite self-possession which characterizes the free being who in projecting himself unfolds the reality of his own destiny." [117] In Bultmann's paraphrase: " To be a man — if I may briefly summarize . . . — is something that uniquely belongs to the individual; and the being of man is a ' possibility of being,' i.e., the man who is involved in care for himself chooses his own unique possibility." [118]

Ontologically, man is a solitary being who finds himself through a resolution of freedom, through history, in an encounter with death and the limiting forces of reality.

For Gogarten, on the other hand, " it is the thou that first discloses the transitoriness of my existence and constrains me to decision." [119] Love is not merely an ontic option, " one possibility for existing authentically among others. . . . On the contrary, love is the *only* possibility of authentic existence. . . . Only in love is man historical." [120]

[116] See David Cairns, *A Gospel Without Myth* (London: SCM Press, Ltd., 1960) , pp. 54 f., for a discussion of the essay of Bultmann to the point we are making.

[117] Thomas Langan, *The Meaning of Heidegger* (Columbia University Press, 1959) , p. 32.

[118] " The Historicity of Man," *Existence*, p. 102.

[119] *Ibid.*, p. 103.

[120] *Ibid.*, p. 105.

For Heidegger, freedom is ontological, love is ontic. For Gogarten, love is ontological, and freedom as such, abstracted from love, is an ontic contradiction — it is sin. Both men cannot be right; yet Bultmann says they are. He claims that we can speak of reconciliation between Heidegger and Gogarten " if we be permitted to say that only where the I decides for the thou . . . is resolution actually realized. The possibility of saying something like this, however, falls outside of existential analysis . . . it speaks about the factual." [121] The difference, maintains Bultmann, is that Gogarten speaks as a theologian of the ontic and Heidegger as a philosopher of the ontological. But if this is the case and love is just another ontic reality, then we do not see that love can be understood, as it is in faith, as the only authentic possibility for man; Bultmann himself knows, and we have seen him state, that love in the Christian view makes ontological claims: " It is not so that man stands in the world as in an empty space [what else is meant by existence as *Sein-zum-Tode*]. . . . It is not so that man must first ask how he stands to another man and what he must do with him. Much rather, my being is from the beginning a being with another. . . . Love is above all no property, no *what* to man, but rather a *how* of his togetherness (*Miteinandersein*) ." [122] That is to say: " Love can be grasped as a possibility of human existence only when [man] can understand himself as already loved." [123] In Bultmann's own words, love, as the Christian understands it, is not a possibility of man's ontological structure as Heidegger views it. It is just not so that " the claim of the man of faith that he alone is free does not compete with the ontological exhibition of man's freedom." [124] One who in faith loves, knows of no ontological depth that is free of or neutral toward love.

To avoid sheer contradiction Bultmann shifts ontological

121 *Ibid.*
122 " Das christliche Gebot der Nächstenliebe," pp. 231, 237.
123 *Ibid.,* p. 241.
124 " The Historicity of Man," p. 107.

ground and betrays, thereby, both the Christian and Heideggerian stances. He states, quoting Heidegger, that " the problem of existential analysis is solely to expose the ontological structure of man's being toward an end." From this he concludes that " the ontic phenomenon of death is only one striking phenomenon in which man's limitation clearly displays itself. And its significance in this regard can also be taken over by another ontic phenomenon that similarly allows man's limitation to become visible — namely, by love." He asks: " Then cannot the encounter with the thou clarify this ontological structure equally as well as death? " [125] Obviously, this proposition is no solution. In the first place, both love and death become ontic, and the question of man's ontological determination is open. This answer begs the ontological question. Secondly, it clearly contradicts the original ontological analysis, whence the problem arises initially. Thirdly, it does not at all answer to the claim of faith that love roots in love. Neutral freedom toward an end is no more capable of love than is freedom in *Sein-zum-Tode*.

How do we choose? There is no synthesis in Bultmann. What, then, does Bultmann mean? Schubert Ogden is unequivocal in his judgment: " Even as man in his inmost selfhood is something radically other and more than the inner and outer world with which he is always related, so also is God as sovereign grace and judgment, or as supreme ' I ' ' infinitely ' and ' qualitatively ' transcendent of the entire created order with which he stands in relation." [126] Therefore, " we must set aside all specifically ' mythological ' formulations because they completely obscure the fact that God's difference from the world is not merely ' quantitative ' but ' qualitative.' " He then points out that existentialism lends itself most adequately to this conception of God.[127] *In sum,* Bultmann's doctrine of

[125] See Heidegger, *Kant und das Problem der Metaphysik,* p. 226. Cited by Bultmann, " The Historicity of Man," p. 109.
[126] From the Introduction to *Existence and Faith,* p. 16.
[127] *Ibid.,* pp. 18 f.

God as "the totally other" is implicit in the existentialist analysis of man who as a being-toward-death transcends the world. Existentialism is not only the hermeneutic tool; it is also the hermeneutic beginning and dogmatic substance of Bultmann's theology.

By way of review, let me return now to the two questions to which the discussion of the freedom of God was in part directed.

The first question, arising out of our discussion of the freedom of man, is whether man loves in freedom or is free in love. We saw, on the one hand, that freedom is openness to the future, that nothing past or present, in past history or in the contemporary world of men and nature, is the judge of an individual's action. Man confronts the past, the world, as if it were nothing, and is thus forced to face the future alone, in the exercise of his own freedom according to its own law. His freedom is as his freedom does. On the other hand, Bultmann also speaks of freedom as love, as openness to every fresh claim of the neighbor. This language means that the norm of freedom is not found in freedom's own potential but in the needs of the neighbor. It appears, however, that this emphasis on love is not the definitive one. Bultmann stresses love when he is most directly responsible to the Bible, but the other emphasis dominates when as an interpreter, as a theologian, he moves away from the Bible in the direction of his own distinctive understanding.

The second question, arising out of our discussion of the gift of freedom ("freedom for freedom") is whether the freedom of God manifest in faith is the ground of, or is dependent upon, the freedom of man, or if perhaps they are paradoxically related. We concluded that Bultmann, as a Christian, is convinced that movement from inauthenticity to authenticity, from bondage to freedom, from the past to the future, is a gift of faith in the word of God freely addressed man in Christ. Faith viewed from this perspective is a radical dependence on the word of God's loving and forgiving presence. Such faith is both confession and trust. But we also noted Bultmann's insistence that faith is a human act, an act of natural freedom. It is that act of freely turning from the past, from trust in one's own achievements, in order to be open for the future, for the gift of grace. In this respect faith is basically an act of freedom upon which grace depends, an act of that very freedom which grace supposedly brings. Here, too, our analysis indicated that this less " orthodox " perspective represented the distinctive Bultmannian thrust.

When we turned to the final section on the doctrine of God we did find support for a final decision, although even at this ontological level the questions and contradictions appeared again. But the view of God as the " totally other " seems to be characteristic and distinctive, and this view justifies our preliminary resolution of the two questions. As the " totally other," God is, above all, the source and author of freedom; he is a God who can be spoken of only in the exercise of that freedom. He is a God who meets us preeminently in his absence, in the mystery of existence. Here, in this mystery, in the nothingness of death, man receives the gift of freedom. Love is an option of this freedom; it is not the essence of freedom. Our first question is answered. Also, a God who is totally other, who bequeaths freedom by virtue of his absence, by being present in death, can hardly be understood to bestow freedom by virtue of his presence in the life of Christ. Freedom is not something bestowed by the gracious presence of another but something elicited by the holy absence of another. Our second question is answered.

Bultmann's emphases on love and the Biblical witness to the freedom of God in Jesus are, therefore, arbitrary and dogmatic. His view of man — his liberation and his ontological structure — neither requires nor allows these emphases. Heidegger is neither blind nor ignorant when he fails to appropriate the Christian witness. The fact of existential inauthenticity, the failure of man to realize his true freedom, is no more an excuse for a turn to the Biblical Jesus than would the betrayal of

Christian faith by a Christian be the excuse for a turn to atheistic existentialism.

We must remind ourselves, however, that Bultmann does
give some theological ground to his concern for the Biblical
emphasis on love and on Jesus as the revelation of God's freedom by contradicting his dominant *theo*logical emphasis on
God as the "totally other." He occasionally understands
God as the one who meets us personally and concretely in
Jesus and who there reveals his love to us and binds us in love
to our neighbor. Were we to move in deductive fashion from
this God of personal love to an understanding of human freedom, we would see that man's freedom is a freedom in radical
subjection to love and that this freedom is bestowed only
through the prior freedom and love of God which is in Jesus
Christ. This line is not dominant in Bultmann's thought.

In conclusion, we must say that Bultmann's theology of
freedom is inadequate. His faithfulness to Scripture is his
own judgment. Speaking theo-*logically*, we must say that Bultmann's frequent recognition of the Scriptural emphasis on love,
and on Jesus, makes the structure of his system contradictory.
Speaking *theo*-logically, we must also say that the effort to seek
structural consistency by moving off center in the direction of
existentialism makes the substance of his system unacceptable.
In other words, as has been argued by the many critics of
Bultmann, the concrete revelation in Christ contradicts the
view of God as the totally other. But let it be granted for the
moment that the existentialist direction of Bultmann's thought
is acceptable. It then appears that it also suffers inner limitations; it is a razor's edge, so that thought which follows its line
must fall off in either of two directions. The difficulty with the
existentialist's approach is suggested when Bultmann substi-
tutes for bondage to the past "the law of one's own spirit."
The problem is: Are we to read "the *law* of one's own spirit"
or "the law of *one's own spirit*"? Do we speak of the *law* of
freedom or of the law of *freedom*? The true existentialist takes
the latter direction — the direction that Bultmann himself

seems to take. If this direction is pushed, man emerges as almost *a se*. This is part of the reason that Bultmann finds it so difficult to talk about God, save in existential terms, save as *man* acts. No structure appears within or transcendent of freedom; logos emerges only as the creature of freedom. The alternative of this radically egoistic tendency is the ontological direction, in which we must speak of the *law* of freedom, a law that roots in a fundamental ontological structure, a structure in which the individual and his freedom participate.[128] Since this route has been taken by Paul Tillich, who is also very sympathetic to the existentialistic and individualistic motifs of Bultmann's position, we turn in the next chapter to examine freedom in the theology of Paul Tillich.

NOTE

There have been two notable attempts by younger American (and, interestingly enough, Methodist) theologians to point the way to a theology based upon the insights of Bultmann. I refer to the late Carl Michalson's *The Hinge of History* and Schubert Ogden's, *Christ Without Myth*. At the time of the writing of his book, Dr. Michalson understood "historical" and "existential" methodologies to be synonymous (see *The Hinge*, p. 9). He was later to develop and modify his position in a book entitled *The Rationality of Faith* (Charles Scribner's Sons, 1963), which he subtitled *An Historical Critique of the Theological Reason,* indicating thereby his intention to go beyond the earlier identification of histori-

---

[128] Roman Catholic interpreters especially point in the direction of ontology. See L. Malavez, *The Christian Message and Myth,* pp. 200 f. See also John Macquarrie's discussion of "Roman Catholic Interest in Demythologizing," in *The Scope of Demythologizing,* pp. 102 f. Giovanni Miegge also has a fine discussion of Roman Catholic criticism in *Gospel and Myth in the Thought of Rudolf Bultmann* (John Knox Press, 1960), pp. 138 f. Miegge notes that there is a group of Catholic scholars who "are rather induced to regard Bultmann's thought as marking a reaction against that exclusive biblicism, the radical distrust of philosophy, which has been dominant in Protestant theology" (p. 141). He cites (p. 142) Fetcher in *Kerygma und Mythos*, V, 77, and Malavez, to whom I have referred above.

cal and existential methods, and move more in the direction of phenomenology (see *The Rationality,* pp. 16–19). While he objected to attempts of critics to reduce his *Hinge* to existentialism (*The Rationality,* p. 18), it is very clear that by his design and in fact, this earlier work is an essay in existentialist theology and is properly considered in the present context.

Whereas Michalson, in *The Hinge of History,* pursues the method of radical existentialism, Ogden, in *Christ Without Myth,* points in the direction of ontology. Both claim to build upon Bultmann and preserve the dependence of faith upon the Christian kerygma. Michalson's work, because it does maintain the existentialist pitch and eschews the ontological, is a better key to what Bultmann is really about than is Ogden's work. Insofar as Michalson does reflect the spirit of Bultmann he also reflects quite dramatically the problems of the position. Michalson agrees with Bultmann that the basic attribute of God is freedom. " The ontological presupposition of God's act of love in Christ is not the nature of love in God, but his freedom to be God." Nothing more ultimate can be said of God than that his freedom is divine and that his divinity is freedom. (*The Hinge,* pp. 167 f.) Man is also radically free. " Man *is* freedom." (P. 98.) Human history, says Michalson, " is human life in the exercise and expression of its freedom " (p. 79). Freedom is first. Decision precedes being; existence precedes essence. " The real enemy of freedom . . . is . . . reason." (P. 85.) As to the relationship between God and man, the relationship of faith, Michalson writes that " the image of God in man is the human possibility for man's relationship to God. That possibility is freedom. . . . It is simply not true that a person first perceives God, and then, as it were, puts himself in relation to him. The effort to establish relation comes first. God made us out of the nothing of freedom " (p. 97). This means that man first discovers himself in his freedom as a being toward death, and then, in faith, discovers that death, and all that limits him is the presence of the hidden God. " To say

that God is present is to say that he is . . . the limit of history,
the boundary, the frontier, the possibility of history." Preaching is significant, therefore, not for what it says, but for the
fact that it calls man into freedom, into decision. The Christian gospel " is a mobilization of decision. It begins not with a
series of facts, but with a call for an act of will " (p. 227).
What has the kerygma to do with Jesus? The Christian is one
who is " inexplicably moved to choose the event of Christ as
the present of God " (p. 165). But the presence of God in
Christ does not refer to a past fact, to " Christ's calculable dis-
placement value in the world." No, the time of divine entry is
" the time of decision. . . . It is the time we are before we
count the time we have " (p. 187).

Michalson thus develops and dramatizes the implications of
Bultmann's view that freedom is the ontological ultimate, so
ultimate that it can hardly account for its duty to love or its
indebtedness to the gracious freedom of God. Michalson's interpretation tends to push Bultmann into the camp of the
" left," best interpreted by Fritz Buri, who sees that for Bultmann the kerygma is not truly necessary. (See Ogden, *Christ
Without Myth,* pp. 133 ff.)

Schubert Ogden would interpret Bultmann in terms of an
ontology. All that is necessary to set forth an alternative to the
individualism and implicit dekerygmatizing of Bultmann's
position (without turning to the mythology of a Barthian
" right ") " is the acknowledgment that the possibility of
Christian existence is an original possibility of man before
God " (p. 140). This alternative will understand that man
is, as Bultmann has insisted, " radically responsible for his
final destiny," because of the " everlasting love of God that
is primordially active in the mighty works of creation, preservation, and redemption " (pp. 141 f.). The " peculiarly
Christian economy of salvation has a definite subordinate role
relative to this primordial purpose and work of God " (p.
143). Consequently, " the only final condition for sharing in
authentic life . . . is a condition that can be formulated in

complete abstraction from the event Jesus of Nazareth" p.
143). Ogden states, rather amazingly, that the Protestant doctrine of justification by faith without works means not only
without my works, but works of any kind, even the works of
Jesus. He does concede that this view has "rarely been seen"
(p. 145). If one is to talk about the authentic life apart from
the peculiarities of the Christian revelation, and yet avoid the
"one-sidely 'anthropological' or 'subjective' way" of Bultmann and the left, one must make use of analogy. This can be
"properly carried out only when Heidegger's analysis of existence is viewed in the perspective of the general ontology it
seems to imply and in which *divine* existence also is appropriately analyzed and conceptualized" (p. 151). Ogden concedes,
as if it were a failure in principle, that Bultmann has not developed this possible alternative. It does seem obvious, however, that for Bultmann — as for Michalson — freedom is the
ontological ultimate. To develop a doctrine of being is to re-
pudiate the entire position. Finally, it is indeed questionable
that the "central conviction of the apostolic witness" is that
"in the event Jesus of Nazareth something of ultimate significance . . . has been manifested," something that quite apart
from Jesus "is the essential reality of every human life"
(pp. 160 f.). Surely the apostolic witness feels that what Jesus
did himself as Jesus is also essential to human existence. It
does not appear that Ogden has given a tenable or convincing
account of the *unique* claims of the kerygma.

We may appraise these divergent resolutions of Bultmannian
theology by observing that Michalson, following the major
thrust of Bultmann's position, grasps the radical dimensions
of human freedom. He succeeds to the sixth day of creation
(riding a bit roughshod over the first five). Ogden's concern
for ontology points to the first five days of creation upon which
the sixth depends, but barely reaches that sixth day itself.
Neither Michalson nor Ogden reaches the seventh day, for in
neither case does God appear in his own terms. He appears
either in statements about human existence or in statements

about the ontological ground of all existence. In terms of freedom: Michalson grasps the freedom of man, but cannot speak about the freedom of God, or of man's relationship in freedom to his neighbor and to creation as such. Ogden can speak of the ontological structures that bind man to his neighbor and to creation generally, but neither man nor God would appear to emerge in any authentic or radical freedom. Since Paul Tillich thoroughly pursues the route Ogden indicates, we turn to see if our premonitions about ontology are correct. We must be aware, of course, that Ogden recommends a process ontology, but we are suggesting that ontology as such is the enemy of freedom, both of the freedom of God and man.

3

PAUL TILLICH: FREEDOM TO BE

BULTMANN'S ANALYSIS of existence led him to the view that the freedom of the Christian is abstract, even though he speaks of a freedom-for and appears to have a notion of the material content of freedom. But in the end freedom, as Bultmann views it, is its own content and norm. Tillich's thinking would break out of this circle. He agrees with Bultmann's starting point — human existence — and for this reason takes seriously the dimension of existence called *freedom*. But he is more impressed with the fact that man *is* than with the fact that man is *free,* and finally views freedom ontologically, in respect to its participation in being. Freedom is an element of being but not being-itself. Tillich does not say that man is free, but that he has freedom.[1]

FREEDOM-FOR

Freedom and Reality

In a most general way Tillich understands freedom as that which gives man the possibility of experiencing the meaningful structures of reality.[2] With freedom one is able to stand off from these essential structures in order to return to them and

[1] Paul Tillich, *Systematic Theology* (henceforth referred to as *S.T.*) I, 182.
[2] *Ibid.*

make them " freely " his own, without at the same time deny-
ing or destroying them.

As *man's* relationship to reality, freedom is a centered act of
the whole self in which " every part and every function which
constitutes man a personal self participates," so that no part of
man could be free and the other bound.[3] As man's *relationship
to reality,* freedom is effected and experienced as " deliberation, decision, and responsibility," aspects that are related as
condition, fact, and consequence.[4] Deliberation is the condition
of freedom because through it a person stands apart from argu-
ments and motives so as to weigh (*librare*) them. As long as
he can weigh them he is not identical with them, but " free."
Should he " decide " to accept them as his own, he may react
as a centered person in " decision " and cut off (*decidere*) un-
wanted possibilities. Since one is free-from in deliberation, and
free-for in decision, his freedom is experienced finally as responsibility, for he is aware that reality has not been put or
forced upon him, but that he has taken it upon himself.[5]

Freedom as centered selfhood also includes freedom of the
self from determination by the externals of the concrete situation in the world. This aspect of freedom rests on the power
of language and its universals to overcome the concrete situation by cutting through to its " deeper levels," to the level of
ultimate reality. Since man would not have freedom over the
world without these universals, they are binding upon freedom and are experienced as " unconditional moral and logical
imperatives." [6]

Beginning with a view of freedom as the centeredness of the
self which enables man to enjoy reality as his own, and not as

[3] *Ibid.,* p. 183.

[4] *Ibid.,* p. 184.

[5] " Since there is no such thing as a motive in abstraction from a person
who weighs the motives, it is a tautology to say that the stronger motive
always prevails. Only the person accounts for what gives a particular motive its strength." (David Roberts, " Tillich's Doctrine of Man," *The Theology of Paul Tillich,* ed. by Charles W. Kegley and Robert W. Bretall,
p. 118; The Macmillan Company, 1952.)

[6] *S.T.,* II, 31.

something alien or heteronomous, we have now come to see that freedom is more dialectical and cannot be viewed merely as centered selfhood, for only as it accepts language and its universals as unconditionally binding can the self be centered, and so free. Furthermore, man can be self-centered only as he is free from his concrete situation in the empirical world, and this can be accomplished only as he transcends the world to its rational depth. A free decision, one in which the self is centered in itself, is therefore one in which the self acknowledges the demands of the reason immanent in its language and then sets itself free from the empirical world by rationally relating to its depths. Freedom is the movement from reason to reason. Reason, the ultimate reality, subjective in the individual, objective in the world, is in a process of becoming through individual freedom. Tillich agrees with Hegel that "ideas are not static possibilities but dynamic forces whose eternity does not prevent them from becoming temporal, whose essence drives them to appear in existence." [7] To "appear in existence" means to be realized through individual freedom. [8] Freedom is therefore "the power to become a symbol for ' the ground of being.' " [9] Being actualizes itself through individual freedom, and the individual is free when he is open to being.

But just as freedom has the power to be a symbol for the ground of being, so it has the power to deny being. Man "has the power of contradicting himself and his essential nature. Man is free even from his freedom; that is, he can surrender his humanity." [10] He is free to forfeit his rational ground and goal. This distinction between rational freedom, or freedom for reason, and freedom from reason is the distinction between true and false freedom. The concept of *freedom-as-such,* merely formal freedom of decision, is an illegitimate abstraction. Free-

[7] *The Protestant Era,* tr. by James L. Adams (The University of Chicago Press, 1948) , p. 13.
   [8] *Ibid.,* p. 118.
   [9] *Ibid.,* p. 123.
   [10] *S.T.,* II, 32.

dom is true only when it is in polarity with destiny, the destiny of reason or being-itself.[11]

Destiny

Just as freedom is the form in which being realizes itself, so also being (or reason) is the material and substance of freedom; it is freedom's destiny. The question of the relationship of freedom to being becomes then the question of the relationship of freedom to its destiny. The concept of destiny has two formal aspects: in the first place, destiny is " that out of which our decisions arise; it is the indefinitely broad basis of our centered selfhood; it is the concreteness of our being which makes all our decisions *our* decisions." In this aspect destiny means that the free subject is not free to determine the subject who is free. Destiny is the self as given. It is " formed by nature, history, and myself." [12] What I am in any moment as the subject of freedom is determined by my past, by my natural and historical environment, and by my free response to these. " Biological, psychological, and sociological powers are effective in every individual decision." Indeed, " the universe works through us as part of the universe." [13] Of course, Tillich does not purpose to say that the subject of freedom is a product of the universe, or the past, as such, but that what man is as the subject of freedom is mediated by the whole of reality. Secondly, freedom has a destiny in the sense that its goal and proper objects are given to it. Without destiny in this second aspect freedom loses its definiteness, its meaning, and becomes arbitrariness.[14] Insofar as the self is in a sense future, something yet to come, it is free to " exist," to stand out of its present condition as destined by the past, " in order to be

[11] " Man is man because he has freedom, but he has freedom only in polar interdependence with destiny." (*S.T.*, I, 182.) As an ontological polarity, all of reality participates in it. Our concern, however, is not with freedom generally, but only with the freedom of man.

[12] *Ibid.*, pp. 184–185.

[13] *S.T.*, II, 42.

[14] *Ibid.*, pp. 62 f., 130.

finite freedom." [15] Freedom is finite because its possibilities are not implicit in its past or present as such and must be ever manifested to freedom as a future destiny.

Destiny is able to provide freedom with its true subject and true objects, with its beginning and end, because it expresses the divine " creaturely self-realization which simultaneously is freedom and destiny." [16] Through his " sustaining creativity " God provides the continuity of the structure of reality as the basis of being and acting without which " finite being would not be able to identify itself with itself or anything with anything." [17] The " sustaining creativity " sustains not only the identity of the centered self, but also its roots in being, so that man exercises his freedom in unity with the whole of reality. God's " directing creativity," experienced as providence, is the activity of God which provides freedom with its proper objects, directing it toward its *telos.* " It is the side of the divine creativity which is related to the future." [18]

The concept of creativity indicates that the true subject and object of freedom — destiny as past and destiny as future — transcend the past and the future through which they appear. It designates the " ' divine condition ' which is present in every group of finite conditions and in the totality of finite conditions." [19] Neither the past as such nor the future as such is man's destiny, but rather the abiding and the universal in man's past as well as the eternal in the future. True freedom is the movement from a " grasping " of the reason of the past toward a rational " shaping " of the future.[20] Freedom lives on the boundary between past and future. It is the form of the present, but a present without its true destiny if not centered in reason and seeking reason, if not moving from reason to reason, from eternity to eternity, from creation to creation. Insofar as the man who is free is always on the move and can never be said to possess himself, he " transcends everything in the

15 *S.T.,* I, 255.   18 *Ibid.,* p. 264.
16 *Ibid.,* p. 256.   19 *Ibid.,* p. 267.
17 *Ibid.,* p. 262.   20 *Ibid.,* p. 76.

historical order, all the heights and depths of his own existence." [21] Yet insofar as he moves from the eternal toward the eternal this nonpossession is not tragic, for he can be said to "participate in something infinite, in an order which is not transitory, not self-destructive, not tragic." [22]

Tillich's theology resembles a symphony in which the basic themes are first stated and then reintroduced in many variations. We found that Tillich could speak of freedom only in terms of its polarity with reason, which appears subjectively as the universals of language and objectively as the rational depth of reality. Formally speaking, freedom can be understood only in correlation with its destiny, which, corresponding to the subjective and objective forms of reason, is both the self as given and the self to be given. The self is given not by the past or the future as such, but by the divine, sustaining, and directing creativity expressed in and through these. Man in his freedom is man in the moment — in the present in which eternity passes out of the past into the future through the mediation of destiny and the divine creativity.[23]

Finally, we should mention the *kairos,* which is Tillich's designation for the moment of freedom filled with eternity. The consciousness of the *kairos* is "dependent on one's being inwardly grasped by the fate and destiny of the time." One is grasped "inwardly" when he is grasped in freedom. Fate and destiny "cannot be demonstrated and forced; it is deed and freedom." *Kairos,* then, is a moment of "unique decision for or against the unconditional." [24]

Tillich's discussions in *Systematic Theology* are carried on

[21] Paul Tillich, *The Shaking of the Foundations* (Charles Scribner's Sons, 1948), p. 22.

[22] *Ibid.*

[23] Paul Tillich, *The Religious Situation,* tr. by H. Richard Niebuhr (Living Age Books, Meridian Books, Inc., 1960), pp. 32 f.

[24] *The Protestant Era,* p. 474. George Tavard states that the term *kairos,* as used by Tillich, "designates the appeal of an historical event to man's free decision," an appeal that is issued by the unconditional dimension of history (George H. Tavard, *Paul Tillich and the Christian Message,* p. 89; Charles Scribner's Sons, 1961).

in such a formal and refined manner that it is easy to lose sight
of the real substance of his meanings. Right now, one might
well ask, just what does this discussion of freedom and destiny,
kairos, past and present, etc., come to? The substance of the
very sophisticated discussion concerning freedom and destiny
in *Systematic Theology* is presented more concretely in the
discussion of "*Kairos* and *Logos*" in *Interpretation of History,*[25] where Tillich indicates that he agrees with Böhme,
Schelling, and to an extent Hegel, that the ultimate reality is
an eternal idea with an abysmal depth, dynamic and ever unfolding in history. It manifests itself subjectively as the given,
logical necessities of the personal subject — the destiny of freedom in the form of the givenness of the self. We spoke in this
connection of the universals of language, which are to be received as unconditionally binding. However, man cannot find
truth or know the eternal by the merely formal pursuit of
these innate ideas and logical necessities. Rather, the eternal
moves on in the world of history, out of the past into the future, and confronts the person as "something foreign . . .
and yet capable of interpretation by the person." [26] In this
sense, history unfolds man's future destiny and presents to
freedom its proper objects. These objects do not lie on the
surface, but are the hidden depths of reality to be grasped and
engaged in an act of interpretation by the subject. Reality is
not the self with its ideas; it is not the empirical world; rather,
it is the rational depth that emerges in the act of interpretation
through the coming together of these two factors in the freedom of the individual. The act of interpretation, the coincidence of destiny as past and future in the freedom of the interpreting individual, is the act in which the eternal idea unfolds itself.

[25] Paul Tillich, *The Interpretation of History,* tr. by N. A. Rasetzki
and Elsa L. Talmey (Charles Scribner's Sons, 1936) , pp. 123–175.

[26] *Ibid.,* p. 142. Tavard's interpretation is clarifying. He states that according to Tillich " history is made of what, in the development of man's
free decisions, is revelatory of the Unconditioned" (*Paul Tillich,*
pp. 86 f.) .

Presupposed in this act of interpretation is the basic decision for the " unconditional," for the fact that the eternal has infinite possibilities which relativize the subject, the object, and every act of interpretation, and which demand, therefore, a constant repetition of the event of interpretation in the free encounter of subject and object. The act of interpretation is what Tillich calls dialectics; it is what Hegel engaged in (although his dialectics suffered the lack of commitment to the unconditioned), and it is the substance of true freedom — freedom subject to its destiny.

Freedom for Destiny

The question that now presses is: What happens to eternity as it passes through the present? What happens to the eternal in view of the fact that it realizes itself through freedom? Stated a bit differently, how free and creative is the event of interpretation? We have come to see that eternity has a history — it is dynamic and living. But is time, finite freedom, or individual personality, also living and dynamic; or, rather, is there any genuine place for individuality in the encounter with eternity?

Tillich answers that God's directing creativity, which takes man toward his future destiny, " uses all factors, both those given by freedom and those given by destiny." [27] In fact, " my freedom participates in shaping my destiny." [28] However, Tillich has stated that destiny is the basis and goal of freedom, that freedom is meaningless without the eternity that passes through freedom out of the past into the future. It would appear then that freedom is not a material factor in man's destiny, and is not taken into account by destiny, except insofar as the future of eternity builds upon the eternal actualized in the past through freedom. Freedom is an ontological element simply because being depends on freedom for its self-realization, and it has neither content nor meaning save in the acceptance of its destiny — the eternity of being-itself. When

[27] S.T., I, 267.　　　　[28] Ibid., p. 185.

freedom becomes anything more than this passive vehicle of destiny and asserts itself as such, it forfeits its essential nature, its unity with being, and brings the "fall" from essence to existence. However, freedom cannot exercise itself without at least a measure of self-consciousness, and thus without the fall. Its actuality or existence is inevitably and at the same time its estrangement and fall.

FREEDOM-FROM

Since freedom exists in a fall from being, it receives from the beginning a negative dimension, and must also be a freedom-from. This negative dimension of freedom is, in traditional language, freedom from sin. However, it is somewhat difficult in Tillich's thought to draw sharply the line between essence and existence, between creation and the fall into sin, because, as we have seen, the fall of freedom seems to be a necessary part of its created nature, so that sin is an expression of freedom as well as that which is alien to it. We ask about the negative dimension of freedom by first considering the "fall."

The Fall of Freedom

The "inevitability" of freedom's fall roots in four aspects of its essential relationship to being. The first is the basic, polar relationship with destiny, which means, as we recall, that freedom does not contain its own meaning.[29] The second aspect is the conscious realization by freedom that if it is limited by destiny it is finite, "related to and excluded from infinity" and, at the same time, participating in nonbeing. The third element is "anxiety," and the fourth is "temptation."[30]

Essentially, in its dreaming innocence and mere potentiality, freedom is open to its destiny. However, in the first moment of self-consciousness, on the threshold of existence, freedom becomes aware of the claim of destiny and of itself as claimed by destiny. A tension arises. Freedom recognizes that its being and meaning lie not in itself but in its polar opposite, in

<hr>

[29] *Ibid.*, pp. 182 f.   [30] *S.T.*, II, 33–36.

destiny. Lacking the unity with destiny which should be the foundation of its decisions, freedom becomes anxious, anxious that if it does exercise itself it will do so without its true destiny and thus fall victim to a partial or alien destiny. But while freedom lacks unity with being and meaning, it appears to be quite one with nonbeing and meaninglessness, such that it has the dubious choice of not actualizing itself and remaining a potentiality for being, or of actualizing itself and also the destructive actuality of nonbeing.[31] Theodore Runyon well states the problem. " To exist is to be separated," and " to the extent that existence is separated from essence it is subject to the attacks of demonic nonbeing." But, to exist and be separated is " to have one's own destiny as a self." [32] Selfhood is to be had only at the cost of meaning and the suffering of demonic threats. Freedom is indeed justly anxious.

The situation is more complicated, however. Nonbeing, and therefore freedom, is not altogether evil. Both nonbeing and freedom are essential elements in the structure of being. Nonbeing is essential to being's life, to its self-consciousness and self-realization. We have already heard Tillich say that " the depth of reality is freedom, the ultimate power of being over itself." Being's ultimate power, its power for life and history, roots in its capacity to become a problem to itself, through freedom and nonbeing. The divine — being-itself — transcends itself through human freedom and nonbeing in order to return to itself in a powerful manifestation of the power of being. Insofar as human freedom is the outward form of this divine self-transcendence, Charles Hartshorne's assessment is correct: " The distinction between God and everything else must fall

[31] E. C. Rust comments on Tillich's position. " Out of the inexhaustible depths of being by which personality and freedom are sustained, the demonic wells up personality." Nonbeing, the demonic, "attacks man at his weakest point, constraining him to his sinful decision by making an appeal to his freedom " (E. C. Rust, *The Christian Understanding of History*, pp. 221 f.; London: Lutterworth Press, 1947).

[32] Theodore Runyon, Jr., *The Immediate Awareness of the Unconditioned and the Interpretation of History in the Theology of Paul Tillich* (Göttingen: Theodore Runyon, Jr., 1958), pp. 36, 39.

within God." [33] This means that in one sense freedom and nonbeing are necessary to being-itself. Room seems to be left for freedom.[34] Insofar as freedom and nonbeing, by the destruction of form and meaning, are the potentiality for new forms, they are not absolutely demonic; to the degree that they resist new forms they tend to be absolutely demonic.[35] David Roberts' comment is appropriate: " Many readers will be baffled by the idea that the actualization of finite freedom is, from one point of view, the *telos* of creation, and, from another point of view, the ruination of creation." [36] It appears that " eschatological fulfillment would involve the obliteration of individual beings." [37]

The anxiety of freedom makes sense, and temptation is inevitable.[38] Freedom's anxiety before the possibility of denied actuality tempts it to elect actuality and suffer alienation from being and a " fall " into nonbeing and an alien destiny. This fall is " the transhistorical quality of all events in time and space." [39] It is the ontological condition that logically precedes history and renders it meaningful, for without the separation of being from itself the dynamic evolution of being which is the meaning of history would be impossible. The fall, then, does not happen in history; it is the very meaning of creation, the ground of history. Reinhold Niebuhr contends that Tillich's identification of creation and fall ontologizes away the fall, so that it is no longer a matter of personal guilt.[40] It seems,

[33] Charles Hartshorne, " Tillich and the Other Great Tradition," *Anglican Theological Review*, 43 (1961), 245.

[34] D'Arcy compliments Tillich for again " making room for freedom." By contrast, " the weakness of Hegel and many other philosophers of history lay in their too formal sequence of ideas which made the work of the spirit inevitably deterministic " (M. C. D'Arcy, S.J., *The Sense of History*, p. 146; London: Faber & Faber, Ltd., 1959).

[35] Runyon, p. 27.

[36] " Tillich's Doctrine of Man," *The Theology of Paul Tillich*, p. 126.

[37] Bernard Loomer, " Tillich's Theology of Correlation," *Journal of Religion*, 36 (1956), 156.

[38] *S.T.*, II, 32.

[39] *Ibid.*, p. 40.

[40] *The Theology of Paul Tillich*, pp. 219 ff.

though, that the problem is even more basic; Tillich not only ontologizes away guilt, he ontologizes away man himself. Man as finite freedom is so constituted that his actuality is his fall; innocence is to be had only at the price of nonexistence. In other words, man exists essentially when he regards his particularity and actuality as nothing and being-as-such as everything — the ultimate concern.

Freedom, as the creative contribution of the interpreter of history, has meaning only as it is overcome in the process of eternity's self-realization. The dignity of the finite and free individual rests not in what he brings to the interpretive task, not the creative newness he expresses in the encounter with reality, but rather in whatever newness the evolving eternal idea brings out of his freedom. It is better to say, then, that eternity creates new meaning through freedom than to say that man through freedom is a creator of meaning.

The Bondage of Freedom

Although freedom actualizes itself in alienation from its true destiny, the polarity of freedom and destiny is nevertheless maintained, for destiny as the true ground and subject of freedom now manifests itself distortedly as inward and arbitrary compulsion,[41] and destiny as the source of freedom's true objects now appears behind the veil of external necessity. Freedom's situation is desperate and ultimately illusory, since despite its self-assertion in the rejection of its true destiny, it nevertheless suffers a threatening destiny that would alienate it from the being it seeks; sin and separation become its fate. Freedom is " imbedded . . . in the universal destiny of existence." [42] Unstructured by the creative power of being, freedom is subjected to the bondage of " the structures of destruction."

The structure of destruction manifests itself relative to the other polar elements in the structure of reality — the polarities

41 " A contingent motive replaces the center [of the self]." (*S.T.*, II, 63.)
42 *Ibid.*, p. 38.

of vitality and intention, and individuality and participation. The basic dimension of personal existence is, however, freedom in polarity with destiny, for freedom has the power to rupture the proper relation between the other polarities, between dynamics and form and individuality and participation. Because freedom is so decisive for the understanding of existence, it is appropriate and characteristic for Tillich to designate personal existence broadly as "finite freedom," implying at the same time the other subjective polarities of individuality and vitality.

Freedom in the narrow sense is the ability of man to stand out of being, to move away *from* being. Vitality is his ability to be free for being, in order to be a living person, a being responsible for new truth and meaning. In his vitality he is free not only to "exist" and stand in himself *out* of being, but also to exist in the sense of standing out of nonbeing *into* being. He is free not only to take his distance from what is, to actualize nonbeing, but he is also free to move from nonbeing toward being. This is what is meant when Tillich states that dynamics or vitality is "meontic," the "potentiality of being, which is nonbeing in contrast to things that have a form, and the power of being in contrast to pure nonbeing." [43] Dynamics is thus another symbol for the fact that freedom is not only responsible to its destiny as the self that is given, but is responsible also for destiny as the *telos,* the self that is yet to be given. Since destiny is the polar opposite of freedom, we could say that freedom in its broader meaning includes the element of vitality.

Now, in the conditions of existence, man is driven in all directions without any definite aim and content. "His dynamics are distorted into a formless urge for self-transcendence. . . . One can speak of the 'temptation of the new.'" [44] At the same time, dynamics abstracted from form are immediately threatened by the abstracted forms which, void of life and appearing now as external law, threaten to rob life of all

[43] *S.T.,* I, 179.   [44] *Ibid.,* II, 64.

vitality. So, in existence a person tends either toward "rebellious outbreaks of dynamic forces leading to chaos," or in reaction, toward "legalism without creativity," or even toward the suppression altogether of dynamic forces.[45] He tends to be extremely liberal or extremely conservative.

The structure of destruction operates analogously in the polarity of individualization and participation. The element of individualization indicates that a person not only exists, and lives, but that he does so in the particularity and concreteness of his individual personality.[46] However, man is not merely an individual; he also participates. He exists individually, concretely, in order to exist in community with the rest of reality through which he participates in being and meaning. Man is genuinely free, free for his true destiny, genuinely creative, creating authentic forms, only when as an individual he seeks reunion with the world around him. Tillich is not a strict idealist because of this insistence that man finds himself and his destiny not by retreat into himself, but by a genuine participation in the world. Because participation is also man's destiny — the polar opposite of freedom — individualization may be understood as a dimension or aspect of freedom. That man exists as a participating individual means that he exists in love, in "the drive towards the unity of the separated." [47] Under the conditions of estrangement, however, love is denied, and the individual tends to shut himself up within himself and refuse participation. The result is that the objective world outside in turn denies individuality and subjectivity, and would reduce the individual self to a mere object, to one of a

45 *Ibid.*

46 *Ibid.*, I, 174 ff.; II, 65 f.

47 *Love, Power, and Justice: Ontological Analyses and Ethical Applications* (A Galaxy Book, Oxford University Press, 1960), p. 25. Heinrich Ott is wrong in contrasting the dynamic ontology of the later Heidegger with a so-called static and unhistoric ontology of Tillich. Carl Michalson also seems overly harsh with Tillich at this point. See *The Later Heidegger and Theology*, Vol. I of *New Frontiers in Theology*, ed. by James M. Robinson and John B. Cobb, Jr. (Harper & Row, Publishers, Inc., 1963), pp. 207, 152 f.

species.[48] Arbitrary freedom is threatened by determinism, formless dynamics by legalism, and nonparticipating individuality by collectivism. Altogether, finite freedom and existence, when it asserts itself as such, suffers oppression by the objective polarities which are its own destiny.

The above discussion of the polar elements indicates that the line of conceptual separation between them is quite fine, and that they could all be subsumed under the notion of freedom. The individual participates through universals, dynamics are effective through forms, and freedom is experienced within the larger structures to which the individual structure belongs. It is significant that in the discussion of the structure of freedom, the terms *freedom* and *individual* are interchangeable. Freedom is the most general category, as is destiny, its polar opposite. Essentially, man is self-related and free when he has an inward vitality that is properly directed and formed, and when, as a discreet individual, he participates in the whole of reality — when, in other words, he " freely " accepts his destiny.

Alienated from the objective polarities, the existing free individual is " estranged from the ground of his being, from other beings, and [thus] from himself "; he exists in unbelief, in the " disruption of . . . [his] cognitive participation in God," in which he actualizes himself without trusting in God.[49] The corollary of unbelief is the pride (*hubris*) in which the self, isolated from the objective polarities, in a freedom without its destiny, exalts itself and becomes its own object.[50] And just as unbelief means pride, so pride means the concupiscence which results because the estranged sinner, now separated from being and meaning, from true objects, is void of meaning and fullness and is driven by an insatiable and unbounded hunger. His " ' poverty ' makes him seek for abundance." [51] In terms of our foregoing discussion of the elements, we may say that believing himself to be a self without objects, the sinner asserts himself against the objective. This is pride. But, void of

48 *S.T.*, II, 66.   50 *Ibid.*, pp. 49 ff.
49 *Ibid.*, pp. 44, 47.   51 *Ibid.*, p. 52.

meaningless content, he covets indiscriminately the objects, and either becomes their slave in order to possess them or tries to devour and possess them without sacrifice.

Man experiences the structure of destruction at the ontic level of finite existence in the form of a loneliness and suffering that leads ultimately to despair and the quest for the new being.[52] In the condition of estrangement man suffers because he exists without his essential selfhood and can possess his essential self, apparently, only with the sacrifice of his existence. Loneliness also typifies his existence, insofar as he exists in his freedom — so-called — only at the expense of community and participation with others. There is, says Tillich, an essential solitude (finite individuality) that is a corollary of free and responsible participation, whereas existential loneliness is a destructive reality and is incapable of relationship. The consequence of suffering and loneliness is doubt — doubt that the self as self is sufficient and that it contains its own goodness and meaning. Doubt drives toward despair, toward " the conflict, on the one hand, between what one potentially is and therefore ought to be, and, on the other hand, what one actually is in the combination of freedom and destiny." [53] In substance, despair is the conflict between existence and essence, between finitude and the infinite. In the moment of despair, in the depths of this conflict, the beleaguered spirit looks for a true freedom, for a freedom from the freedom of existence and a freedom for what Tillich calls " the New Being."

In sum, from what is the Christian free? In the first place, he is free from being. To be free means to stand out of being in order to make the choice of being. It means to be free from one's destiny so that it may be destiny and not an external fate. It means to stand apart from the world as an individual in order to participate personally, individually, in its reality. It means to be vital, to have possibilities for the future and to be the means by which new forms of being are actualized. There is, therefore, in man's essential freedom for being also an

[52] *Ibid.*, pp. 66–78.   [53] *Ibid.*, p. 75.

essential freedom from being. In this vein Tillich designates the essential individuality of the finite person as solitude, to be distinguished from its existential counterpart of loneliness. However, essential freedom — freedom-for and freedom-from — is only a potentiality. Existential, actual freedom is already so free from being and free for itself that it has become its own enemy; henceforth, freedom-from must include a freedom from that freedom which has alienated itself from its destiny in being. Certainly, true freedom will have the form of freedom from a heteronomous fate and necessity, from external law, and from the power of a collective and objectified world. But since these threats to freedom are imposed as a result of freedom's self-centeredness, the final need is for a freedom from freedom itself — a new freedom in being that Tillich designates as " the reality of the New Being."

FREEDOM FOR FREEDOM

Freedom and Jesus as the Christ

While existence tends to separate the polar elements and destroy the structure of reality, life is never mere existence; existence itself is in polar tension with being; it lives in being so that the structure of being is manifest now as the structure of destruction. Freedom's destiny is its bondage. This fact that freedom still has a destiny, that freedom's sin and arbitrariness are also a matter of destiny, " does not make man's consciousness of guilt unreal; but it does liberate him from the unrealistic assumption that in every moment he has the undetermined freedom to decide in whatever way he chooses." [54] Consequently, " no act within the context of existential estrangement can overcome existential estrangement. Destiny keeps freedom in bondage without eliminating it." [55] This situation demands not a new decision of the will but a new will, not a new expression of the existing structure of man's being but a new structure of being, a new being itself. This

[54] *Ibid.*, p. 57.   [55] *Ibid.*, p. 78.

New Being will not be altogether new and unconnected with the one who receives it, for it is actually a new manifestation of man's original and essential being, the being against which existence has revolted and in which existence has any being or meaning at all.[56] The New Being reunites freedom with its true destiny. This is New Being not only because it reaches beyond the limits of existence but also because it goes beyond the conditions of mere essence, where being is potential but not actual.[57] It overcomes finite freedom, freedom's arbitrariness, by rooting it in being. The New Being also overcomes the law, for under the conditions of existence essential being stands over existence, judging it as a law, but when one participates in the New Being essence is " taken into his existence and actualized in it." [58] That is, the New Being is taken up into freedom. In this reconciliation of freedom and destiny history comes to its end, so that " nothing qualitatively new in the dimension of the ultimate can be produced by history which is not implicitly present in the New Being in Jesus as the Christ." [59] Freedom can never be more free than by its participation in the New Being.

This entrance of the ultimate into existence through Jesus as the Christ is a fulfillment " in principle " insofar as " no other principle of fulfilment can be expected. In him [Jesus as the reality of the New Being] has appeared what fulfilment qualitatively means." [60] It is relevant to the question of freedom to ask why this end or fulfillment must be only " in principle." We have seen how freedom's actuality meant estrangement from essence. Does this mean that the actuality of essence in the New Being *de facto* is possible only when freedom is over-

[56] *Ibid.*, p. 79.

[57] *Ibid.*, p. 119. " The New Being is new in so far as it is the undistorted manifestation of essential being within and under the conditions of existence. It is new in two respects: it is new in contrast to the merely potential character of essential being; and it is new over against the estranged character of existential being." (*Ibid.*)

[58] *Ibid.*

[59] *Ibid.*, pp. 119 f.

[60] *Ibid.*, p. 119.

come, and that as long as free, finite existence endures, the New Being must remain actual only " in principle " — *de jure?* Is the law overcome by essence coming into freedom or by its overcoming freedom?

The New Being has appeared in Jesus " as the Christ " inasmuch as in him essence has appeared undistorted in the conditions of existence. Therefore, if there is an essential freedom in the conditions of existence it is here, in Jesus as the Christ. Because Tillich's ontological analysis of freedom seems to make any real, actual unity of finite, existential freedom with its essential destiny inconceivable, close attention must be given to the Christological question of the unity between Jesus of Nazareth as finite freedom with his reality as a manifestation of being under the conditions of existence. The same close attention will also be given to the concept of faith, in which the believer appropriates the New Being, to see if it is indeed appropriated by and contained within the finite freedom of the individual believer.

The Freedom of Jesus

Tillich does insist that Jesus, in his finite, free existence, bears the New Being. He states that " only where existence is most radically existence — in him who is finite freedom — can existence be conquered." [61] The New Being is expressed in the totality of Jesus' personal existence — in his words, his deeds, and his sufferings.[62] It is *expressed in* these; it is not identical with any one aspect as such — word, deed, or suffering.[63] With this emphasis Tillich seems to be saying that we cannot separate the manifestations of personality from the personal cen-

[61] *Ibid.,* p. 120.
[62] *Ibid.,* pp. 121 ff.
[63] By stressing that the New Being is expressed in the totality of his being — in his words, works, and sufferings — Tillich rejects: (1) liberal theology which apotheosizes the teachings of Jesus into a new law, (2) pietistic and Roman Catholic traditions which do the same with Jesus' life and work through conceptions of the *imitatio Christi,* and (3) atonement theories, such as Anselm's, which separate Jesus' sacrifice from his being as the Christ.

ter, that we cannot separate the expressions of freedom from freedom itself, and that the center and subject of this personal expression is the New Being. However, a closer examination does not make it so evident that Tillich's concern is for the personal center, the freedom of Jesus. He says that it is " not his actions but the being out of which his actions come [that] makes him the Christ." But " the being out of which his actions come " is not his *personal* being, for "without the continuous sacrifice of himself as a particular individual under the conditions of existence to himself as the bearer of the New Being, he could not have been the Christ." [64] Jesus is Christ without his actions, without his individuality — without his finite freedom. Evidently Jesus' real freedom is his freedom to surrender freedom. When one really encounters Jesus of the Gospels, " it is an occasion of the encounter of the New Being with the forces of estrangement, not some specific psychological behaviour which is involved. . . . The word ' being ' points to the fact that this power is not a matter of someone's good will but that it is a gift which precedes or determines the character of every act of the will." [65] It is not a matter of personal freedom, of dynamic, creative individuality, but of a " power " that " determines." The New Being indeed is not Jesus' words, deeds, or death; nor is it his psychology, his " character structure," nor his " good will." [66] It is not his centered self. It is not his freedom.

This impression is strengthened by Tillich's examination of the conquest of estrangement by the New Being in Jesus as the Christ.[67] The style of this section is itself instructive. Here, as everywhere, Tillich speaks of Jesus *as the Christ,* indicating that Jesus, the free individual as such, is not the Christ.[68] Til-

[64] *S.T.*, II, 123.
[65] *Ibid.*, p. 125.
[66] *Ibid.*, p. 124.
[67] *Ibid.*, pp. 125–135.
[68] Tillich commits the genetic fallacy by insisting that since the concept of " the Christ " was first distinguished from Jesus by the early Christian community, it was a theological slip for the church to make the simple

lich also consistently uses the passive voice with reference to
Jesus. He states, for example, that the New Testament portrays
Jesus " as the one in whom the conflict between the essential
unity of God and man and man's existential estrangement *is
overcome.*" [69] In Jesus the polar tensions of existence " *are*
eternally *conquered.*" [70] Apparently, then, John the Baptist
misunderstood when, according to the Fourth Gospel, he
pointed to Jesus and said, " Behold, the Lamb of God who
takes away the sins of the world." Not because Jesus is free, but
in spite of his freedom is he the Christ. The paradoxical character of Jesus' being consists, says Tillich, in the fact that " *although he has only finite freedom* under the conditions of time
and space, he is not estranged from the ground of his being." [71]
Tillich understands a paradox as that which transcends all
human expectations, and the expectation for finite freedom is
estrangement.[72] Obviously, freedom is not a factor in Jesus'
existence as one who is reconciled. His personal vocation is
thus passivity — passion. Accordingly, Jesus did *not* remove his
personal center from the divine center; he did *not* elevate himself; he did *not* express worldly desires. " He rejects the term
' good ' as applicable to himself in isolation from God and puts
the problem in the right place, namely, the uniqueness of his
relation to God. His goodness is goodness only insofar as he
participates in the goodness of God." Whenever something
positive is affirmed concerning Jesus as the Christ we have an
instance of rationalization in which a " religious statement of
existential-symbolic character is transformed into a theoretical
statement of rational-objectifying character." [73] The only

---

identification — Jesus Christ. Surely it is possible that this identification is
no mistake, but an act of theological responsibility that affirms the Christological truth of the unity of the divine and the human in the person of
Jesus.

  [69] *S.T.*, II, 125. (Italics mine.)
  [70] *Ibid.*, p. 127. (Italics mine.)
  [71] *Ibid.*, p. 126. (Italics mine.)
  [72] *Ibid.*, I, 57.
  [73] *Ibid.*, II, 127.

affirmations about Jesus affirm his lack of positive goodness. We affirm his finitude, namely, his participation in nonbeing. We affirm the reality of his temptations, namely, the threat of nonbeing over him. Finally, we do affirm the reality of the New Being, namely, the victory of being-itself over nonbeing through Jesus' transparency to being-itself, through his not exercising his finite freedom.

Our attention focuses for the moment on the question of Jesus' temptations. We ask, first, if Jesus is really tempted, and second, if the victory over temptation is truly Jesus' victory. In other words, is Jesus actually the unity of existence and essence; is he really free to sin and not to sin, *posse peccare, et posse non peccare?* Are actual freedom and actual essence compatible? Tillich answers in part that " since Jesus as the Christ is finite freedom, he also confronts real temptation. Possibility is itself temptation." [74] Furthermore, Tillich expressly rejects the Monophysitic heresy that denies the real humanity and temptations of Jesus. Jesus has human, finite freedom; he is subject to temptation and free to sin. However, it is not so clear that Jesus also has what might be termed " infinite freedom," freedom over temptation, freedom for God, truth, and meaning. While Tillich guards against Monophysitism, it seems as if his success is Nestorian, for Jesus' humanity seems entirely separated from the divine reality of redemption. He is suspicious of Jesus' real humanity because of the fear that Jesus' rejection of his temptations would thus be contingent upon the decision of an individual man. It is absurd, on the one hand, to contend " that the universal cause of the human predicament was contingent upon the wrong decision of an individual man," and on the other hand to contend that salvation is contingent upon the right decision of an individual man. " There is no undetermined contingency in the negative and the positive situation of mankind, but there is the unity of freedom and destiny under God's directing creativity." [75] The

[74] *Ibid.*
[75] *Ibid.*, pp. 130 f. J. Heywood Thomas, viewing the problem of Jesus

idea of the polarity of freedom and destiny would be helpful if it were a genuine polarity, but the foregoing references indicate that freedom has only a negative and passive part to play. The New Being is not an achievement of freedom and destiny, but of destiny in and over freedom. Being and not Jesus is savior. In support of this line, Tillich analyzes Jesus' personal psychology, stressing Jesus' "doubt about his own work, as in his hesitation to accept the messianic title, and, above all, his feeling of having been left alone by God without God's expected interference on the Cross." [76] His exegesis is quite dogmatic, and when he speaks of Jesus' "doubt about his own work" he has somehow penetrated the depths of Jesus' spirit in a way reminiscent of the liberal quest. He states that Jesus enjoyed a *"permanent unity with God"* which enabled him to elevate his doubts, his finitude, anxiety, ambiguity, and tragedy "into the truth which transcends every finite truth." Such a truth, if it were imaginable, could not by definition in any way involve Jesus himself. Consequently, "no traces of fanaticism are present in the biblical picture. Jesus does not claim absolute certitude for a finite conviction. He rejects the fanatical attitude of the disciples toward those who do not follow him. In the power of a certitude which transcends certitude and incertitude . . . , he accepts incertitude as an element of finiteness." [77] While the concept of a finite being holding an infinite certitude is itself difficult, such does seem to appear in Jesus' imperious call of disciples, in the demand of unqualified devotion to him, in the apparently "fanatical" rejection of official Judaism, with the fact that he taught "as one who had authority" and not as the scribes and Pharisees who as such had no immediate authority. It helps little for

---

as the Christ from an epistemological perspective, points out that Tillich's neglect of history — i.e., his neglect of Jesus' own life and historical decisions — means that "the doctrine of Jesus as the Christ cannot be fully maintained" (*Paul Tillich: An Appraisal*, p. 88; The Westminster Press, 1963).

[76] *S.T.*, II, p. 132.
[77] *Ibid.*, p. 134.

Tillich to occasionally proof-text, as when he quotes Jesus in the Fourth Gospel: "He who believes in me does not believe in me, but in Him who has sent me." [78] One need only cite John 3:16 and refer to the characteristic "*egō eimi*" passages of the Fourth Gospel. It is too easy and not too clear to say that Jesus' finite and immanent incertitude is transcended by an infinite certainty. The Biblical picture suggests a man in whom the infinite is present, such that his finite decision and deed, his finite freedom, is at once infinite and ultimate. Or, better stated, he appears as one whose humanity is also divine.

In his discussion of the Christological symbols Tillich expressly rejects this possibility of finite God-manhood. His analysis " discloses that the term ' divine nature ' is questionable and that it cannot be applied to the Christ in any meaningful way; for the Christ (who is Jesus of Nazareth) is not beyond essence and existence. If he were, he could not be a personal life living in a limited period of time, . . . tragically involved in existence. The assertion that Jesus as the Christ is *the personal unity* of a divine and a human nature must be replaced by the assertion that in Jesus as the Christ *the eternal unity of God and man* has become historical reality. . . . We replace the inadequate concept ' divine nature ' by the concepts ' eternal God-man-unity ' or ' Eternal God-Manhood.' Such concepts replace a static essence by a dynamic relation." [79] Jesus does not have a divine nature; rather, he reveals the nature of the divine.

This passage demands clarification. The traditional language speaks of *personal* unity and of *two natures*. The changes Tillich proposes touch both aspects. On the one hand, he would eliminate the static concept "nature," and on the other hand, the category of the personal. In effect he does not really change the first statement at all; rather, he proposes something quite other. He seems to object to the static unity of the two natures in the person of Jesus, but his proposed change speaks of eternity, and not of Jesus. Furthermore, it is questionable whether the traditional concept of the union of

[78] *Ibid.*, p. 126.   [79] *Ibid.*, p. 148.

the two natures is so static as Tillich suggests, for it referred
to a personal unity, and the Greek *physis* (nature) connoted
more than a static, physical-like substance. It was a broader
concept that did not exclude the dynamic element.[80] But in
any case, what was a Christological statement, a statement
about Jesus (*personal*) is now an *ontological* statement about
being and eternity. Tillich raises our question for us: " The
question now arises as to whether the replacement of the two-
nature theory by dynamic-relational concepts does not remove
the important idea of ' Incarnation.' Is not a relational concept
a return from a Christology of Incarnation to a Christology of
adoption? " [81] This might be the case if the dynamic-relational
concepts had to do with a concrete, personal, historical relation between deity and Jesus as a historical person with finite
freedom. But Tillich appears to have neither an adoptionist
nor an incarnational Christology. As to the latter, he asks how
we can make sense of the idea that the Word *became* flesh.[82]
He answers that the incarnation of the Logos is " his total
manifestation in a personal life. . . . As Protestantism asserts
the justification of the sinner, so it demands a Christology of
the participation of the Christ in sinful existence, including, at
the same time, its conquest." [83] Conquest means determination,
as we have seen, albeit through freedom. As Tillich expressly
states, God-manhood is " an objective structure and not a state
of man "; therefore, it is neither a state of Jesus nor a reality
in his freedom.[84] It may be said that the New Being partici-

[80] Paul Althaus, for example, points out that the Greek word *physis*
(nature) , while it does connote the physical, is at the same time an inclusive concept which designates what German means by *Wesen* or *Seinswe-
sen*. Therefore, it may be used by modern theology as a protection against
an ethical reductionism. (*Die Christliche Wahrheit*, II, 223 f.; Gütersloh:
C. Bertelsmann, 1949.)

[81] *S.T.*, II, 148.

[82] " It is natural that the question should arise concerning how something which *becomes* something else can remain at the same time what it
is. Or did the Logos otherwise disappear when Jesus of Nazareth was
born? " (*Ibid.*, p. 149.)

[83] *Ibid.*, pp. 149 f.

[84] *Ibid.*, p. 150.

pates in existence *and conquers it*.[85] Tillich's theology does not allow for the freedom of Jesus. The resurrection is not the overcoming of the negation of Jesus and his freedom. " Certainly, it is not the death of an individual man [that is overcome in resurrection], no matter how important. . . . The negativity which is overcome in the Resurrection is that of the disappearance of him whose being was the New Being [obviously distinct from individuality or freedom]. . . . And, since the conquest of such transitoriness is essential for the New Being, Jesus, it appeared, could not have been its bearer." [86] However, apparently inexplicably, the church did regard Jesus the man highly enough to write Gospels. The explanation for this is not to be found in Jesus, but in " an ecstatic experience " of Christians in which " the concrete picture of Jesus of Nazareth became indissolubly united with the reality of the New Being. He is present wherever the New Being is present." [87] Why this should be the case is not clear, to say the least. Jesus, we have learned, could not have been the bearer of the New Being. Evidently embarrassed by this contradiction, Tillich takes back what he has said by observing that this presence of the concrete picture of Jesus of Nazareth " does not have the character of a revived (and transmuted) body, nor does it have the character of the reappearance of an individual soul; it has the character of spiritual presence." [88] Here Tillich quits, leaving the reader to imagine what he means by " spiritual presence."

Faith and the Gift of Freedom

Having considered Jesus as the reality of the New Being, we now ask about the appropriation of the New Being in faith, which, says Tillich, " is the state of being grasped by the New Being as it is manifest in Jesus as the Christ." [89] Like many

85 *Ibid.*, p. 114.
86 *Ibid.*, pp. 156 f.
87 *Ibid.*, p. 157.
88 *Ibid.*
89 *Ibid.*, III, 131. Though the discussion that follows is based largely

words in Tillich's thought, faith is a word that does double
duty and for which there are several synonyms. Faith is "ultimate concern" or "the courage to be." Jesus is the Christ because he freely accepted his destiny in being-itself, because he
was ultimately concerned, because he had authentic faith.
Faith is thus another word for freedom. It is as universal as is
freedom. Just as in the conditions of existence, freedom remains, although in subjection to a false or partial destiny, so
also faith remains, even though it has substituted a penultimate for its ultimate. But also, when by grace the New Being
is manifest and freedom is united with its destiny, so faith is
properly directed toward and authentically concerned for the
ultimate. Faith thus designates both a basic structure of man
under the conditions of existence and estrangement, and his
experience of the New Being. The difference between the two
types of faith is the relative difference between partial and
more perfect forms.[90] It follows from this discussion that faith,
as a basic structure of finite existence, cannot, even in its absolute form, be *essentially* related to any particular finite existence, such as Jesus of Nazareth; it is a general reality and
possibility. This same point was made by our Christological
analysis, which demonstrated that the reality of Jesus as the
Christ does not attach to his personality or to his particular individuality.

The question, then, of the gift of freedom shifts from a consideration of Jesus as the Christ to an examination of faith.
For the Christian, faith is bestowed by grace through the mediation of the symbol of Jesus as the Christ, but it is faith or
the New Being that is given, and not Jesus himself. By the

---

upon Tillich's *The Courage to Be* (Yale University Press, 1952) and *The
Dynamics of Faith* (Harper & Brothers, 1957), faith is also the subject of
important sections of *S.T.*, III (see pp. 129 f.). Yet here Tillich directs his
readers to *Dynamics of Faith* for a discussion of faith (*S.T.*, III, 129). He
might well have mentioned in addition *The Courage to Be* inasmuch as
he defines faith also as courage (*S.T.*, III, 133).

90 Tillich designates these two types of faith — which are distinguished
not only as partial and more perfect, but also as general and particular —
as "formal" and "material" (*S.T.*, III, 130 f.).

grace of God (being-itself) Jesus serves, as a miracle does, to mediate faith that is received in a moment of ecstasy, a moment in which the individual realizes that which is beyond all the possibilities of existence. Granted that the Christian experience of faith roots in the witness to Jesus as the Christ, we are directed nevertheless to the question of faith as such and its freedom.

The essential elements of faith are indicated in the following passage in which Tillich discusses the dynamics of faith in terms of " the courage to be ": " Since the relation of man to the ground of his being must be expressed in symbols taken from the structure of being, the polarity of participation and individualization determines the special character of this relation as it determines the special character of the courage to be. If participation is dominant, the relation to being-itself has a mystical character, if individualization prevails the relation to being-itself has a personal character, if both poles are accepted and transcended the relation to being-itself has the character of faith." [91] From this we may extract the following tentative definition of faith. Faith is a relationship to being-itself, which is both mystical and personal, participating and free, and yet one in which participation and freedom are transcended in faith as " the courage to be." Our task now is to understand what it means to say that the relation of faith transcends subject and object in " the courage to be," that " in the act of faith that which is the source of this act is present beyond the cleavage of subject and object." [92]

In order to answer this question, it is helpful to distinguish three elements of faith: (1) the individual believer, in polar tension with participation, (2) the existential context, and (3) the essential content. The first element is experienced as the structure of the relationship, the second as anxiety, and the third as courage. Altogether, faith is the structure of the individual in which courage is overcoming anxiety. Now, true or

[91] *The Courage to Be,* pp. 156 f.
[92] *The Dynamics of Faith,* p. 11.

absolute faith may be distinguished from less adequate forms, those forms which it includes and transcends, by comparing it with these lesser forms relative to each of these elements. We can speak of the anxiety it conquers, of the courage it gives, and of its structure relative to the polarity of individualization and participation. In this analysis it will help to remember that Tillich also defines faith as " the state of being ultimately concerned." This expression reflects very well the structural element, the tension between and unity of individualization and participation, between subjectivity and objectivity, between the quality of concern and the object of concern. In this general sense, faith is universal, for every man is concerned about the ultimate, about the ground of his being. Absolute faith, however, is not universal. In *The Courage to Be,* Tillich shows that every man is related to the ultimate, but that not every man has a relationship of " faith " (meaning authentic faith) .[93] We may explain the difference and note the dialectic movement from the lower forms of faith to the higher forms and to absolute faith first with respect to the structure of faith, the subject-object polarity.

The Polarity of Faith

In the lower forms of faith, the ultimate is identified with the penultimate — the ground of being with an element in the structure of being. We may still speak of faith, however, because in such acts the individual is nevertheless concerned for the ultimate. In one form of such faith the individual affirms himself as a part and seeks to find ultimacy through participation at the expense of the pole of individuality and freedom. It is an act of freedom in which freedom surrenders itself to the absolutized pole of participation. Its inadequacy rests, however, not so much in its surrender of freedom as in the fact that it does not transcend the pole of participation for the ground of being. All forms of modern collectivism, racism, nationalism, etc., are expressions of this type of faith.[94]

[93] *The Courage to Be,* pp. 156 f.   [94] *Ibid.,* pp. 90 ff.

Against this absolutizing of participation existentialism protests on behalf of the self and freedom.[95] In its most radical
form it does this at the expense of all participation so that the
individual and his freedom are all, *a se*. This faith, in which
one finds the ultimate as oneself, is valid as a protest against
the affirmation of oneself as a part; however, as an expression
of ultimate concern it is lacking, for it elevates to ultimacy the
pole of individuality and freedom. This is to say that neither
type of faith, affirmation of oneself as a part or as oneself, could
be called authentic faith, for each sacrifices the ground of being for an element of being. Insofar as each type is a threat to
the other, their claims to ultimacy are ever in jeopardy, and
the quest for true faith, for being-itself, remains.

True faith by contrast is not an affirmation or elevation of
the self at all, either as such or as a part; it is the condition of
being grasped by the ground of being. Therefore a distinction
is made between being-itself, or the ground of being, and the
structures of being. The object of faith is neither the self
nor its world; rather, it is the ground of both. The subjective
and objective elements, which otherwise tend to separate, are
held together by their unity in this transcendent ground and
by the fact that this ground of being manifests itself through
them. If the individual polarity is stressed, then we may speak
of personal faith; if the pole of participation is stressed, then
we may speak of faith as mysticism. In personal faith such as
is found in the elements of the Jewish-Christian tradition, the
religious experience will be expressed as " a personal encounter
with God." [96] Personal faith, says Tillich, suffers inner contradictions and limitations, which reveal at the same time its
authenticity. The lowest forms of faith are inwardly consistent
and therefore have to be judged and brought down from the
outside, by the threat of an equally consistent and wholly contradictory form. But personal faith, since it is a being grasped
by the ultimate, relativizes its own forms and is inwardly driven
beyond itself to absolute faith. That is, personal faith is the

[95] *Ibid.*, pp. 123 ff.   [96] *Ibid.*, p. 160.

PAUL TILLICH: FREEDOM TO BE 101

effort to understand in subjective and personal terms the experience of being grasped by the reality which transcends subject and object. Its limitation is its failure to comprehend that while God does stand " in the divine-human reciprocity " he does so " only as he who transcends it and comprises both sides of the reciprocity. He reacts, but he reacts to that which is his own act working through our finite freedom. He never can become a mere object. This is the limit of the symbols of reciprocity." [97] In these terms Tillich objects to Brunner's concept of faith as encounter or " fellowship " with God. " If God is more than one side of a fellowship [and he is], the category of 'fellowship' loses its ultimacy . . . and the question of transpersonal categories arises." [98]

Mysticism is therefore an advancement upon personal religion, for it does express itself in transpersonal categories, in terms of the pole of participation. " In mysticism the individual self strives for a participation in the ground of being which approaches identification." [99] In the mystical experience one draws power of self-affirmation from the experience of the power of being-itself with which one is united. It is an experience of true participation in which the subject-object relationship is overcome. It is not an experience *within* the categories of being, but rather *through* them in such a fashion that they are transcended.

With mysticism we move closer to " absolute faith," but before examining this concept it is in order to retrace our steps to examine the four types of faith with respect to the anxiety they conquer and the courage they express. Faith moves dialectically through these four types to absolute faith because of

[97] Paul Tillich, *Biblical Religion and the Search for Ultimate Reality* (The University of Chicago Press, 1955), p. 81. This book is generally dedicated to the task of overcoming the limitations of personal faith.

[98] *The Theology of Emil Brunner*, ed. by Charles W. Kegley (The Macmillan Company, 1962), pp. 101 f. Emil Brunner responds to Tillich: " My thinking is oriented differently from that of Tillich. I do not ask philosophically if in this concept, ' Encounter,' there are still other relationships contained than the I-Thou " (p. 334).

[99] *The Courage to Be*, p. 157.

the failure of each stage and type of faith to deal adequately
with anxiety and to provide ultimate courage. Faith holds together anxiety and courage, nonbeing and being, in such a
way that courage prevails. In existence as such, anxiety and
courage coexist but so that anxiety prevails over courage. As
faith approximates absolute faith the balance is shifted in the
other direction so that courage overcomes anxiety.

The Courage of Faith

Let us examine now these elements, courage and anxiety,
more carefully in the context of faith. In anxiety, man experiences the negation of nonbeing. In courage, man accepts the
possibilities of being. Speaking in terms of freedom, freedom
in existence is tempted by nonbeing; in faith it is open to being
in spite of nonbeing. Courage, then, is freedom set free, is man
as he is liberated for freedom's genuine possibilities. " Courage
is the self-affirmation of being in spite of the fact of nonbeing." [100] Anxiety, as fear of nonbeing and meaninglessness,
has no real object except that object which is " the negation of
every object " and " which by its very nature cannot be known,
because it is nonbeing." [101] There are three basic forms of anxiety, determined by the nature of being. " Nonbeing threatens
man's ontic self-affirmation, relatively in terms of fate, absolutely in terms of death. It threatens man's spiritual self-affirmation, relatively in terms of emptiness, absolutely in terms of
meaninglessness. It threatens man's moral self-affirmation, relatively in terms of guilt, absolutely in terms of condemnation." [102]

The first anxiety roots in the threat of nonbeing at the point
of the polarity of individuality and participation. Separated
from the structure of reality, the finite, individual self is threatened relatively in its simple existence by the world of objects
external to it.[103] It is the fear of complete loss of self implied
by biological extinction. The many contingencies of man's

100 *Ibid.*, p. 155.
101 *Ibid.*, pp. 36–37.
102 *Ibid.*, p. 41.
103 *Ibid.*, p. 45.

spatial, temporal existence are no longer experienced as the source of true destiny but, rather, as a forbidding fate. Ultimately, it is in death that nonbeing threatens the very existence of the individual self.

The second anxiety is due to the attack of nonbeing upon the polarity of dynamics and form. It is the anxiety about one's "spiritual self-affirmation" — about his ability to express his power and dynamics meaningfully.[104] Its relative expression is the anxiety of emptiness — anxiety about the meaningfulness of the concrete expressions of the creative spirit. Ultimately, it is the anxiety of the meaninglessness of the creative spirit as such.

"Nonbeing threatens from a third side; it threatens man's moral self-affirmation. Man's being, ontic as well as spiritual, is not only given to him but also demanded of him. He is responsible for it."[105] That is to say, man is *free* for his destiny. This third anxiety attacks this polarity of freedom and destiny. Nonbeing threatens freedom relatively with guilt and ultimately with condemnation. In every moment of its expression, in every moment of moral awareness, guilt is present and "can drive us toward complete self-rejection, to the feeling of being condemned — not to an external punishment but to the despair of having lost our destiny."[106]

With this discussion of anxiety we have reviewed and amplified dimensions of our earlier discussion of freedom's bondage in order to see now what its liberation from this bondage entails.

The first level of faith, that faith which affirms the self as a part, is especially effective in providing courage against the anxiety of death and meaninglessness. The individual finds life and meaning by losing himself to the apparently enduring life and meaning of the group. This life is had, however, at the price of individuality, so that it is questionable whether the individual could speak of it as "my" life. The courage afforded in this manner prevails until the rise of the consciousness of guilt which discloses the reality of the individual and

[104] *Ibid.*, p. 47.   [105] *Ibid.*, p. 51.   [106] *Ibid.*, pp. 52 f.

problems not to be solved by participation.[107] (The soul that sins, it shall die.) There is no courage in participation as such to deal with guilt, and so there arise individualistic types of faith in which is sought the courage to bear guilt, the courage of despair. Existentialism is the most thoroughgoing expression of the courage of freedom and individuality in the face of the anxiety of guilt. It knows " no exit " from freedom. It calls for an act of courage indeed, and is valid as a protest against the courage to be as a part. However, it is threatened by the anxiety of meaninglessness. " Man can affirm himself only if he affirms not an empty shell." [108] In sum: " Neither self-affirmation as a part nor self-affirmation as oneself is beyond the manifold threat of nonbeing," because the courage to be is not self-affirmation at all, but " the state of being grasped by the power of being-itself." [109] Thus, by transcending both freedom and destiny and individuality and meaning, authentic faith is enabled to overcome anxiety at all points of its attack.

In the first expression of authentic faith, faith as " being grasped by the power of being-itself," the relationship with being-itself is understood in terms of a personal encounter with a personal God. The " grasp " is experienced as the appeal of forgiveness by a personal God, and it issues in the courage to accept oneself — not as oneself but " as accepted in spite of being unacceptable." It is a mighty expression of the courage to be oneself against the anxiety of guilt. However, it is not justification of one's accidental individuality, nor is it merely the existentialist courage to be a self, inasmuch as it speaks also to the anxiety of meaninglessness by relating the individual not only to himself as forgiven but also to the meaningful other who forgives. Yet, this type of faith is limited because its efforts to understand the experience of being grasped by the power of being in personal terms submits this power to the ontic categories which themselves are subject to the attacks of nonbeing. In other words, it solves the existential problem of non-

107 *Ibid.*, p. 94.   108 *Ibid.*, p. 152.   109 *Ibid.*, pp. 155–156.

being and anxiety by removing it to the transcendent where it becomes God's existential problem. We have already seen how, in the conditions of existence, freedom is threatened by destiny, dynamics by form, and individuality by participation, etc. When God is understood as personal, he is grasped within these ontological elements, and we find that his personal existence suffers the same anxiety of meaninglessness. His transcendent individuality seems incapable of meaningful participation. His freedom is not reconcilable with his justice, nor his power with forms of meaning. This faith, like existentialism, cannot take on the full threat of meaninglessness — " the power of nonbeing in its most radical form." [110] No, faith must move beyond faith as personal encounter, for the object of ultimate faith transcends the individualization-participation polarity; it transcends personal categories.

In Tillich's appraisal of personal faith we approach the answer to our question — does salvation, the realization of essence in the conditions of existence, do away with or establish freedom? We learn that individuality is accidental, that, for example, in the psychoanalytic situation " the healer . . . does not stand for himself as an individual but represents the objective power of acceptance and self-affirmation." [111] We are also told that the power of nonbeing in its most radical form is the anxiety of meaninglessness, so that personal confidence, individuality, and finite freedom, which are the gifts of acceptance in personal encounter, are secondary to the courage that overcomes meaninglessness — the courage of absolute faith. Thus salvation really has to do not with individuals but with " objective power " which affirms the self, though not the self in its " accidental individuality." [112] Socrates understood that courage did not involve the affirmation of " accidental subjectivity." He realized that " the self which the executioners will destroy is not the self which affirms itself in his courage to be." His was an expression of absolute faith, an " affirmation

of himself in his essential, indestructible being." He knew that
his essential self belonged to a transtemporal order.[113] Quite
incompatible in Tillich's thought are " objective power " and
" accidental subjectivity," the literal self which executioners
can destroy and the essential self which is transtemporal. In a
word, being and freedom appear antithetical; they are, as we
have seen all along, related to each other as nonbeing and
being.

We must move on, then, from personal faith to faith as
mysticism, which brings us to the threshold of absolute faith.
Mysticism does not suffer the limitations of personal faith. It
does overcome, as we have noted, the subject-object polarity.
Its limitation, however, is that it achieves this goal without
true courage, in ignorance of the threat of meaninglessness. It
transcends all specific contents (such as God as personal) " not
because it doubts them or has found them meaningless; rather
it deems them to be preliminary." [114] In other words, it enjoys
the fruits of absolute faith — participation in the ground of
being — but without absolute courage. Neither personal faith
nor mystical faith provides a full salvation, a sufficiently radical courage. Personalism cannot conquer meaninglessness;
mysticism avoids it.

Absolute Faith

Absolute faith is not personal encounter, and it is beyond
faith of the mystical type. In absolute faith " mystical experience and personal encounter are identical." This means that
absolute faith has no special content. " It is simply faith, un-
directed, absolute." [115]

There are three elements in absolute faith. First, the awareness of the power of being " in face of the most radical manifestation of nonbeing." [116] That is, the awareness of meaning
in meaninglessness. Second, the awareness of the dependence
of nonbeing and meaninglessness on being and meaning.

113 *Ibid.*, pp. 168 f.   115 *Ibid.*, pp. 173, 176.
114 *Ibid.*, pp. 177–178.   116 *Ibid.*, p. 177.

Thirdly, the acceptance of being accepted.[117] This experience of absolute faith can readily be translated into ontological terms as the experience of the dialectic of being in its movement from thesis (being-itself), to the antithesis (nonbeing and freedom), to its synthesis in the New Being. In the first aspect of faith, one is grasped by being itself; in the second aspect, nonbeing is seen in its debt to being, as being's own self-transcendence; in the third aspect, faith experiences being's return to itself when it accepts nonbeing and takes it back up into itself.

Absolute faith is an event of immediate awareness. " It is as immediate and as much beyond doubt as the self is to the self." [118] (Which is to say that it is as much beyond doubt as is doubt itself.) It needs to be immediate, since all that is mediated participates in nonbeing and is overcome in the experience of absolute faith. Therefore, in absolute faith the self is transcended. Absolute faith " *is* the self in its self-transcending quality." [119] Insofar as faith rests upon the immediate awareness of the unconditional it has the character of certainty. However, insofar as faith is received by a finite being (suffering the limitations of nonbeing) it has the character of doubt.[120] The word " faith," as opposed to knowledge on the one hand and ignorance on the other, implies this unity of certainty and doubt. " There is no faith without participation," and " faith would cease to be faith without separation." The situation of man, says Tillich, " its finitude and estrangement, prevents man's participation in the ultimate without both the separation and the promise of faith." [121] Faith is therefore a movement from doubt to certainty, from finitude to infinity, from freedom to being. Insofar as it is a move away from the finite, free self, faith is experience as " ecstasy," as " standing outside one's self," which points to a state of mind which is extraordinary, in the sense that " it transcends the basic condition of

[117] *Ibid.*
[118] *The Dynamics of Faith*, p. 17.
[119] *Ibid.*
[120] *Ibid.*, pp. 18 ff.
[121] *Ibid.*, pp. 99 f.

finite rationality, the subject-object structure." [122] Corresponding to the inner ecstasy is the outer "shock" when one encounters the "stigma" of finitude, when one encounters the world in its finitude and so under the judgment of being-itself.

To the degree that faith is ecstasy, beyond the possibilities of selfhood, it is also beyond finite freedom. Indeed, ecstasy could be understood as the experience in which the objective polarities — destiny, form, and participation — are so overwhelming that the subjective pole, roughly designated "finite freedom," is overcome and the polar distinction itself is also overcome. This is why absolute faith is "beyond" subject and object. This is also why Tillich designates absolute faith as "the courage to be." This courage is had in the experience of "the God above God" — the God above the personal God of theism, the God of absolute faith who "unites and transcends the courage to be as a part and the courage to be as oneself." [123] The courage to be is therefore never "something separated and definite," i.e., personal and concrete. Yet, says Tillich, in the courage to be, the self "receives itself back. For the power of being acts through the power of the individual selves." [124] In what sense does one receive himself back through the ecstasy of absolute faith? Certainly, to the degree that the self is delivered from any absolutized finite reality — whether the self as a part or the self as self. But on the other hand, Tillich does not allow us to think that the self is returned so that it may be joyously and confidently affirmed in courageous acts of finite freedom. No, what really returns, the subject that really receives itself back, is being-itself. So, in absolute faith, the self is "grasped" by the "power of being-itself." "The courage to be" is just that, the courage to be — not the courage to be oneself, not the courage to enjoy one's accidental individuality, not the courage to be free. This is the meaning of Tillich's statement concerning the faith of Israel, that "election and destruction are bound together, so that no finite being, group, or individual may consider himself more than a medium of

[122] *S.T.*, I, 111 f.   [123] *The Courage to Be*, p. 187.   [124] *Ibid.*, p. 188.

the mystery of being. If, however, a group or single individuals endure this tension, their destruction is their fulfillment." [125] But then, of course, it is not " their " fulfillment; it is being's fulfillment. This is the meaning and promise of faith, not only in a teleological but also in an ontological sense. In faith freedom ends, for faith is the " fulfillment of reason," not finite, " autonomous " reason, but " the depth of reason " ecstatically experienced and symbolically expressed.[126]

In our ontological analysis we saw that freedom and being are incompatible. We also saw that Jesus must become transparent and die in order to manifest essence in existence. And now we see that man must lose himself in the ecstasy of absolute faith in order to be "grasped by the power of being." Tillich's theology does not seem to carry the burden of freedom, if by freedom we mean a spontaneous and dynamic expression of finite selfhood. Freedom for Tillich is at best the possibility of choosing being-itself by a sacrifice of the person who chooses. Tillich's God does not appear to be the God-man, the incarnate God of Jesus Christ, whose fulfillment is the resurrection of the man Jesus and so the glorification of finite existence, but rather one whose fulfillment is the death of the finite and the reappearance of being-itself.

If this is the logic of Tillich's thinking, it should become manifest in the development of his eschatology. But before I consider this, I should underline two implications of the preceding analysis. First, Tillich's thought is ambiguous; while my analysis suggests that " freedom " and finite existence are lost to the destiny of infinite being, Tillich nevertheless insists on the pole of freedom. The second is that my statement is therefore interpretive as well as analytic, a deliberate choice to read Tillich in the light of what I feel is a dominating tendency.[127] I make these two observations because of the fact that

[125] S.T., I, 143.
[126] The Dynamics of Faith, p. 77; S.T., I, 84.
[127] In a fine review of Tavard's Paul Tillich and the Christian Message, Prof. Thomas Langford calls attention to the fact that Tillich can be read in two ways — in terms of his ontology or his understanding of existence.

Tillich in *Systematic Theology*, Vol. III, does explicitly take a line (not, I feel, anticipated or justified by Vols. I and II) that appears to answer some of the criticisms raised in this discussion.

Eschatology and Freedom

This latest development is most strikingly apparent if one compares what Tillich says about the resurrection of Jesus in *Systematic Theology*, Vol. II, with what he says about the resurrection of man in Vol. III. In the first instance he says, as we have seen, that in Jesus' resurrection " certainly it is not the death of an individual man that is overcome." [128] That which is present in the resurrection does not have the character of " the reappearance of an individual soul." [129] In Vol. III he writes in contrast that the " Resurrection says mainly that the Kingdom of God includes all dimensions of being. The whole personality participates in Eternal Life." He continues by saying that " the Christian emphasis on the ' body of Resurrection ' also includes a strong affirmation of the eternal significance of the individual person's uniqueness." [130] The substance of this shift in emphasis is to give to finite freedom an ultimate significance that appears to raise serious questions about the entire structure of Tillich's system. We have seen how his earlier ontological commitment seems thoroughly to relativize and finally exclude freedom. Do not the later developments place in radical jeopardy the ontological premise with which he began?

We indicated that the " early " Tillich understands by finite freedom any moment of decision in which the self is centered,

---

He suggests that Tillich begins methodologically with the existential but concludes valuationally with the ontic, and that any conclusion as to which is the dominant note is difficult to arrive at. Obviously, I have chosen the ontological route of interpretation, as have both Langford and Tavard.

[128] *Supra*, p. 96.
[129] *S.T.*, II, 157.
[130] *S.T.*, III, 412 f.

yet in which the self becomes a symbol transparent to the emerging depth of being. The moment of true freedom is one in which being-itself and not the free individual appears. Indeed, whenever finite freedom is *self*-conscious, it alienates itself from being, falls into nonbeing, and becomes in its actuality or existence the antithesis of being. Consequently, a free decision is paradoxically one in which the free individual is both centered and overcome, just as the result of Jesus' centered life is not his resurrection but the overcoming of his finite, free, centered self through the appearance of the reality of the New Being. Finite freedom, thus conceived, is merely a formal category which gives actuality to being, but which, in itself, is a negativity overcome by the being that it actualizes.

In Vol. III, Tillich states, along the lines of the preceding volumes, that in eternity all negativity is overcome. The negative becomes manifest as " the unambiguously negative." [131] But at the same time he states that " every finite happening is significant for God." [132] Since finitude is by definition being limited by nonbeing, it is difficult to envision the overcoming of all negativity and the preservation of finitude at the same time.[133] To make this point stand, theology must, says Tillich, " try to combine the doctrine of eternal blessedness with the negative element without which life is not possible and blessedness ceases to be blessed." [134] In short, the final goal of life is both the overcoming of finite existence and its fulfillment. In terms of the concept of freedom Tillich now insists that freedom is not simply the means by which the essential is actualized, not simply " a return to what a thing essentially is," but also an event that actualizes something new in time and space and thereby " adds something to essential being." [135] Between creation and fulfillment, " between beginning and end, the new is created. For the divine ground of being we must say

131 *Ibid.*, p. 397.
132 *Ibid.*, p. 398.
133 Thomas, pp. 127, 132.
134 *S.T.*, III, 404 f.
135 *Ibid.*, p. 400.

both that the created is *not* new, for it is potentially rooted in the ground, and that it *is* new, for its actuality is based on freedom in unity with destiny, and freedom is the precondition of all newness in existence." [136] Providence, which directs history, is not a heavenly design or blueprint, for such a conception "restricts the element of contingency in the processes of history to the extent that destiny annihilates freedom. But the texture of history includes the contingent, the surprising, the underivably new." [137] Accordingly, the Kingdom of God — the goal and fulfillment of history — includes not only political and social aspects, but also the personalistic. It gives "eternal meaning to the individual person," and to the decisions of his finite freedom.[138]

In sum, whereas heretofore Tillich seemed to tip the ontological scale in favor of the polarity of destiny instead of freedom, in favor of being instead of becoming, it now appears that he intends to balance the scales.[139] On the one hand, he says that personalities "are significant when more is embodied in them than a transitory occurrence within the universal process of becoming." That is, personalities are significant when they are more than mere instruments and transparent symbols of being's becoming. On the other hand, "without the revelation of human potentialities [that is, potentialities rooting in the essential ground] . . . historical accounts would not report significant events." [140] In short, the final and eternal product of history is given both in the essential ground and in the creative possibilities of finite human freedom.

There are two conclusions which might be drawn from this development in Tillich's thought. First, that he has shifted from an earlier ontological commitment to a more personalistic (incarnational?) view, in which the ultimate is not the

[136] *Ibid.,* p. 398.
[137] *Ibid.,* p. 372.
[138] *Ibid.,* p. 358.
[139] *Ibid.,* p. 402. Here Tillich speaks of the "ultimate unity of freedom and destiny."
[140] *Ibid.,* p. 304.

abstraction of being-itself, but the concrete reality of being in finite freedom. In any event, freedom appears no longer to be just an instrument or element of being (note how Tillich prefers in the third volume to speak about dimensions instead of elements of being), but as a cocreator of the final reality of the Kingdom, as itself the ground of being. In this respect, Tillich's thought suggests not only the panentheism of Whitehead and Hartshorne,[141] but also the personalistic thought of Nicolas Berdyaev and even Karl Barth.

A closely related second observation has to do with the conception of nonbeing. Tillich has shown that nonbeing is the antithesis of being, as well as the condition of finite freedom. Now, since finite freedom is not finally overcome in eternity, there must be, as Tillich himself stated, a proper and essential nonbeing, in which case Tillich must ask what then is negated by the victory of being in the Kingdom when essence overcomes the ambiguities of existence?[142] Earlier he could state, as he did, that finite existence — being limited by nonbeing — is overcome. (Similarly, in the resurrection the New Being overcomes the individual personality of Jesus.) Now, however, Tillich must offer another solution, perhaps suggested by Barth's concept of the good negativities or the " shadowy " side of existence.

Again, let it be said that it would be a misunderstanding of this study and of Tillich himself most certainly if the reader were to understand by these conclusions that there is no presentiment of the third volume in the other two.[143] The point is that the main thrust of the first two is belied and challenged by a surprising personalistic note which is not often sounded earlier but upon which the entire work comes to an end. Tillich himself seems, implicitly at least, to agree with the gist of

[141] " One could call this system eschatological pan-en-theism." (*Ibid.*, p. 421.)

[142] *Ibid.*, p. 399.

[143] See Thomas, Ch. VII, " History and the Kingdom of God," where he points out that the new element in the third volue of *Systematic Theology* does indeed come to partial expression in earlier writings.

the preceding criticisms of the view of freedom developed in *Systematic Theology*, Vols. I and II, and other earlier writings.

THE FREEDOM OF GOD

Tillich refers to the freedom of God when he speaks of the grace by which the believer comes to faith and freedom. It is true, he observes, that " we decide," and that " we believe we are able to decide"; however, " after the decision we realize that it was not our own power but a power which decided through us. If we make a decision for what we essentially are, and therefore ought to be, it is a decision out of grace." [144] The grace implicit in faith has also been indicated by the understanding of faith as the experience of " being grasped by the power of being-itself," in such a way that being-itself is both subject and object of the experience. Faith is grace because it is finally not so much an act of finite freedom as an event of being-itself in which the self is ecstatically transcended. In religious symbolism, salvation is an act of the freedom of God.

Tillich asks whether, when we say that grace is an expression of the divine freedom, we mean that it roots in the contingency of God's " free will." This kind of language is, in Tillich's judgment, highly symbolic, reflecting the subject-object polarity within which theism moves and which is transcended by the God above God. Freedom in God is really the corollary of the separation of being from being-itself. Viewed ontologically it is the power of being to transcend itself in nonbeing and return to itself in the victory of the New Being. It is a symbol of the dynamic, historical nature of God. Viewed from the perspective of existence or finitude, the freedom of God expresses the relativity and contingency of the finite, the fact that as such it is *non capax infiniti*. Ontologically, the freedom of God is his positive power to resist and overcome the threat of nonbeing and finitude.

Without nonbeing and finitude God would not be free; he " would not even be self-affirmation but an immovable self-

[144] *Biblical Religion and the Search for Ultimate Reality*, p. 67.

identity." [145] So in a sense God owes his life, his freedom, to finite existence, insofar as it participates in nonbeing. "God loves and knows himself through the love and knowledge of finite beings. Nonbeing (that in God which makes his self-affirmation dynamic) opens up the divine self-seclusion and reveals him as power and love." [146] Consequently, the "freedom" of God cannot have, for Tillich, the sense that it traditionally bears. It cannot suggest that God's relationship to man has an aspect of contingency and spontaneity, so that it could be designated properly a matter of "election" or decision. "God is called 'free,' but he is free not in arbitrariness but in absolute and unconditional identity with his destiny, so that the essential structures of being are not strange to his freedom but are the actuality of his freedom. . . . They [symbols of the "divine life"] imply God's ultimacy in which the polarities of being disappear in the ground of being, in being-itself." [147] The church is a "called" community in the sense that it is set apart from the world, but not in the sense that there has been an eternal and "free" decision on its behalf. Indeed, it is perhaps more to the point to speak of the calling of God, inasmuch as man's finitude, his freedom and existence, is a call to God, a summons to life and action occasioned by the threat of nonbeing. Grace, or God's freedom, from man's side appears almost ominous — a divine self-seeking through the overcoming of finitude and existence.

In sum: The freedom of God means that man, insofar as he is or has being, depends on God, and that God is "free" to move out of himself, unto himself, by taking nonbeing into himself. God's "freedom" is not to be understood as "free will," as a spontaneous, gracious decision or election. It is just another symbol for the concept of God as the dynamic ground of being and history.

[145] *The Courage to Be,* p. 179. [146] *Ibid.,* p. 180. [147] *S.T.,* I, 244.

4

KARL BARTH: FREEDOM IN CHRIST

BULTMANN AND TILLICH have in common an existentialist approach to theology in which they begin methodologically with man, his existence and freedom. Karl Barth, on the other hand, begins not with man as such, but with God as he is revealed to the church in Jesus Christ. In view of Barth's basic theological orientation I have chosen to ask first about the freedom of God, then about the freedom of the Christian.

THE FREEDOM OF GOD

Karl Barth's understanding of " Christian freedom " accents the word " Christian "; [1] it is a view of freedom which is determined by the faith that in Jesus Christ, God reveals himself as Lord.[2]

" Christian " Freedom

This means, for Barth, that God's freedom and Lordship are " Christian "; faith's understanding cannot separate God from Jesus Christ. The statement of this inseparable union finds its most emphatic and characteristic expression in Barth's interpretation of the doctrine of election, which maintains that God exists only in the eternal, free, and gracious decision in which

[1] Barth states that a person's Christianity is primarily " his belonging to Jesus Christ." *Die Kirchliche Dogmatik*, IV, 3, 601 (523) .

[2] I, 1, 323 (351) .

he binds himself to Jesus, and in him to all men.³ Predestination, or eternal election, is therefore an act in which God first
of all determines and binds *himself* by electing for himself another (Jesus Christ) to become the limit of his freedom and
the very context of his eternal existence. And within this limit
God indeed exists in the full realization of all his attributes,
in his omnipotence, in the fullness of his deity. God is so committed to Jesus that Jesus must be thought of as the beginning
of all God's ways, as the content of his abiding will, and as the
goal of his every act.⁴ Jesus is " the electing God." ⁵

Not surprisingly, Barth rejects the traditional Calvinistic
conception in which predestination is abstracted from the revelation in Jesus and becomes an inscrutable decree hidden behind Jesus of which Jesus and the grace in him are only one
expression.⁶ Barth maintains that according to the New Testament the eternal will of God is identical with Jesus; Jesus is the
eternal presupposition, the alpha and omega, of the whole cre-
ation.⁷ Barth admits that not many passages regarding predestination and election are explicitly Christological, but he
maintains that we are not thereby excused from reading them
in Christological perspective.⁸ The New Testament, says Barth,
understands that God has Jesus in mind first of all, and whatever else he does is for the sake of Jesus.⁹ It witnesses to Jesus
as the alpha and omega — the word in the beginning, which
as such is the source, substance, and purpose of God's every
word and will. In Jesus, God is free and the creator of freedom.
Freedom, therefore, the freedom of God and whatever other

³ II, 2, 101 f. (94 f.) .
⁴ II, 2, 151 ff. (140 ff.) .
⁵ " Jesus Christ is the electing God. We need ask about none other than
him. We will meet in the depths of the Godhead none other than him.
There is no deity-as-such." II, 2, 123 (115) .
⁶ II, 2, 161 f., 169–172 (149 f., 156–158) .
⁷ It was the error of orthodoxy that " the work of God with its center
in Jesus Christ was for them one thing, the eternal presupposition of this
work another." II, 2, 162 (149) .
⁸ II, 2, 165 (152 f.) .
⁹ II, 2, 125 (116) .

freedom there may be, is limited by Jesus. Hans Urs von Balthasar illustrates Barth's viewpoint with the hourglass, the top representing God, the bottom his creation, and the narrow throat Jesus — the point where the two parts meet. As God is not outside the relationship to the creation through the one man, Jesus, so also man and creation are eternally bound to God in and through that one man.[10] What does not come from Jesus is not from God; and what does not come to man from Jesus cannot come to man. Beyond Christ is that existence which God has rejected — nonbeing, *das Nichtige*, the devil. A freedom from Jesus is in truth a slavery unto death.

Jesus is not only the electing God, the beginning of all God's ways. He is also " the elected man," the goal and fulfillment of God's eternal will.[11] He is the event in which God's eternal will is actualized. The creation comes from Christ, and it is fulfilled in him.[12] As Jesus is at the beginning and in the middle, he is also at the end. Jesus is " the promise and its recipient." [13] Whatever comes to man in the freedom of God and in the fulfillment of his eternal will comes first of all to Jesus as *the* elected man. When God elects Jesus, he elects not only an eternal will (Jesus as the electing God) but also a temporal fact (Jesus as the elected man) .[14]

Barth resorts to these linguistic extremes because he is convinced that not only do they point to the heart of the gospel, but that also they defend true doctrine against misconceptions — the non-Christological interpretations of divine and human freedom in orthodox Calvinism and Lutheranism, and in philosophical versions of the same in modern Protestantism. Generally speaking, he is endeavoring to correct deterministic

[10] *Karl Barth: Darstellung und Deutung seiner Theologie* (Olten: Hegner Bucheri, 1951) , p. 210.

[11] II, 2, 124 ff. (116 ff.) . This double aspect of Jesus, as the beginning and end of God's ways, is examined in the useful book by Robert W. Jenson, *Alpha and Omega: A Study in the Theology of Karl Barth* (Thomas Nelson & Sons, 1963) .

[12] II, 2, 125 (116) .

[13] II, 2, 336 (306) .

[14] II, 2, 387 (352) .

constructions of God's freedom on the one hand and existentialistic, indeterministic constructions of human freedom on the other hand.[15] Traditional Calvinism tends to abstract God's eternal will from the grace manifest in Jesus, and to attribute salvation instead to the determination of an abstract and arbitrary will. But Barth understands the gospel to declare that Jesus is not an expression merely of *a* divine intention, but rather the incarnation of the source of *all* intentions. On the other hand, traditional Lutheranism tends to think of the faith of the Christian in abstraction from the faith and obedience of the man Jesus, and so throws the individual back upon his own abstract and arbitrary freedom and existence. But to say that Jesus Christ is the elected man is to state that the fulfillment of election is also God's work, once for all achieved in Jesus. As the electing God and the elected man, Jesus is the believer's assurance of the eternal grace and the eternal power of God.

The most extreme expression of this Christological orientation is Barth's reference to Jesus as the "pre-existing Godman."[16] Certainly Barth is not insensitive to the idealistic tone implicit in such a notion, and elsewhere in the *Church Dogmatics* he generally speaks more moderately, claiming that Jesus preexists as the eternal purpose, goal, or aim of God.[17] In this vein he writes that God "is the God whose action is directed by his desire to have fellowship with man."[18] Jesus exists eternally as an intended actuality: "God's merciful will (as realized and revealed in Jesus) to take the side of his crea-

[15] II, 2, 64–82, 113–123, 136–157 (60–76, 106–115, 127–145). Barth writes in his Gifford Lectures that "the true mystery of Predestination is neither the secular mystery of determinism nor the equally secular mystery of indeterminism, but the holy and real mystery of Jesus Christ" (*The Knowledge of God and the Service of God*, tr. by J. L. M. Haire and Ian Henderson, p. 79; London: Hodder and Stoughton, 1938).

[16] II, 2, 118 (110). Note that the English translation fails to translate literally Barth's German — "*der praeexistierende Gottmensch Jesus Christus.*"

[17] Jenson is not altogether correct when he says that Barth is not being rhetorical when he speaks of Jesus' preexistence. (*Alpha and Omega*, p. 67.)

[18] *The Knowledge of God*, p. 20.

ture against the darkness (*das Nichts*) . . . was from eternity." [19] From the beginning God is not "neutral," for he exists eternally in his "convenanting will," in his will to be incarnate in Jesus.[20] That God created the universe in Jesus Christ means that "Jesus Christ was the meaning and purpose of the creation." [21] Jesus, he says, is "the divine disposition which precedes all history, indeed the creation of the world." [22]

Barth maintains that the fundamental lines of his thinking are Biblical, perhaps even in some of the extreme statements. In support he frequently cites the Prologue to the Fourth Gospel, especially John 1:1 and 1:15.[23] According to Barth, the Evangelist so radically identifies Jesus of Nazareth with the eternal Logos that it is proper to say that the Word is divine because it is Jesus.[24] In Colossians, Paul says that Jesus "is before all things, and in him all things hold together." [25] Barth's language is not unscriptural; certainly he is essaying to understand the very heart of the Scripture message — the good

[19] III, 3, 89 (79).

[20] IV, 1, 37 (36); III, 3, 38 f. (33 f.).

[21] III, 4, 43 (40 f.).

[22] IV, 3, 269 (234). Eduard Buess objects to Barth's doctrine of predestination because it tends to deny history. He argues that to designate Jesus "the electing God" is to forget that God is the subject of salvation and that Jesus is the means, and that there is a history between God's statement of purpose and its fulfillment. ("Zur Praedestinationslehre Karl Barths," *Theologische Studien*, Heft 43, 50 f.; Zollikon-Zürich: Evangelischer Verlag, 1955.) This is not an uncommon criticism of Barth's doctrine. See G. C. Berkouwer, *The Triumph of Grace in the Theology of Karl Barth*, tr. by Henry R. Boer (London: The Paternoster Press, 1955), pp. 250–259. Balthasar makes a similar point when he states that Barth does not allow "all the necessary room between creation and covenant" (*Karl Barth: Darstellung und Deutung*, p. 254). Despite the legitimacy of this type of objection to the extreme statements of II, 2, it is evident from the many citations above that Barth's view is not so undialectical as often appears. Balthasar concedes this when he reminds us that Barth's tendency toward idealism is in tension with a steadfast emphasis on the historical revelation of Jesus. See Balthasar's discussion, "Idealism and Revelation," *ibid.*, pp. 229 ff.

[23] See II, 2, 102 ff. (95 ff.); IV, 3, 265 ff. (231 ff.).

[24] II, 2, 105 (98).

[25] Col. 1:17. The same "high" Christology is found in Eph. 1:9-11, and Heb. 1:3, for example.

news that salvation in Jesus is rooted in eternity. The doctrine
of election is the sum of the gospel in its affirmation that our
salvation is decreed from the foundation of the earth [26] and
actualized once for all in Jesus.

Twofold Freedom

God determines from the beginning that the beginning and
end of his ways shall be those of Jesus. What does this mean?
The answer to this question lies in Barth's understanding of
the office of Christ which reveals a twofold freedom of God.
Jesus, as God's eternal Word, fulfills two responsibilities, allowing Barth to speak of a double decree in God's eternal will. In
the first place, Jesus is one who calls all men unto himself, so
that when God takes Jesus as his eternal existence form, he
takes upon himself mankind.[27] When he elects mankind in
Jesus, he also elects for himself the creation and preservation
of mankind as well as the burden of mankind's sin — the judgment, damnation, and rejection which are its due. He elects the
cross, suffering, and death for himself.[28]

The other, the positive and primary side of the double de-
cree — the reason for it all — is manifest in the fact that while
Jesus called men unto himself, he also gave himself to men.
God elected, therefore, not only man for himself, but even

---

[26] II, 2, 11, 25 (11, 24).

[27] II, 2, 340 f. (309 ff.).

[28] II, 2, 215, 217–221, 384–391 (195, 197–200, 349–354). Most of Barth's
critics stumble here. For if Jesus is eternally elected to bear man's sins,
then is not sin already justified as the necessary presupposition of gracious election? Berkouwer states that "it cannot be denied that Barth . . .
thinks in this direction" (*The Triumph of Grace*, p. 251). It is for this
reason, says Berkouwer, that Barth must speak of the ontological impossibility of sin (p. 256). Hans Küng recognizes the problem, but calls attention to the dialectical nature of Barth's theology, so that Barth wants
to say that Jesus is both an eternal word from God and a divine word in
response to the historical fact of sin. " *Zweifellos ist die Rechtfertigung
eine Reaktion auf des menschen Sünde, ein Dennoch und Trotzdem auf
diesem Zwischenfall.*" However, " *sie ist vielmehr 'die von Gott selbst voll-
zogen Behauptung, Durchsetzung seines Bundes mit dem Menschen.'* "
(*Rechtfertigung*, p. 33; Eisedeln: Johannes Verlag, 1957.)

more, himself for man. He elects man's sin that man might become a Son.[29]

Eternal Salvation

Barth is emphatic: the doctrine of election announces that salvation in Jesus is eternal. The doctrine can be viewed from two perspectives, formal and material.

From the formal perspective, salvation is seen as eternal. The eternal God really stands behind Jesus. On the other hand, the eternal is a Savior; Jesus stands ever before God. In sum, the doctrine of election designates a dimension of the Christian experience of salvation through Jesus and a dimension of God's relationship to Jesus.[30] It is because it says both, that Barth protects himself from obvious pitfalls. If the doctrine of predestination were merely a statement about God, then it would altogether relativize the historical event of Jesus and faith in him. Our salvation would then be an eternal verity, of which history is simply the temporal revelation.[31] On the other hand, if the doctrine of predestination be merely a mythological representation of the experience called salvation and not a statement about God, then salvation must finally be understood not as salvation at all, not as the work of a savior, but as an act of man himself in fulfillment of the law of his own na-

[29] II, 2, 183 (167). Predestination is God's eternal decision to liberate man from damnation to the disadvantage of God. It is the determination of God to liberate man by becoming himself the one who is lost, abandoned, and rejected — the lamb slain from the foundation of the world.

[30] This double perspective runs throughout Barth's theology. J. L. Leuba, for example, says that Barth's theology may be read systematically for *what* is said, or prophetically, as " *l'annonce du jugement et de la grace de Dieu* " (" Le Problème de l'Église chez M. Karl Barth," cited by Henri Bouillard, *Karl Barth*, III, 285; Paris: Aubier, 1957).

[31] This is the way Berkouwer reads Barth's doctrine. " His conception leaves the impression that everything has already been done, all the decisions have been taken, so that one can hardly say that the *historical fall* and the *historical reconciliation* are at issue, but only the *revelation* of redemption in history." (*The Triumph of Grace*, p. 250.) So also Regin Prenter: " *The Gospel of the universal predestination is not the good news, for it denies our temporal life.*" (Karl Barths Umbildung der traditionellen Zweinaturlehre," *Studia Theologica*, XI, 87; Lund, 1958.)

ture. God becomes but another word for man's inmost and highest potential. When Barth says that Jesus is the electing God, he guards against this humanism. When he says that Jesus is the elected man, he guards against a Gnostic Docetism. Balthasar rightly notes this dialectic in Barth's teaching when he reminds his reader that Barth's statements about God are always at the same time statements of him who exists in faith in Jesus.[32]

From the material perspective, the doctrine of eternal election voices the assurance of salvation that our God is eternally a *Savior* and that our *salvation* is eternal.[33] God is eternally a covenanting God, a gracious God; and man is from the beginning God's covenant partner. Sin is, in these terms, inconceivable, an " ontological impossibility." Protestant students tend to criticize this material affirmation because it leaves no freedom to God. Brunner, for instance, objects to Barth, insisting that " God has freedom in Jesus Christ to elect, and outside of Jesus to reject." Otherwise, " then neither in God nor in man is an ' Either-Or ' possible." [34] Catholic critics, on the other hand, tend to criticize Barth's emphasis, not for its limitation upon God's freedom, but for its implicit denial of man and the immanent freedom he possesses apart from and as the condition of salvation. Thus Balthasar, after defending Barth at other points of typical criticism, protests that " the priority of Christ in no wise demands [as Barth tends to insist] that the

[32] " In order to answer the charge of Gnosticism, Barth has only to point to faith. . . . Faith means the end of an impossible neutrality, and therewith the end of the possibility of a purely theoretical consideration of the truth [of election]." (Balthasar, p. 231. See the entire section, " Das System und das Existentielle," pp, 230 ff.)

[33] This is why Berkouwer calls Barth's theology a " triumph of grace." It is a triumph because of the formal implications of the doctrine of election.

[34] Emil Brunner, *The Christian Doctrine of God: Dogmatics, Vol. I,* tr. by Olive Wyon (The Westminster Press, 1950) , p. 314. See also Berkouwer, p. 252, where he takes exception to Barth's apparent denial of the " step-wise " character of God's work and the freedom and life of God. So also Robert Jenson claims that Barth denies to God the freedom of his wrath. (*Alpha and Omega,* p. 160.)

whole work of creation must necessarily be pressed painfully
into a Christological scheme." [35] Hans Küng makes the same
point when he asks if Barth's view finally touches man in his
historical existence. "In fact, is not man as God's covenant
partner finally omitted?" [36] This question, of the freedom of
man in the light of God's eternal freedom in Christ, is the subject of the next sections of this chapter. Here it is in order to
indicate in a general way how Barth answers these Protestant
and Catholic critics. Barth's overall answer is his theological
method, which requires that he think out the implications of
faith afresh at every one of its loci and not proceed deductively
from any one theological statement or principle. Thus, while
faith in Jesus obliges Barth to think of God's eternal will, it
does not allow him to deny the significance of Jesus' history for
this reason. Faith is always faith in Jesus and at every point in
its self-understanding it must return to Jesus.[37] As a matter of
fact the doctrine of election means little more or less than that
theology is always reflection upon faith in Jesus, for Jesus is
always (eternally) between man and God; he has the name
that is above every name. Applying this principle, Hedinger
defends Barth's views of the freedom of God against the Protestant critics who feel that Barth jeopardizes it. He quotes
Barth himself, who rejects Berkouwer's attempt to reduce theology to the principle of grace, contending that it is not grace,
but Jesus that is faith's concern.[38] Then Hedinger notes,
against Berkouwer, Brunner, and Buess, etc., that Barth does
distinguish between God in himself and God in Christ, i.e.,
that while God elects Jesus, he truly *elects*, i.e., he is *freely* in
Jesus and Jesus remains God's *free* choice.[39] As regards the

[35] Balthasar, p. 253.
[36] Küng, pp. 100 f.
[37] See I, 2, 972 (869), where Barth likens theology to the circumference
of a circle which is formed by moving out from the center and not by a
movement from one point on the circumference to the next in a way that
would invariably throw the circle out of shape. Theology cannot move
from the doctrine of election to the doctrine of justification without re-
turning first to the revelation itself.
[38] IV, 3, 198 f. (173 f.).
[39] Ulrich Hedinger, *Der Freiheitsbegriff in der Kirchlichen Dogmatik*

denial of man's freedom, it is a thesis of this section that Barth's theological method has not been adequately understood by most of his critics, and that Barth does indeed give room to the creature, not because grace presupposes it, but because Christ in his prophetic office, in his witness as the Spirit, demands it. This thesis waits the next sections for its development.

Relative to the freedom of the Christian man, the doctrine of predestination as developed by Barth means that freedom is radically dependent upon and directed toward Jesus. Just as Jesus is the realm of God's freedom, so he is the creator and limit of all other freedoms. We turn now to ask if the Christian is free under these conditions and, if so, how?

FREEDOM-FOR

The doctrine of election declares that Jesus is the beginning and end, the ground and goal of man's freedom. The freedom of the Christian man is therefore a freedom for Jesus. To be free for Jesus is, as we have observed in the first section, to be free for an *eternal will* — for a divine purpose that is from the beginning. It also means to be free for an *actual fact,* a fact that happened once upon a time. It means further to be free for a *present word* — a word that is being spoken now. And finally, it means to be free for a *living Spirit,* which saves now and will save unto the end. Stated somewhat differently: freedom for Jesus is freedom for an eternal word spoken from the beginning; it is freedom for the word made flesh and spoken once upon a time; it is freedom for the apostolic words spoken in the church; it is freedom in a creative word spoken by the Christian through the Spirit to the world.[40] We must now consider these forms of the Christian's freedom-for.

Karl Barths (Zürich: Zwingli Verlag, 1962) , pp. 56 ff. See also the author's Drew University dissertation, " Freedom in the Theology of Karl Barth " (1955) , p. 51.

[40] The scope of Jesus' significance is indicated by Arnold B. Come when he writes: " Christology for Barth includes everything from the original creative decision and action of the Father to the ultimate eschatological redemption of mankind by the Holy Spirit " (*An Introduction to Barth's* Dogmatics *for Preachers,* pp. 133 f.; The Westminster Press, 1963) .

I. Freedom for God's Eternal Word in Jesus

Original Freedom

The first and most obvious implication of the fact that Jesus is God's eternal will and word is that the freedom wherein God creates is the freedom of Christ, so that whatever he creates has no other ground or goal than Jesus. God in Jesus is the only possibility, the only content of man's created and true freedom; he is man's " ontological determination." [41] Originally, in his created nature, man is " from God " (von Gott her) and " toward God " (zu Gott hin) .[42] Whatever else man's freedom may be, it is first of all his freedom to be loved and favored by God. Also, since it is original, man's relationship to God can only be one of freedom — spontaneous and " natural."

Since God's love is first, the very ground of creation itself, then God in his election of man through his love is not dependent upon man's created nature, and man, in his created nature, has nowhere to stand and nothing wherein to trust except in the love of God which is his beginning.[43] He may not presuppose his created being, even in its depth, nor any ontology as a logical or epistemological a priori.[44] Man is elected to

---

[41] III, 2, 160 (132).

[42] III, 2, 167 ff,. 207 ff. (140 ff., 174 ff.).

[43] Herein lies the explanation of how Barth can maintain that man does not cease to be man even though his sin be total. By his act of sin man cannot forfeit his humanity which is primarily his calling and existence in God's act of grace. " Man cannot . . . ontologically speaking become Godless." IV, 1, 534 (480). Thus Barth can say that Christ precedes Adam and that Adam is a type of Christ. Adam " precedes Christ merely as a shadow and an example. He is only apparently the first. The first is Jesus Christ " (A Shorter Commentary on Romans, tr. by D. H. van Daalen, p. 62; John Knox Press, 1959).

[44] In IV, 3, the section entitled "The Light of Life," pp. 40–188 (38–165), Barth outlines an ontology and discusses the natural and immanent truth (light) of life. He grants that there is an immanent dialectic in life, a " relative opposition," which must not be confused with the contrast between the Creator and the creature, IV, 3, 164 (145). Whatever freedom man has relative to the world (and thus dependent upon the world) " cannot possibly be confused or compared with the freedom of the Creator and

be an object of God's love before he is created. Here logic falters before the faith it would understand, for the very idea of " election " requires an object of election — a humanity existing in a being which as such subsists outside the electing will with a capacity to respond to that will.[45] Nevertheless, says Barth, this logic may not be pressed. The question about *who* is elected is a vain one " because that which precedes the being of man as a being summoned by God's word is God and his word alone, God . . . in Jesus." [46] The only humanity which God's eternal word presupposes is that of Jesus Christ; Christ precedes Adam. To understand Barth's thinking here it must be remembered that he never abstracts himself from his stance as a believer; his logic is *faith's* logic. The believer knows *himself* to be elected from eternity; yet, even as an elected believer, nay, just because he is an elected believer, he knows that his election is not at all contingent upon what he is outside of and apart from his election. Like a drowning man in the arms of his rescuer he is not constrained to ask about his own potentialities. The Christian knows that while he is *called,* he is called as the one who already *is elected* from eternity, even before he is formed in his mother's womb. This position does not indicate that Barth is a pure idealist, ignorant of the common-sense facts of man's existence as a body-soul entity; nevertheless, he insists that this entity (man's " *Sein als Natur-und-*

Lord, nor with the freedom which he sends man from afar." IV, 3, 168 (148) .

45 So Barth maintains that God's revelation presupposes that there exists distant from God a world *in which* he can reveal himself and someone *to whom* he can reveal himself. See III, 1, 103–107 (94–99) . Balthasar insists that Barth has introduced a conception of being and nature in distinction from grace, and a concept of analogy that is inconsistent with Barth's emphasis on the primacy of gracious election. (See Balthasar, pp. 136 ff.) However, Balthasar himself indicates that Barth's system really reaches its peak in the doctrine of election, where Barth excludes the concept of nature outside of and apart from grace and the election of grace. " *Ursprung aller Erwählung, unter und über des keine frühere, keine hoherer . . . gibt . . . ist Jesus Christus . . . in dem . . . alle Schöpfung grundgelegt ist ' vor Grundlegung der Welt.' "* (P. 188.)

46 III, 2, 180 (151) .

Geisteswesen ") , which is apparently presupposed in the call, " is, in relation to his human nature itself [his nature as a being in the eternal election of grace] only a *materia inhabilis et indisposita*. His human nature is not based upon it, nor is his human nature to be explained from it." [47] In other words, there is no natural " point of contact " or " natural theology." As regards his nature outside grace, man is *ex nihilo*. His righteousness is not in him, but between him and God.[48] The righteous man does not live from himself but from God and for God; this is what it means to be free for Jesus as God's *eternal* word and will.

Responding Freedom

Because man from the beginning is from God and for God, he has no freedom but to move out of himself and take that which God has for him; he exists in an answer to God's grace. His freedom, says Barth, is an actual " answering " of God (*eine Verantwortung*) and not simply an " answerability " to God (*ein Verantwortlichkeit*) .[49] There is no ground for mere " responsibility," since responsibility is a state in which one is only a potentiality for response as if the word of grace were yet to be spoken and man's potentialities had a prior existence. Yet, the gracious word of God is first and man has no potentialities prior to or outside his existence in grace and the response to grace. Whatever structures man may bring to the re-

---

[47] " The existence of man is an elected existence (*Aufgerufen sein*) which, outside God's word, has nothing prior to itself." III, 2, 182 (152) . " There is . . . an actual pre-existence of man as one called out by God — namely, in God's decree and to this extent in God himself, that is, in God's son, insofar as this one is the uncreated image of mankind who is destined to become one with God, the ' first-born of the entire creation.' " III, 2, 186 (155) .

[48] The ultimate meaning of whatever light shines in the creation as such is a " Why? ", a radical why that contains no hidden " Because." It is not a mask that hides a face. IV, 3, 169 (149) .

[49] III, 4, 51 (47) . Note also that just as Barth objects to the word *Verantwortlichkeit* so also he objects to the word *Freiheit*, because the suffix *heit* suggests a condition, a state, rather than the movement that is genuine freedom. III, 2, 233 (195 f.) .

sponding process, their capacity for grace exists only within and primarily for the actual responding itself. Because the act of responding which is the meaning of freedom for God's eternal will is the first and basic act of existence, it has the quality of spontaneity symbolized and experienced as " joy " and " gladness " (gerne). The substance of the celebration of the Sabbath, the day in which man remembers that he exists by the work of grace and not by his own work, is " joy, the celebration of a festival." [50]

Freedom for the eternal word of God is a response, a joyful movement outward toward the grace of God which alone is in the beginning.[51] While man is above all a free, joyful, God-ward movement, he nevertheless is; in this movement he expresses his own nature and created " response-abilities." [52] The first of these is knowledge, knowledge of the eternal gracious election to which he indeed responds. This ability to understand is not a presupposition of freedom but is, rather, a possibility created by the grace of God and the response of the subject to that grace.[53] This basic act of knowing is also a self-

[50] III, 4, 73 (68).

[51] " Behind ' Thou,' ' He,' and even . . . ' mine,' ' thine,' and ' his ' there stands always, unannounced but necessary, the human self and thus human freedom, a freedom which we can take for ourselves and which cannot be given and actually is given only by God because God alone is originally free." III, 2, 231 (194).

[52] Again we are brought back to a very problematic aspect of Barth's theology — namely, the question of analogy. We have seen Barth insist that God does not presuppose in his dealings with man any independent capacity — any analogy of being. But, given the relationship to God, the outward movement which is true faith and freedom, then within this freedom man does manifest abilities. So Barth speaks of an analogia fidei — the analogy of being to God when being exists in faith. The analogy of faith makes use of what Barth calls the analogia relationis, the analogy between the relationship of man to God and the relationship of man to man. This analogia relationis actually becomes an analogy of God, a speech about God, when it is in a relationship to God, when it is an analogia fidei. For a discussion of this aspect of Barth's thought, see Come, pp. 142–149.

[53] Faith as the invitation to knowledge is the theme of Barth's work on Anselm. There Barth insists that faith does not presuppose or depend upon knowledge for its existence, but rather knowledge exists only in faith. " It

knowledge — knowledge of oneself as actual and true only in the response to grace.[54] Responsible knowledge, knowledge in *der Verantwortung vor Gott,* is the "basic act of the reason which God has given man . . . it is prior and superior to all other knowledge,"[55] and because it is first it is free and natural, and is the basic "illumination of the reason."[56] In effect Barth is rejecting a Cartesian *cogito ergo.* Faith knows no abstract "*cogito,*" but only the concrete "*Christus ergo cogito.*" It contains the truth of all truths, "the truth, the universal truth which creates all truth . . . , the *prima veritas,* which is also the *ultima veritas.*"[57] As the knowledge of the first and universal truth about all reality and life it is not an objective or abstract knowing, but a subjective self-knowledge; it is "living knowledge" (*Lebenserkenntnis*).[58]

Existence as an answer to grace also enjoins an active response of the free will; it establishes existence as obedience. Life is thus not only a gift (*Gabe*), as signified by the Sabbath and the gift of the knowledge of God; it is also a task (*Aufgabe*). Man is placed under the obligation of choosing himself before God, and it is a true and free choice that is obliged.[59] The decision of will thus called forth is not one among others behind which the true ego neutrally resides; no, the decision

---

is not the existence of faith, but rather . . . the nature of faith that desires knowledge." (*Anselm: Fides Quarens Intellectum,* tr. by Ian W. Robertson, p. 18; John Knox Press, 1960.)

[54] "I find myself, I find that being which I am through God's word, contained in the fulfillment of the act of responding, in that outward step." III, 2, 213 (178).

[55] III, 2, 212 (178).

[56] III, 4, 80 (73).

[57] Karl Barth, *Dogmatics in Outline,* tr. by G. T. Thomson (Philosophical Library, Inc., 1949), p. 26.

[58] *Ibid.,* p. 25.

[59] "It is . . . the law under which I stand, the law of my freedom, and thus the law by which I have to establish myself as the person I will be, the law by which I have to choose my only possibility as prescribed and obliged in my knowledge of God." III, 2, 215 f. (181). Thus, just as the Sabbath speaks of the gift of God, so do the six days speak of the obedience of man.

for God's word is one of " to be or not to be " [60] — a decision so radical and comprehensive " that no question remains regarding the way back, that the willing individual already exists in his decision and thus no longer knows or possesses himself in any sort of neutrality." [61] The most concrete expression of man's freedom for obedience is confession, the act in which grace is acknowledged before God and man.[62] If a man is " one who is free before God," then he is free to confess and to live accordingly.[63]

Finally, freedom as existence in answer to God has the character of an invocation (*Anrufung*).[64] When one hears the word of grace he can and must respond, giving his life — his mind, his will, his deed — in answer. But he can do so not with a complacent self-confidence, but only by invoking the grace and mercy of God to accept the offering; it is not within man's power or freedom — or within the created situation as such — to make the offer acceptable.[65] The man who knows the word of grace and is obedient to it knows that he is worthy and acceptable only through grace itself.[66] His existence is one of thanksgiving.[67] Prayer is therefore essential to existence and is primarily a petition, the " utterance of a lack and a need " and " the expression of the certainty that the thing needed . . . is

[60] "When I choose and decide in obedience I venture not only my thinking and doing, but rather myself, my whole self. . . . I venture outward into the new realm of my future, and let go of the 'I' that I was in order to strive toward the 'I' that I will be. I walk the road ordained before my beginning and upon which I can travel only as an active, participating subject." III, 2, 216 (181).

[61] III, 2, 217 (182).

[62] Confession " is the obedience which corresponds to a calling that rests upon free election." III, 4, 93 (85).

[63] III, 4, 79 (73).

[64] III, 2, 222 ff. (186 ff.).

[65] " He can indeed arise and go to his father; he cannot, however, enter his father's house with his own being and deed. That the circle be closed . . . does not lie in his hand." III, 2, 224 (188).

[66] " If God is gracious to him, then it is immediately precluded that man should ever be in the position to oblige God, and to make himself acceptable and pleasing to God." III, 2, 226 (190).

[67] III, 2, 198 ff. (166 ff.).

to be found in God." [68] The ground of prayer is the " freedom of man before God," the freedom that rests in the assurance of divine " free-grace." God's gracious will is " so superior, so majestic, so clear that it makes the prayer of men immediately necessary. It is man's ground, his permission, his necessity." [69] Man must go out of himself; he must move out toward God — not because he has power or freedom to approach God, but because he is confident that God's grace will receive his petition and invocation which are his very life.

A summary designation of the freedom of man in the hearing of the word of his eternal election is "history" (Geschichte). History occurs when the creature experiences some other, something new, something beyond all possibilities of his nature.[70] It occurs in the meeting and decision between man and God. History is therefore originally Heilsgeschichte — a meeting with the creator and savior of life. History is thus to be distinguished from a mere state or condition (Zustand), whereas in history something really new happens (geschieht); in a Zustand there may occur a modification or evolution, but not the radically new. The meeting between the Creator and the creature, between God and man, is not a possibility of and within the creaturely condition as such; when such a meeting does occur then something really new to the creature happens; there is genuine history.[71]

The relationship between man's eternal election and the freedom that it bestows upon man is symbolized in the Creation narratives of Gen., chs. 1 and 2, the exposition of which is the substance of Church Dogmatics III, 1, the first part of Barth's doctrine of creation.

Freedom in Creation

The Yahwist narrative in Gen., ch. 2, symbolizes the aspects of this original freedom of man as a living response to grace. The garden represents the realm staked out by God for man,

[68] III, 4, 99 (91) .   [70] III, 2, 189 (158) .
[69] III, 4, 102 (93) .   [71] III, 2, 188–194 (157–162) .

the realm of grace. The tree of life is the divine testimony that this space is elected for man by God and that it is the good, original, and thus only possibility of life for man. Adam has no need to eat the fruit of this tree because his very life denotes participation in that which the tree represents.[72] In the second tree, the tree of the knowledge of good and evil, Adam is offered the privilege and necessity of accepting and affirming his election and life in the garden. God, by forbidding him to eat of the fruit of the tree, tells Adam that his life and his righteousness are God's decision and that it is not for Adam to eat the fruit of this tree in order to know good and evil and be able to decide himself what his life is and shall be. Adam's acceptance of this prohibition is his obedient, free existence in the hearing of God's word and in the acceptance of God's decision.[73] God prohibits Adam from eating of this tree, not because he is jealous of his prerogatives, but because man's existence can be sustained only by God's grace and preserved by this same grace from the evil which threatens it from the outside.[74] Were Adam to know as God knows and to be responsible for good and evil as God is responsible, he, who is not God, would forfeit the ground of his being and the hope of his survival. Therefore, God's demand is the promise of grace.[75] It reserves to God the care of man.

However, inasmuch as God's word speaks to Adam and forbids him to eat, it also gives him the freedom to obey and accept his election.[76] Within the limits of an existence from God based upon election and to God in the hearing of his word (existence in the garden with its trees) Adam is free to affirm, accept, and acknowledge this his being. Because Adam in the garden is thus limited by the divine freedom he is *non posse peccare,* but because he is free to accept these limits he is *posse*

---

[72] III, 1, 291 (256).
[73] III, 1, 296 (260).
[74] III, 1, 297 ff. (261 ff.).
[75] III, 1, 300 (263).
[76] "Here man is given elbow room; he is granted freedom." III, 1, 300 (263).

non peccare. His freedom is directed and limited and, for this reason, true freedom.[77]

The Priestly account of Creation reaches its climax in the same basic understanding of human existence — as " a movement from God to God," as existence based upon election, and as existence in the hearing of God's word. Genesis, ch. 1, deals more with the creation, the cosmos as such, than it does with the relationship between the cosmos and its creator. The P story views the created cosmos as the " outer ground of covenant," as the physical possibility of covenant, and the J story pictures creation within the covenant designated by Barth as the " inner ground of creation." But the P story does not end with the outer ground as such; it shows by its account of the Sabbath rest of God that the Creation is not complete with man's creation in the sixth day. No, the sixth day — man's day — looks to the seventh, or God's day.[78] Creation not only comes from God and is based upon his election but also is created for God, to be and to abide in relationship to him. God's Sabbath rest with his creation in the seventh day defines man as existence with God, as existence in a free answering to God's grace.[79]

That man is *free* within the limits of God's *eternal will* helps us to understand Barth's discussion of the law of God. The law or commandment of God is the form in which the eternal will of God confronts man; it is the form of grace and as such it is both a claim upon man and a decision over him.[80] It is a

[77] III, 1, 300 f. (263 f.) . See also p. 431 (376) . Barth writes that man " is not given elbow room on the brink of the abyss; it is not a place in the center between obedience and disobedience." And again, that the tree of knowledge means " this and only this, that man is presented the possibility of obedience as *the* possibility, as the possibility of a free decision." (III, 1, 301 (264) .

[78] III, 1, 245 f. (217 f.) .

[79] The meaning of the Sabbath is " that the creation, and above all man, rests with God on this seventh day of creation, and thus is freely, joyously, and happily at rest with itself." III, 1, 245 (217) .

[80] The following discussion is a brief indication of the direction in which Barth develops the foundation of Christian ethics. See II, 2, 564–875 (509–781) .

decision over man because it confronts him with the *eternal decree* of God which is the original decision about man. Accordingly, God's law does not claim man merely from the outside; rather, it goes to the heart of man to tell him who he really is by this eternal decision and to establish him in this decision.[81] It tells man not only what is demanded but also of whom the demand is made.[82] It is radical because it reaches and binds man himself, and leaves intact no a priori existential self-understanding.[83]

God's law lays claim to man because it not only *tells* man who he is according to God's eternal decision, but also *invites* or *claims* him for this decision. The invitation claims man because it is the call of man's true self. As such it actually grants man permission to be himself. In this vein Barth says that God commands or claims us as " the God in whom we *may* believe," i.e., as the God who has done for us what we cannot do for ourselves — electing us for existence with him. " We must learn . . . what God wants with us and from us only from what He has done for us." [84] Because God's law speaks of what God decides and does *for* us it lays so radical a claim *upon* us. It is the claim of our authentic selfhood.

Barth's criticism of Lutheranism is apparent here. Against Lutherans, he insists that law follows the gospel and gives expression to it. The law is not so much a demand for an obedient decision that presupposes a sinful and penitent existence in need of gospel and grace as it is the word of a decision that reveals and bestows the gospel of man's new humanity in God's

---

[81] II, 2, 704 (633 f.).

[82] " God's law is . . . the truth from which man, whether he knows and will know it or not, ever comes and from which he can never escape." II, 2, 572 (516).

[83] II, 2, 702 (632). Barth's criticism of Lutheranism is apparent here. He claims that the gospel precedes the law and that the law expresses the gospel. That is, the law is not so much a demand for the decision and obedience of an existing penitential sinner in need of grace and gospel, as it is a decision which creates a new being and on the basis of this gospel claims the new man for this gracious decision.

[84] II, 2, 621 (560).

elect-man, Jesus. On the basis of this gospel, the law then demands and claims from man an obedient decision.

In summary, God's law is a decision over a man because it
"changes, brands, and qualifies" the man it binds and
claims,[85] because it puts him under the aegis of grace. God's
law is a claim because it calls forth from man an active acceptance of himself as thus decided upon. So God's commandment to Adam not to eat of the tree of knowledge effects God's
decision that Adam is to live by God's grace, and claims Adam
for this decision by giving him the freedom of obedient trust.

The fact that God's decision is also heard as a claim establishes freedom. Barth states that the form of the commandment is a gift of freedom, a "permission," the "granting of a
very definite freedom," [86] because it allows man himself to be
and do what in fact he is; it allows him to be, by his own
decision, what he is by God's decision — elected from the beginning in Jesus.[87] "Should . . . means may. . . . But then,
immediately, may . . . means *should*." [88]

Freedom for Man

Jesus is the man who is for God.[89] Jesus is also the man who
is for other men.[90] Since Jesus is just as essentially "for the
other man" as he is "for God," so the man who lives from
and for him is radically with his fellowman. Man is in an
I-thou relationship, in a movement from "thou" to "thou"
("*vom Du her*" and "*zum Du hin*").[91] He cannot say "I"
without at once relating himself to and distinguishing himself
from "thou." Humanity is basically, essentially, and necessarily "togetherness with fellowman" (*Mitmenschlichkeit*).[92]
Corresponding to this essential togetherness is a radical dependence of "I" upon "thou" and "thou" upon "I." I
need you, I need your eye, your ear, your hand; I am *vom Du*

85 II, 2, 702 (632).
86 II, 2, 650 (585).
87 II, 2, 652 f. (587 f.).
88 II, 2, 669 ff. (682 ff.).

89 III, 2, 64 ff. (55 ff.).
90 III, 2, 242 ff. (203 ff.).
91 III, 2 256 (215).
92 III, 2, 296 (247).

her. Conversely, your needs claim me; you claim my eye, my ear, and my hand; I am *zum Du hin.*[93] I am dependent upon you as I am dependent, *mutatis mutandis,* upon God. I live for you and with you, in hearing your word, as I live in the hearing of God's word. This I-thou relationship is the other essential dimension of my freedom.

Relationship to "thou" is the limit of *freedom* because it discloses to me my only possibility — that of being together with my fellowman.[94] I am freely with my fellowman when I am gladly with him, rather than neutrally or indifferently. This "gladly" (*gerne*) is of the essence of humanity, the *conditio sine qua non.*[95] Man is with his fellowman as surely as he is with God, as surely as he comes from God's eternal word spoken in Jesus Christ. Consequently, he can no more regard his fellowman as a burden than he can regard God as a burden. Spontaneous, free existence with my fellowman is the only possibility that I have as a creature of God's eternal will. So when Barth considers in detail the commandment of God the Creator, the commandment that comes to man as he is in his "togetherness with his fellowman" (*Mitmenschlichkeit*), he does so under the heading "Freedom in Fellowship" (*Freiheit im Gemeinschaft*).[96]

In sum, relationship to Jesus as God's eternal will is indeed one of freedom — joy and spontaneity — inasmuch as it is the original and only possibility of human existence. And, on the other hand, the context of man's true joy and freedom can be none other than Jesus of Nazareth. So when the Christian meets the claim of God upon him in Christ he receives it as a grace, as the possibility of freedom, as a permission, because it expresses the divine, eternal, and only true decision concerning the na-

93 "And this is the humanity of the human being — this his total determination as a being in the encounter with the being of a thou, as a being with his fellow man, as togetherness (*Mitmenschlichkeit*) ." III, 2, 296 (247) . See pp. 296–324 (247–269) .

94 III, 2, 322 f. (268 f.) .

95 III, 2, 319 (266) .

96 III, 4, 127–366 (116–323) .

ture of man. In the free response to this claim man comes to himself; his knowing and his willing are established and called forth. But he is called out not only in his personal abilities, but above all else, in his togetherness with his fellowman, for the Christ in whose service is perfect freedom is the Christ who is eternally the brother of all men. There is no freedom for him that is not at the same time freedom in a radical I-thou relationship with the neighbor. To have radical freedom *for relationship* to Jesus and the neighbor, and in relationship to Jesus and the neighbor *radical freedom* — this is the meaning of freedom for Jesus as God's eternal will.

II. FREEDOM FOR JESUS OF NAZARETH

We asked about freedom in view of the fact that in Christ faith meets God's eternal, gracious will. We now ask what it means for freedom that this gracious will is also *actualized* in Jesus. Before we hear Barth's answer, he would have us hear very clearly and unequivocally the fact concerning which we inquire — the fact that the free man is an actuality, once for all, in Jesus of Nazareth.[97]

An Actual Freedom

To appreciate Barth's discussion we must refer to the doctrine of sin which is the concern of our section on freedom as freedom-from. It need be noted at this point only that the existing man, the man whom Christ calls brother, is the man who crucifies Christ — the man who exists, therefore, in a freedom, if it may be called that, which is quite other than that which Jesus actualized.[98] The actualization of man's created freedom in Jesus offers, therefore, the bonus of the victory and

[97] This actuality of the free man in Jesus is the subject of the section in the *Church Dogmatics* entitled "The Liberation of Man." See IV, 1, 634–678 (568–608). (Note that Barth's translators render *Freispruch* as "pardon.")

[98] Thus Barth, speaking of the salvation history which is the life of Jesus, says that it has a *terminus a quo* (sin) and a *terminus ad quem* (righteousness). It is a *creatio ex contrario*. IV, 1, 639 f. (573 f.).

KARL BARTH: FREEDOM IN CHRIST 139

freedom of man over the powers of sin. In Christ, man is restored to the freedom he possesses as the creature of God — a freedom to be *from* and *for* God — and he is also given the freedom to be *with* God in fulfillment of the covenant and to share with God victory over the devil, sin, and death.[99] This new man — created, completed, and conquering — is actual; he exists in Jesus.[100] In himself, the believer is a sinner. Altogether he is *simul peccator et justus:* in himself, *peccator;* in Jesus, *justus*. As Paul has stated it classically in Rom. 7:24-25: "Wretched man that I am, who will deliver me from this body of death? Thanks be to God through Jesus Christ our Lord." [101] The fulfillment is in Christ; the believer has the promise, and the two may not be confused.[102] As Christians seek out the justified man, the man who is actually free, they look in vain to themselves in contrast to pagans and nonbelievers, for even as they see themselves they see more urgently the need for Christ. There is only one answer: the justified man is to be found only in Jesus Christ. Just as the justified man is found only in Christ, so is the free man found in him. Thus Barth speaks of the justification of man in Christ as also "the liberation of man" (*des Menschen Freispruch*).[103] Man's freedom is first of all the freedom of the man Jesus. There, in the life, death, and resurrection of Christ, "occurs his [man's] transition from his existence as the old man to his existence as the new man." [104] In this his new humanity, man is free, "free for the law of his humanity, free to live on the basis and within the protection of this law; he is free to live as the one who is just." [105]

99 Karl Barth, *Die Geschenk der Freiheit* (Theologische Studien, Heft 39; Zollikon-Zürich: Evangelischer Verlag, 1953), p. 13.
100 Karl Barth, *Die Wirklichkeit des neuen Menschen* (Theologische Studien, Heft 27; 1950), p. 8.
101 IV, 1, 649 (581 f.).
102 IV, 1, 663 (595).
103 IV, 1, 634 ff. (568 ff.).
104 IV, 1, 635 (569).
105 *Ibid.*

Freedom of Humility

But we come again to the question: What does this actuality
of freedom in Christ mean as regards the concrete freedom
of the Christian man — the believer himself? And Barth has
one answer — the freedom of faith. " Faith is itself the simple,
humble, but also altogether positive answer to the question of
the reality and existence of the man justified by God." [106] And
faith is " a free, human *act*." [107] Faith is the freedom given to
existing man by virtue of the fact that his essential humanity
and true freedom exist first of all in Jesus of Nazareth, in his
humanity and in his freedom.

Broadly speaking, faith is an inclusive concept designating
the totality of the life of the Christian community, and the individual Christian in the world. But in its central aspect it is
justifying faith, the act in which man realizes that his justification is in Jesus; and this act is above all else humility. Even
though it is the believer who believes, " when he believes he
knows that he no longer has anything to offer when it comes to
something in which he can be proud." In this respect, man is
" no longer relevant." [108] Faith is altogether faith *in;* it is absolutely determined by its object, Jesus, who does for man what
he cannot do for himself. Faith owes nothing to its own subjectivity and activity.[109] It is altogether a reaching out to and
a following after its object. The believer knows that he is not
saved " by faith " but " through faith." " What is *sola fide* but
a weak, yet necessary, echo of the *solus Christus?* " [110]

Faith is humility not only because it is directed exclusively
toward its object, but also because it is grounded solely in its

[106] IV, 1, 685 (614).
[107] IV, 1, 846 (757).
[108] The Christian believer " does not experience, confirm, or understand
himself in abstraction, in and for himself (man is above all not for himself,
rather, Jesus Christ is for him), but rather from and toward what he is in
Jesus Christ." IV, 1, 708 (633).
[109] IV, 1, 705–707 (631–633).
[110] IV, 1, 706 (632).

object. Faith must be grounded in its object because in faith one is unaware not only of the insufficiency of the self, but also of its actual enmity to the grace which is its object. If man is a proud sinner, whence the humility of faith? [111] The humility of faith roots in the discovery of sin vis-à-vis Jesus, but even more it roots in Jesus — in the great sufficiency of his deed.[112] " If Jesus Christ, and the God who is in Him, exist for him [the believer], then what can be the meaning of the sum of his own thoughts, words, attitudes, undertakings and accomplishments by which he is something in and of himself? He can expect from them absolutely nothing, nothing from his own works, where his justification is concerned. If his eyes are on Jesus Christ, on the history of his own salvation as it has occurred in Him, how then can he, in addition, also have an eye for himself and his works? How can he have any interest in them?" [113] No, in view of the actuality of his liberation in Christ, and in view of his own sin, faith as radical humility is man's only possibility and true freedom. " Faith is the liberation man experiences in the encounter with Jesus Christ. . . . Faith is life in the freedom which is given to man on the basis of the order of righteousness that is created and realized there." [114]

Faith is freedom because it is a possibility that apart from the gift of Christ man would not possess, and because when it is received, it is accepted as the only possibility.[115] In light of the grace of Christ it is inconceivable that one should not be free to believe.[116] Faith is spontaneous and enjoyed as a privilege, and cannot be viewed as a work or a task; obedience cannot be its first dimension. It is also no self-elected humility, for the electing self in this instance would be the prideful self, and the humility a pseudohumility, expressing itself in such manifestations as skepticism, defeatism, and the like.[117] It is

111 IV, 1, 833 (745 f.) .

112 IV, 1, 690 f. (618 f.) .

113 IV, 1, 705 (631) .

114 IV, 1, 708 (634) .

115 IV, 1, 834 (746) .

116 IV, 1, 836 (748) .

117 IV, 1, 691 (619) .

also not a forced humility, a "self-humiliation, retreat, or self-denial forced upon man through fate and circumstances." [118] True humility is "confident despair" (*getroste Verzweiflung*).[119] Only he who trusts fully and confidently in another can despair in true humility of self. The man "in Christ" is the only man who can despair of man "in himself."

The humility of faith is expressed in the fact that it actualizes nothing new. "It changes nothing; as a deed of man it is only the confirmation of a change that has already occurred." [120] It is first of all a cognitive event and not a creative one. It is cognitive in three dimensions — as recognition (*Anerkennen*), cognition (*Erkennen*), and confession (*Bekennen*). The prior factuality and actuality of its object makes faith first of all an act of recognition and acknowledgment. Faith does not create its object; it does not recreate the activity that it presupposes. It is a recognition of the actuality and the sufficiency of its object; it is trust.[121]

Faith is not only an acknowledgment that its object exists and is adequate, but also a knowledge about its object — knowledge about Jesus Christ. Faith is invited to know because Jesus has form (*Gestalt*) and is therefore an opportunity for learning. There is no acknowledgment of Christ that does not become theology immediately.[122] And this is decisive, not that or how much the believer knows, but that the one whom he acknowledges in faith is knowable and invites understanding.[123] The knowledge sought in him is genuine knowledge, *recta cognito;* that is, it takes place within definite limits — namely, within the church and under the norm of Scripture. Yet, while it is genuine and definite, this knowledge is also manifold and preliminary — manifold because of the riches of Christ and because of the uniqueness of each knower, and preliminary because of the depth of Christ's riches and be-

[118] IV, 1, 692 (620).
[119] *Ibid.*
[120] IV, 1, 839 f. (751 f.).
[121] *Dogmatics in Outline*, pp. 15–21.
[122] *Ibid.*, pp. 22–27.
[123] IV, 1, 852 (762).

cause of the shallowness of each knower. Consequently, the knowledge of faith cannot be identified with the assent to dogma or theology. Like faith itself, faith's understanding — theology — is free. Faith is always in search of theology; it is always *fides quaerens intellectum*.

A Living Freedom

The knowledge of faith is not an abstract, objective knowledge that leaves the knower unmoved, for in the first place it is not the whole of faith but, rather, is an element in the *act* of faith. It is a knowledge that arises out of and leads immediately to the act, an act of the whole self, for it knows that its object is directed toward and claims the whole man. To know Christ in the act of faith is to know oneself in this act.[124]

Truth as living reality is symbolized as confession. Confession is " the decision in which men have the freedom to be publicly responsible for their trust in God's word and for their knowledge of the truth of Jesus Christ." [125] It is " the act in which man relates himself to God as is appropriate to God." It takes place " in a stepping out of neutrality towards God, out of any disavowal of the private sphere, into resoluteness, responsibility and public life." Generally speaking, confession is " that movement in the act of faith in which the believer stands for Jesus, and indeed now ' *nach aussen* ' . . . in relation to men." [126] There is no question here of motivation or teleology; it is not an action that is constrained or bound by external purposes.

Barth speaks of faith as freedom for confession and as freedom from questions of motivation and goals when he writes to the Hungarian Christians regarding their duty within their trying circumstances under communist rule: " Everything will

[124] " Does there not follow from this knowledge necessarily a wholesale shaking up of human existence, a radical decision of my existence in its relation to myself and to the world? " IV, 1, 857 (766 f.) .

[125] *Dogmatics in Outline*, p. 28.

[126] IV, 1, 869 (777) .

now depend on your being inspired with a joyful confidence
in the possibility of thinking, judging and deciding spiritually,
instead of strategically and tactically, in the practical problems
that confront you." [127]

It is important to see Barth's emphasis on the "pointless-
ness" of faith as confession. One does not confess Christ in order to make Christians, in order to build a new social order or
to condemn an existing one. One confesses only because the
word of God comes to him in the totality of his experience and
demands a total response — a response of man as one who
stands not only for God but also with his fellowman. Here is
also the great liberty of the Christian man and the Christian
church; they are responsible to no one but God and they are
therefore dependent upon no conditions other than the hearing of God's word for the privilege and duty of speaking for
Christ. The man in the church is truly not responsible — not
responsible for the occurrence of God's will.[128] That is to say,
one can be Christian wherever he is, because to be a Christian
necessitates only the hearing and confessing of God's word.
The church does not *need* to be against or for anything in order
to be the church; it does not *need* to be communistic or capital-
istic, nor *need* it be against these as such.[129] It *need* only confess itself, its faith, wherever it is. The church need do this
and only this simply because in itself it brings nothing and is
nothing; in Christ it is everything, and in the confessing of
Christ it is powerful and free. The most dangerous thing that

[127] *Against the Stream: Shorter Post-War Writings, 1946–1952*, ed. by
R. G. Smith; tr. by E. M. Delacour and Stanley Godman (London: SCM
Press, Ltd., 1954), p. 121.

[128] "'Thy will be done' . . . I don't have to trouble myself in the
least about that, because it's not my concern. I am not responsible. . . .
He cares for you. And precisely in this freedom, in this ultimate responsibility, we have then also as a foregone conclusion the freedom to hear
God's revelation." I, 2, 300 f. (275).

[129] "All other masters, teachers, leaders and lords laden and saddle us
with responsibilities, i.e., with questions which we are to answer from our
own knowledge, with obligations which we are to satisfy with our own
willing and doing, and with programs which we are to execute by our
efforts." I, 2, 299 (274).

an apostate society can do is to make it necessary for the church to do nothing but confess; but that society may be quite safe from the church where the church is not only allowed but encouraged to be busy and anxious about many things. The American society would appear to have little to fear.

Implicit in faith as confession is the freedom of the believer from fear — fear of the world to which he confesses. He is not afraid, because he believes in the God who has overcome the world.[130] Of course, this trust, knowledge, and confession are all acts — *acts* of knowing, *deeds* of knowing. What else could they be, inasmuch as that which they know is the transformation of the whole man into the freedom of God? To know God's word and to confess it means to trust it and to be taught by it.

A New Freedom

Faith is first of all a radical humility — a cognitive and not a creative or significantly new event. But as there is a " first of all," there is also a " last of all," an aspect in which faith is creative and the source of something new. There is something new in the very fact that faith occurs. " There also belongs to the alteration of the human situation which Christian faith can merely confirm, the obvious fact that this confirmation takes place, that there are . . . individual, Christian subjects." [131] And there is something new in the manner in which this new fact occurs, namely, as an analogy or likeness of Christ. " He confirms himself as a Christian in that he can and will exist in a likeness to Jesus Christ, to his death and resurrection, through a heartfelt *mortification* and a *vivifica-*

---

[130] To the Hungarian Church, Barth writes: " If you have no *fear* of the ill will of your government — and why should you? — whether you stand or fall rests in the hands not of your government but of your Master who is Lord of all — then you need not fear a decision which may please or at any rate not displease the new regime." (Italics mine.) The fear of which Barth speaks here is the fear of what the West might think if the church were to appoint Bereczky its Bishop. (*Against the Stream*, p. 123.)

[131] IV, 1, 840 (751 f.) .

tion." [132] That is, in the humility of faith, and in the creative occurrence of faith, in passive trust and creative knowing, the believer is a mirror of Christ.[133]

It is too little to say that nothing new happens in faith, as if the believer were untouched or unrelated to what he believes. And it is too much to say that everything happens in faith, so that faith becomes identical with its object.[134] In making this latter point Barth sets himself firmly against Bultmann [135] and insists that while the man of faith is an analogy of Christ, he is only that — penultimate and not ultimate. Faith can no more be identified with the eschatological event, as in Bultmann's Protestant theology, than can the elements of the Mass be identified with Christ as in Rome's Catholic theology.[136]

In sum: The freedom of faith is the freedom to live in the knowledge of one's created and true freedom as it is actualized in Christ. It is primarily and first of all humility, a relationship determined wholly by its object.[137] This is a freedom because it is not possible apart from its object Jesus Christ and because it is the only possibility in view of its object. In this its primary aspect faith is not a creative act; it changes nothing. It is, rather, a cognitive act, determined by a change that has already occurred. On the other hand, insofar as faith does occur in fact, and insofar as it occurs in humility and cognition, it is creative, effecting something new — namely, a rebirth of the Christian believer such that he becomes an analogue of the original change toward which faith is directed. In

[132] IV, 1, 860 (769).
[133] IV, 1, 862 ff. (771 f.).
[134] IV, 1, 864 (773).
[135] See the note in IV, 1, 857 f. (767 f.).
[136] IV, 1, 858 (768).
[137] Evangelical theology " is *modest* because its entire logic can only be a human *ana-logy* to that word [Jesus Christ]. . . . In short, theology is not a creative act but only a praise of the Creator. . . . Likewise, theology is *free* because it is not only summoned but liberated for such analogy " (Karl Barth, *Evangelical Theology: An Introduction,* tr. by Grover Foley, p. 17; Holt, Rinehart and Winston, Inc., 1963).

faith man finds his life by losing it for the life he has in Christ.[138]

The line of distinction between the two dimensions of freedom we have been discussing needs clarification. The question may be stated as follows: What is the difference between freedom for God's *eternal will* in Jesus and freedom for *Jesus* as God's eternal will? Another way of identifying the problem is to ask about the difference between creation and redemption, between created and Christian freedom. If I understand Barth correctly, there is no final separation or synthesis of these two aspects. Insofar as Jesus is the eternal word for which man is created, the hearing of that word in faith should be the original, creaturely, and creative freedom. But insofar as sin enters, and the believer is a sinner, the freedom of faith is not the original, creative event, but rather a secondary and humble acceptance of the actualized original in Jesus. The two aspects of freedom taken together mean that the freedom of faith is both an original expression of man's created nature and yet also a witness to the fact of his sin and redemption. The original freedom of man that one exercises in faith is a reality in

---

[138] As Barth's doctrine of predestination appears to swallow up the historical deed of Christ, so now his doctrine of the person and work of Christ appears to eliminate the event of faith and reduce faith and the work of the church to relative meaninglessness. This judgment is rather unanimous among Barth's critics. Jerome Hamer criticizes Barth's Christocentrism by contending that " in order to go to the heart of the debate, the theologian ought to grasp the *human moment in the very act of faith* " (*Karl Barth*, tr. by Dominic M. Maruca, S.J., pp. xxxvii f.; The Newman Press, 1962). Faith conceived as merely cognitive is questioned testily by Arnold Come: " Because he [Barth] sees God accomplishing his own glory only in Jesus Christ, Barth quite naturally describes the ultimate service of the creature as its being a wall that echoes back God's own voice, or as a mirror that reflects God's own image to himself for his own self-glorification. Such language is wholly indefensible " (*An Introduction to Barth's* Dogmatics, p. 155). Fortunately this language is Come's, not Barth's. Berkouwer states that " in Barth's theology the triumph of grace makes vague the seriousness of the human decision " (*The Triumph of Grace*, p. 279). So also Balthasar feels that Barth's tendency toward a Christological system sharply undercuts the reality and significance of faith and church. (*Karl Barth: Darstellung und Deutung*, pp. 257 ff.)

faith only as it is first of all a reality in Jesus — which is acknowledged by the noncreative humility of faith.

The problem can be viewed from another perspective. Barth
has stated that according to God's eternal decree man is created
for Jesus, that his being *for* Jesus is the basic dimension of his
created existence. Man is " toward God " (*zu Gott hin*), and
because God has elected Jesus from eternity to be the realm of
his existence, man as creature is at the same time " toward
Jesus " (*zu Jesus hin*). If we underline the preposition and
read *toward* God in Jesus, then man's creative freedom may
be viewed as his movement in a direction, the goal of which is
Jesus. Only in redemption and faith does man arrive at the
goal. As a creature, man (like Israel) is en route; as one who is
redeemed, he (like the church) has arrived. This is one of
Barth's explicit answers to this question: " Salvation is more
than being. Salvation is the fulfillment, and indeed, the highest, most sufficient, first, eternal fulfillment of being. . . . Created being as such needs salvation . . . ; it can only move
towards it. . . . Salvation, fulfillment, perfected being means
— and this is what created being does not have in itself — a
being in participation in the being of God from whom he
comes and to whom he goes." [139] Hedinger symbolizes Barth's
meaning with concentric circles, the inner circle representing
created freedom which points to and is taken up by the outer
circle of redemptive freedom.

The limitations of this idea of redemption as fulfillment are
apparent, the primary one being the Biblical notion of creation as good! Thus Barth also insists that creation is good and
not in need of salvation, that originally man is not only en
route to God but also with God. He is not only en route to
Jesus, but with Jesus. Such appears to be the spirit of Barth's
understanding of the " real man " in his anthropology. There
he states many times over that " every man as such is the fellow
man of Jesus."[140] Man " is together with Jesus; that is the con-

[139] IV, 1, 7 (8).   [140] III, 2, 157 (134).

crete form of his togetherness with God." [141] Because man is
"ontologically determined" by the fact that "amongst all
other men, one is the man Jesus," human existence means "to
be together with God." [142] Consequently, sin — Godlessness — is
"ontologically impossible." [143] At the end of his discussion of
the "real man" he makes it clear that the reality of the real,
created man, is not merely his capabilities (*Fahigkeiten*)
which are the phenomenal aspects included in the reality of
man and studied by philosophy, but the actual man. [144] What
then remains? In what sense can the actuality of redemption
in Jesus and the freedom of faith be other than or more than
the freedom of the creature? Or, from the other side, must we
not conclude that those who do not believe in Jesus are not
creatures in an essential way? Has Barth not identified creation
and redemption and reduced the two concentric circles to
one? From one side of the coin creation — existence outside
faith — is by definition sinful and incomplete, in need of salvation. Is its sin not therefore justified? On the other side, it appears saved, one with God and Jesus from the beginning, so
that there is no justification for the redemptive event of Jesus.

We can answer to the first objection to the extent that we
distinguish in Jesus between the fact that in him God is with
us, and the fact that in him God with us overcomes sin. It is
with regard to the first of these facts that Jesus is the fulfillment of creation, insofar as man who is originally *toward* God
is now *with* him. The second objection brings us back to the
beginning of our discussion, to the dialectic of faith which
asserts that Jesus is both eternal and temporal, so that the redemptive event is both original and eternal and yet repeated
temporally and decisively in Palestine two thousand years ago.

Very simply, Barth's theology poses a dilemma, all sides of
which he both exposes and explores. The dilemma results from
his efforts to combine incarnational and atonement theolo-

[141] III, 2, 168 (140) .   [143] III, 2, 166 (139) .
[142] III, 2, 161 (134) .   [144] III, 2, 236-241 (198-202) .

gies, east and west, ontology and history, so that Jesus is both the eternal word and the historical deed. The separation of these two tendencies is fatal for faith, but their unity is also fatal to a systematic theology. Again, we see why Barth does church (faith) theology and not systematic theology. And as we move on we see the problem compounded by the fact that in addition to the ontological and the historical there are also existential and creative aspects to faith which make synthesis and system even more impossible.

III. FREEDOM FOR JESUS THE WORD OF GOD

Jesus as Prophet

In our last section we discussed the freedom of man in the light of the once-for-all actuality and factuality of the achievement of Christ. We found that this event is also the actual, once-for-all event of man's acquittal, liberation, or *Freispruch*.[145] Therefore, the believer's freedom cannot but be the freedom of faith, understood as a humility that itself changes nothing because it is wholly determined by the change which is effected once for all by Jesus. We noted, however, that in a secondary way a second change does occur – in the fact *that* faith takes place, and that it is a mirror of its object. In Vol. IV, 3, Barth gives specific attention to this positive dimension of faith, something he can and must do for the reason that Jesus Christ is not only a once-for-all event of the past, but also an ever-occurring event of the present. He who *was* king and priest is *now* also the prophet. In its substance Christ's work is complete; in its form it ever continues. So also, in its substance faith is humility before the accomplished fact but in its form it is creative and active participation. As king and priest, as a past fact, Jesus is the electing God and the elected man, both word and response. As prophet in our time, and in our world, he is word only, and the Christian is the response. In light of Christ's past work as mediator man's freedom is

[145] IV, 1, par. 61, 573–718 (514–642).

above all else his acquittal *(Freispruch)* in Jesus himself which has its reflection in the humility of faith. In the presence of Christ's prophecy the believer's freedom is a creative participation of the created self; it is his own private *Befreiung,* or liberation. Faith, as humility before Christ's accomplished work, is comprehended altogether in the category of Christology, but when we speak of faith in relation to Christ's ongoing prophecy, we move in the direction of anthropology, and so also into a new dimension of freedom.[146] If Christ is prophet, if he wills to be acknowledged and glorified by man, then man has a calling and a very positive role to play.[147]

Jesus, who is the prophet of his own work, the light upon his own life, which is also the life of man, enters into his prophetic office through a twofold Parousia — his return in resurrection and again in the Spirit.[148] With the resurrection, yesterday's " fact " becomes today's " factor." [149] And in this respect, he who comes as the same one who was before, also " comes new in the Easter event." [150] And now that " Jesus Christ is raised from the dead no man who has ever lived or ever will live is or will be the same as he would be had Christ not been raised." [151] However, this resurrection faith presents us with a difficult theological question — namely, that if his death and resurrection were effective once for all, what can be added by his venture into prophecy? What is added by talk? The question is complicated further by the fact that the resurrection as witness to Jesus' life and death seems relatively ineffective. If Christ is declared to be Christ in a definitive way by the resurrection, if by the resurrection Christ becomes once for all a factor in the life of

[146] IV, 3, 318 (276).

[147] IV, 3, par. 71, 553–779 (481–680).

[148] IV, 3, 337 ff. (292 ff.).

[149] The fact and problem of the prophetic office of Christ arise first of all because of the resurrection, and the need to take it seriously. For Barth, the resurrection, " the Easter-event — as the revelation of the nature and work of Jesus Christ in his past life and death — is his *new coming as the one who has come before."* IV, 3, 335 (291).

[150] IV, 3, 335 f. (291 f.).

[151] IV, 3, 344 (298).

all men, why is this factor not everywhere effective? Why are not all men Christian? Why were only a small band in the beginning chosen to be witnesses? Why did not Christ's first appearance in resurrection " overwhelm everything like a tidal wave "? [152] These questions are Barth's, and they are legitimate, he feels, because they arise out of resurrection faith itself. The answer, which he proposes after rejecting several common and unacceptable alternatives, is simply that Christ wants to be a factor in the existence of man. The apparent failure of Christ's prophecy in resurrection, the fact that it has " not yet " realized its goal, " has its foundation in that it is Jesus Christ's good will . . . to be short of the goal, *en route*, so that nothing remains to the creature who is [already] reconciled to him than to take his situation earnestly and to exist in a proper correspondence to it. The ' not yet ' obtains not because the darkness still remains . . . but because it is his good will to confirm himself . . . as a victor in faith against the darkness." [153] In a word, Jesus' delay is man's opportunity. Man's role is positive (as opposed to the merely cognitive and passive) not only because Christ as prophet calls man, but also because he gives man time for a response — a time between Jesus' first Parousia in his resurrection and his final return at time's end.

But there is another dimension to the answer indicated when Barth speaks of Jesus' " good will to confirm himself." Jesus wills not only to witness through his resurrection, but also through a second Parousia — his return and presence as the Holy Spirit.[154] The time between beginning and end, man's time, has, says Barth, its own peculiar glory, the glory of Christ's presence in his Spirit, and this presence is every bit as real, authentic, and full as the others.[155] This, says Barth, is the deeper answer to the question of the reason for the " not yet." [156]

152 IV, 3, 365 (316).   155 IV, 3, 416 (360).
153 IV, 3, 380 (330).   156 IV, 3, 416 ff. (360 ff.).
154 IV, 3, 403 (349).

In sum: man is called because Christ as the resurrected one calls and waits, because he would give time to man and glory for his own spiritual presence.

The Call of the Christian

This positive dimension of the freedom of faith is established by Christ's prophetic call — a call that Christ brings to man through the message and mission of the church. This saving work of Christ by which he establishes this dimension of freedom will be discussed in the section on freedom for freedom. For now, it is our concern to examine the resulting freedom itself.

In the first place, Barth would disabuse his readers of notions which belittle this positive and personal dimension of the freedom of faith. Thus, while it is true that the one who calls has already reconciled all men, and while the calling of the individual Christian is received first of all as the calling of all men that binds the Christian to the church and humanity as such, nevertheless, the Christian's calling is *his* calling, the calling of his particular and concrete existence.[157] No Christological considerations may be allowed to take away from the historical actuality of the event of this private call. Nor may any fear of mysticism, pietism, etc., detract from the personal experience and reality of the call.[158] Indeed, Christ is *de jure* for all men, but by his call he becomes *de facto* only for the Christian.[159] The humility which is proper to faith must not jeopardize faith's seriousness; the fact of my reconciliation in Christ must not gainsay the fact that I am en route to salvation in response to Christ's call. The fact that Christ has acted does not alter the fact that he continues to act. While my reconciliation on Calvary's cross is a fact, so also is my calling now in Christ's church.

The calling of the Christian is also a genuinely spiritual experience.[160] Certainly it is mediated by the witness and

[157] IV, 3, 570 (496).
[158] IV, 3, 572 ff. (497 ff.).
[159] IV, 3, 321 (278).
[160] IV, 3, 576-579 (501-503).

kerygma of the church but it is nevertheless effected directly by the immediate speaking of Jesus himself, who is now present as the Holy Spirit. It is the special glory of the Holy Spirit that the Christian does not move from resurrection to final glory in a vacuum, *remoto Christi*.[161] No, Jesus is immediately and actively present, and spiritually experienced, as the Christian moves down the road from Easter to *eschaton*.[162] It is this real experience of the Holy Spirit that gives faith its positive dimension and establishes the Christian in his calling.

The event of calling means a radical change in the believer's existence in which he becomes himself an analogy of Christ. In his calling the Christian does not have merely the knowledge of reconciliation, but this knowledge is itself a reconciliation.[163] We might say that in the event of calling, three histories come together — the history of the reconciling act of Jesus, from Bethlehem to Easter, the history of the calling of Jesus, from Easter to *eschaton*, and the history, from faith to fulfillment, of the reconciled and called Christian. The change wrought by the prophecy of Christ is that the Christian is established in the history of his faith, and inasmuch as this history has its beginning, it is an unique, once-for-all change requiring that John Wesley, for example, date his conversion in his own lifetime. (Inasmuch as it is a change made possible by him who once for all reconciled all men on the cross, Kohlbrügge is correct in dating his conversion in the first century.) [164] However, conversion is conversion to a history, a history in which the believer is ever on the move from the lie and deception of sin to the knowledge and truth that is the light and word of Christ.[165] The content and goal of this history of the Christian appears then to be nothing more, nor less, than the Christian life itself, life *unico cum Christo*.[166] The believer is put on his own feet and established in his own history in order to be with Christ *de facto* and not merely *de jure*, and so

161 IV, 3, 400 (346) .   164 IV, 3, 574 (499 f.) .
162 IV, 3, 402 ff. (348 ff.) .   165 IV, 3, 575 f. (500 f.) .
163 IV, 3, 247 (216) .   166 IV, 3, 621 ff. (540 ff.) .

thereby to become a true analogy of Christ.[167] Barth would say something about this life, without at the same time reducing it to other terms, so that no matter how it be described it is finally life *with Christ*. He considers several traditional and popular alternatives, each of which finally results in a reduction of the Christian life to its effects.[168] The only satisfactory characterization of the Christian life is " existence in the execution of . . . duty." [169] Duty is the basic category because it gives the proper glory and honor to the one who calls and maintains the dimension of the Christian life that makes it a *Christian* life.[170] And there is only one duty which is at the same time *unico cum Christo,* namely, the duty to witness.[171] Paul was called to be an apostle, a representative, a spokesman, for Jesus.[172] Jesus lives in, actualizes, and speaks the will of God for man, so when one is called to be with him, one is called to be a fellow worker and spokesman with him of God's love and Kingdom. The Christian is not " a mere observer of his Lord, and thus not merely a dead instrument moved and

[167] IV, 3, 616 (536).

[168] The alternatives considered by Barth are: (1) The eschatological view, which understands existence with Christ as freedom from the world. But this, says Barth, is an effect and not the substance of Christian existence. (2) The moral view, according to which the Christian life means a new ethos of inner and outer behavior. This view has the value of giving positive content to the Christian life, but finally it also relativizes Christ in favor of his effect upon the Christian. (3) What Barth designates as the " classical view," which finds the significance of the Christian life in the experience of salvation. Aside from certain inner problems connected with this view, it is contradicted by Scripture which regards the personal blessings of the Christian life as preparation for and the fruit of the Christian calling. In the last analysis, each of these views reduces life with Christ to life with the benefits of Christ. IV, 3, 640–658 (557–573).

[169] IV, 3, 658 (573).

[170] Barth reminds us that Paul was called not primarily to be free from the world, to live the good life, or to enjoy the fruits of salvation — but simply to perform the duty given him by Christ. He is free from the world because he is free for Jesus. He is to live a righteous life because his duty demands it. He is to enjoy the fruits of salvation as instruments of his duty. IV, 3, 657 f. (573 f.).

[171] IV, 3, 660 (575).

[172] IV, 3, 677 ff. (591 f.).

used by the Lord. . . . He is, in his place and in his function,
no less free than his Lord." He is free to obey and to serve his
Lord just as his Lord is free " to claim, accept, direct, and
rejoice in the Christian's service." [173] This does not mean that
the Christian in his calling is a substitute for Christ, witnessing
in his absence. No, this duty is performed by the grace of him
who calls, by virtue of the presence of the Holy Spirit, and
through the gifts bestowed by the Spirit. In the performance
of his duty and in his witness the Christian realizes his unity
with Christ. The Christian is called and he personally witnesses; but he is a cooperating (*mitwirkendes*) subject, not an
absolute subject.[174]

As Paul has said, " I live, yet not I, but Christ." When the
Christian remembers that his witness is effective because Christ
is with him, and that the Christ who is with him is the Christ
who was with him and all men once for all on Golgotha's hill,
he will not for one minute confuse his history and witness with
the history of Him through whom and to whom he witnesses.[175]
For all its creativity and meaningfulness, faith that fulfills itself
in witness grounds itself in a humble petition of Christ, *the*
Priest, King, and Prophet. And yet Christ lives " also in another form in the Christian. In this form too he lives for the
world, for all men — as their mediator, head, and representative, the new and true Adam — even in this form. But in this
form certainly not in all men, but only in the one called by
him — the Christian." [176]

The event of the believer's faith is a positive event because
Christ as prophet speaks a word that is meant only for the believer, and because Christ wishes to accompany the believer in
the glory of his spiritual presence. Therefore, the calling of the
Christian is a true experience in the Christian's own time and
place; it is an event that changes his life, establishing it in a
history or life with Christ — a life in which the Christian becomes an analogy of Christ by fulfilling his duty as witness.

[173] IV, 3, 690 (602).　　[175] IV, 3, 693 (604).
[174] IV, 3, 687 (600).　　[176] IV, 3, 694 (605).

This is a history *unico cum Christi*. It must now be added that although this is a history with Christ, rooted in him, and sustained by him, it is nevertheless a genuinely human history. In his encounter with and calling by the Lord Jesus, Paul is not lost, or overwhelmed, but rather "precisely through this calling he is put on his own feet vis-à-vis Jesus, and as apostle of Jesus is established in his own freedom and movement." [177] Barth must therefore at last, but not least, speak of the calling of the Christian as "the liberation of the Christian" (*die Befreiung des Christen*). He may speak of faith as a "determination of man in his ' private existence.' " [178]

The Liberation of the Christian

In its first aspects faith is the freedom of humility before Christ, in its second aspect freedom with Christ, and now it may be spoken of as "the liberation [or freedom] of the Christian." [179] In its first two dimensions the freedom of faith is a Christological category; but in its third dimension it is an anthropological category, speaking not only of Christ, but also of the Christian himself. In the preceding discussion of the question of the structure of the Christian's unity with Christ we saw that this structure could not consist primarily of the personal enjoyment of the benefits of Christ's salvation, that these benefits are unto the end and the result of that which is essential to the unity with Christ, namely, service with Christ as his witness. Now, with the centrality of duty established, the dimension of personal, private salvation, the "liberation of the Christian," may be given direct attention.

Accordingly, the work of God is not external and alien to man, but becomes "experience," an "element" in the life of the Christian. [180] Faith is not only a knowledge of Christ, but also a new being in Christ. [181] Insofar as this experience of salvation, or conversion to a new being, is for the sake of the duty

177 IV, 3, 243 (213).
178 IV, 3, 742 (647).
179 IV, 3, 742 ff. (647 ff.).
180 IV, 3, 744 (649).
181 IV, 3, 745 f. (650 f.).

and service of witness to Christ, the experience is secondary. Yet, insists Barth, the experience is necessary. Orthodox Protestantism failed to see what pietism so rightly discerned — that a witness without experience, a witness without a life, a witness without freedom, is severely limited. A witness to the fact of salvation is not convincing if this fact is no factor in the life of the Christian. If Christ is a judgment upon sin in the world, a witness to Christ who does not submit to this judgment in his own life is unconvincing. But above all, if the word is good news, a joyful word, it can hardly be testified to without a smile, without a life lived in the joy, peace, and freedom of salvation.[182] The liberation of the Christian, the experience of the salvation, is necessary for the fulfillment of the service of the Christian.

The personal freedom experienced by the Christian is thus the freedom not only to acknowledge and to follow Christ, but to *be* himself " an image and analogy " of Christ and of " the great and perfect transition, the liberation of the world and of all men, which God has accomplished in Jesus Christ." [183] The Christian is free, he exists in joy and peace, inasmuch as he is delivered from the disintegration of a will oriented toward a fragmented world and is established in the integrity of the will that wills one thing — the will of Jesus Christ. He is free inasmuch as he is delivered from self and the world so as to live for other persons. He is free from the self-alienation that roots in the law and in the need to prove and justify himself, because he is free for the justification and righteousness given him by Christ. He is free from his own impotence and indolence; he is free to act and to live through him who is raised and now lives for him; he is free from the dialectic of the moral-immoral, the essential-existential. He is free for the dialectic of forgiveness and gratitude, to exist from that which is essential, toward and with that which is essential. He is free *from* the confidence in the good and the good will that overcomes the bad; he is free

182 IV, 3, 754 f., 757 f. (658 f., 660 f.) .
183 IV, 3, 760 (663) .

for the righteousness of God and the power of the grateful will that overcomes both the good and the bad will. It all may be summed up by saying that he is free from anxiety, and free for prayer.[184]

The freedom of the Christian man, his inward reflection of the glory of Christ, is a beginning thing — a movement toward the prize of the upward call in Christ. Not only is it a beginning thing, but it is also a secondary thing, an accompaniment of and a witness to Christ. But nevertheless, it is a theme of the highest importance. It is proper and responsible to ask, " How is it with your heart? " [185]

Certainly the most concrete and essential expression of the freedom of the Christian for Jesus as prophet is the freedom he has in the church to explicate (*explicatio*) Scripture in exegesis and apply (*applicatio*) it in proclamation. The Christian is not only free to be one *with* Christ (*unico cum Christi*) and to speak *to* him, but he is also free, as we have seen, to be *like* him and to speak for him. This freedom for Scripture is discussed by Barth in the " Prolegomena " to the *Church Dogmatics* under the heading " Freedom in the Church," especially in the subsection " Freedom Under the Word." [186] Freedom under the word, says Barth, is the " readiness and willingness to be responsible ourselves for the understanding of the Word." [187] We do not *possess* this freedom; in ourselves we *are* not responsible; rather, we are *given* this freedom and are *made* responsible.[188] In its substance this freedom is the freedom to clarify Scripture in exegesis and interpretation (*ex-*

---

[184] See IV, 3, 759–772 (662–673).

[185] IV, 3, 777 (677).

[186] This entire section, " Freedom in the Church," deals directly with what might be called Barth's hermeneutics. The first subsection, " The Freedom of the Word," will be touched upon in the last section of this study (" Freedom for Freedom ") inasmuch as it is the freedom of the Word which sets man free *for* the Word. In this part of our discussion it is appropriate to consider the second subsection, " Freedom Under the Word." See I, 2, 779–830 (695–740).

[187] I, 2, 780 (696).

[188] I, 2, 781 (687).

plicatio et applicatio).[189] We *must* clarify Scripture because of its humanity; we *may* clarify it because of the clarity of its divinity.[190] Its humanity invites us to this task and engages our humanity — our conceptions, thoughts, convictions, and, yes, our philosophies, just as the divinity of the Word redeems our humanity — our words, thoughts, and philosophies — so that they indeed speak for him. Freedom means therefore activity, and not sheer passivity, and demands that we take up Scripture into our language and not simply reiterate and repeat the language of Canaan.[191] However, the language we employ is subordinate to the language of the Bible, and the content in our language must give precedence to the content of the Bible — Jesus Christ.[192] It must be underscored here (although it is the concern of the last section on " Freedom for Freedom ") that the success of interpretation or the actuality of the Christian's freedom for the word roots in and is evidence of the freedom of the word. The effective subordination of our words is finally not the result of hermeneutic skill but of God's power.

The concern of this study does not call for a further examination of Barth's hermeneutics, except for a brief note and comment upon the practical steps involved in the exercise of the church's freedom in the Word to interpret and apply the Word.[193] The first is " observation " *(Beobachtung)* or exegesis, in which the reader, by means of the historical-critical method asks *what* is said and *of what* it is said.[193] Admittedly, this involves ultimately a preunderstanding of what generally can happen, but this preunderstanding is no law and must be prepared to yield to the word of Scripture if necessary. The second step is reflection, in which the word passes over into the thinking of the exegete to become his own word. It is not to be denied that this means a philosophical expression, yet it must be one in which philosophy is subject to the word and is used

189 See I, 2, 780, 799, 815 (696, 712, 729).
190 I, 2, 799 (712).
191 I, 2, 802, 805 (715, 717 f.).
192 I, 2, 807 (720).
193 I, 2, 810–830 (722–740).

self-consciously, hypothetically, and not as the thing-in-itself. The last phase, which leads to the witness of the church in proclamation, is the event of the church's appropriation and application of the Word in its own witness and responses, in both its inner and outer life of devotion and witness.

In sum: to be free for Jesus as prophet is to be free for Scripture — in exegesis, interpretation, and application, and the success of this enterprise, the event of this freedom, is a concrete witness to the glory of God and the freedom of the Word.

A few words in summary are in order. We have seen Barth develop the discussion of freedom to show that the dimension of freedom relative to the Christian's calling comes first of all to the individual who must then express it in and through the church, whereas the ontological freedom, the liberation that the Christian has in Christ through his once-for-all act from Bethlehem to Easter, is initially the freedom of Christ, the apostles, and the church. In this prophetic dimension of Christology we are at last on the threshold of anthropology, and so Barth concludes his study of the calling of man with a discussion of the " private experience " of the Christian. But even in its private dimensions the freedom of faith is freedom *in Christ*. As humility, it is altogether a Christological phenomenon, a bowing before the work of Christ. As the service of witness, it is a creative act of man, yet an act whose content is altogether determined by the Christ to whom it witnesses. And as the experience of liberation, it is not only an act of man and an expression of his very being, yet his being not as a concrete particular individual but his being as one *in Christ*. He has not yet entered fully into the realm of anthropology.

In a word, the full range of Barth's Trinitarian theology is yet to be developed; he has yet to realize fully the implications of the work of the third Person of the Trinity, the Holy Spirit.

IV. FREEDOM IN THE SPIRIT

In the Christological context the Spirit does not receive its own glory; it is seen altogether in its procession from Christ, and not in its own peculiar hypostasis. While the Holy Spirit does indeed speak of Christ to man, it also speaks its own voice, and to man in his own spirit. We would expect that should Barth have been allowed to write the final volume of his *Church Dogmatics* another "new" Barth might have appeared. Brunner spoke of a new Barth when Barth made clear his decision to view theology in light of the once-for-all event of man's reconciliation in Christ. So thoroughly did Barth speak in these terms that critics found it difficult to see how Barth could be anything but a univeralist who made meaningless the calling and witness of the church, and the urgency and significance of faith. Now we have seen that in connection with the prophetic office, faith, an act and event in the life and experience of men, must be taken seriously. Man in his freedom is not only hidden with God in Christ, but actualized in the life of the Christian. So when Barth moves to consider the Holy Spirit and the life and work of the Christian and church, must he not say *man* with a seriousness that is yet to be detected? Is not my witness as a Christian also *my* witness? What difference do *I*, in my uniqueness and creative possibilities, make to God? Inasmuch as God's spirit comes to *me*, am I not only privileged, but obliged, to take myself earnestly?

In his discussion of Christ as "the light of life," Barth does not deny that there are lesser, creaturely lights in the cosmos which, while they are not the lights that speak of God and thus also the last word about man and his world, are nevertheless true lights with their own worldly, immanent truth.[194] The brightest of these lights is the light of man himself. The lights of the cosmos shine in the polarity of subject-object, in a dynamic rhythm born of the world's inner contradictions and created imperfection, so that object sheds light upon subject and subject upon object. There is, however, an imbalance which means that finally the world, the object outside, addresses man, the subject, with a question.[195] It issues a call to

[194] IV, 3, 122 ff. (110 ff.) ; 153 ff. (135 ff.) .
[195] See IV, 3, 158–171 (140–151) .

man and his freedom, making him responsible for the cosmos. The world cries to man for humanizing.[196] For this reason, man has his own freedom, his own creative possibility and responsibility; he has the humanity for which the cosmos waits.[197] True, this freedom and creative possibility are powerless to shed light on the ultimate question concerning the ground and meaning of man and the cosmos. The ultimate answer is provided by the word of God which finds its fulfillment and expression in Jesus. But when this word is spoken, is not man then established in his cosmic responsibility, in a freedom to realize creatively his humanity and so to begin the deliverance of the world from its groaning and travail? [198] To this responsibility the Spirit calls, and unto its achievement, the Spirit sustains. Perhaps it is in this direction that Barth's theology would have moved were Barth to have been allowed the time. In any case, it is in this direction that the "theology" of Nicolas Berdyaev does move, permitting us to view it not so much as a correction but as a development of Barth's view of freedom.

196 IV, 3, 167 (147).

197 IV, 3, 169 (149). "It is certainly not insignificant . . . that in and with all these [creaturely] lights still another light becomes and is visible, namely . . . the light of the unanswerable question ' Why? ' that shines over the one and the many."

198 Although Barth does speak of man's responsibility for the cosmos, he fails to develop the implications. The hope of the cosmos appears to rest altogether in the accomplished work of Christ and not at all in the creative freedom of the Christian who lives from the Christ event and in the Spirit of Christ. The future redemption of man and the cosmos referred to by Paul in Rom. 8:21-23, consists in the coming revelation of Jesus. "Nothing needs to be added to our salvation, which has taken place in Jesus Christ. ' It is finished.' " (A Shorter Commentary, p. 101.) The Spirit provides hope only as it discloses the past achievement of Christ. "Faith is hope inasmuch as it knows the promise and cleaves to it." (Ibid.) See also the Church Dogmatics, where Barth says that the life of the Christian in the Spirit is only a "preliminary one." IV. 3, 773 (674). If the life is only a preliminary one, then has the spirit really received its proper glory? Barth states that in the doctrine of reconciliation he comes to the edge of anthropology; it does not appear that he steps into it.

FREEDOM-FROM

We have summed up the meaning of Christian freedom as freedom for Jesus. However, inasmuch as men reject Jesus before they accept him, are against him before they are for him, are Adam before they are sons of Christ, they evidently exist in a condition from which they must be set free if at the same time they are to be free for Jesus. This condition, since it is the opposite of freedom and must be called a bondage, is nevertheless experienced and claimed as some sort of freedom.

True freedom is a freedom for Jesus, who, as we have seen, is the expression of God's eternal will, the actuality of that will, the living witness to that actuality, and also its abiding presence. According to these dimensions of the Christian's freedom we may speak of corresponding dimensions of bondage and freedom-so-called.

Freedom from the Devil

If Jesus is God's eternal will, the alpha and omega of all his ways and of all creation, then from the outset all other possibilities are excluded from God's creature. Therefore the " freedom " with which man rejects Jesus, the bondage in which he regards himself free of Jesus, is impossible. Man's original and only freedom is his being *non potest peccare* — not able to sin. Freedom is not the arbitrary freedom of choice.[199] Man has no freedom to sin; it is an " ontological impossibility." [200] He comes from and for Jesus Christ. He may be compared with a passenger in an airplane who lives only as he is upheld and surrounded by the airplane, whose deliberate effort to " free "

---

[199] Ulrich Hedinger asks (and answers in Barth's words) : " Why is the *liberum arbitrium* treated with so little seriousness in Barth's theology? Because Jesus Christ ' is not at all a mere alternative or opportunity given to man, not merely a demand upon him,' a choice *à prendre ou à laisser* placed before him. The other ' alternative is as a matter of fact removed in Christ.' . . . The necessity of faith stands objectively, ontologically for all men " (*Der Freiheitsbegriff*, pp. 16 ff.) .

[200] *Against the Stream*, p. 189.

himself of the plane is sheer madness — as was Adam's fall and the freedom of man from Jesus.[201] Now, God did, as we have seen, give Adam *freedom* for his word, and in this freedom which is called into being by God's word there lies the " impossible possibility " of sin — the possibility that freedom might opt what the garden does not possess, an alternative other than God's word. It is the failure of idealistic and secondary forms of Christianity to seek to give sin a place, for example, as the price of maturity and freedom. This denies the nature of sin as sin. There could be no meaning in the justification of the sinner by Christ if his sin is as such already justified in creation.[202]

Since Jesus is God's eternal will, " freedom " from Jesus is impossible, and the effort to find the essence of freedom in man's relation to the world is also impossible, inasmuch as the world, the creation as such, comes after and for Jesus who is the firstborn of all creation. Man's place is the boundary line between God and the world, where he is free from confusing himself with either. His is the sixth day of creation, standing properly between the fifth and the seventh, between the world and God, above and of the world with and under God.[203] It is impossible that man would be so proud as to feel free to play God, to work on the Sabbath, and that he should be so lazy as not to live up to his humanity and fulfill the responsibilities of his six days.

Freedom for God's eternal will means freedom from the impossible and freedom from the world. In substance, man's original freedom is a freedom for God or it is nothing. And when man rejects Jesus, he betrays just that, a freedom for nothing, and therein a delivering of himself over to that nothingness —

---

[201] " So also, man's trespass is not to be deduced from the positive expectations for the freedom which God gave man." III, 1, 303 f. (266) .

[202] " Sin belongs nowhere; it is without authentic potential and has not the slightest claim to reality." IV, 1, 455 (410) .

[203] We have already observed that Barth regards the world — the creation as such — a *materia inhabilis et indisposita* when the substance of man's being and freedom is the question.

des Nichtige, or the devil.[204] *Das Nichtige* is not a neutral negative (the *ouk on* out of which God created); it is, rather, that to which God says no. It is defined and given its negative constitution and reality as that to which God says eternally " no " when he speaks his eternal " yes " to creation in Jesus. It has its being, if it may be called such, in God's will that it not *be*. It has a place that is no place.

Man has, on the other hand, a true and proper place, and within this place, between God and his creation, freedom. Through this freedom *das Nichtige* gains entry to the created realm where it does not belong. Having illicitly entered the realm of reality, he takes covering behind its " shadowy " side and claims the relative and good negativities of life as his own, and through them says no to God, to his creation, and so also to the dimensions of man's true freedom.[205] For example, the fact that man is eternally distinguished from God, the fact that he *is not* God and is subject to finitude and death, is claimed by the devil. To this good negativity which is the condition and possibility of life *with* God (as opposed to life *as* God), the devil adds his own evil " no," so that death comes to mean not only *not* God but also *not* good. Thus man's not being God becomes a problem, a threat to and a judgment upon him and no longer a promise and a grace.[206] His not being God appears now to mean that he is not with God, neither from nor for God, and his original freedom for God is lost.

In a similar fashion the fact that man *is not* his neighbor is made problematic and not good. No longer is his distinction from his neighbor a gift of freedom from and for the neighbor but a limitation that must be overcome.[207] Barth sees this spirit

---

[204] See III, 3, 327–425 (289–368). Barth's doctrine of the devil ought not to be taken too seriously. He is not so much saying who or what the devil is, as he is what it is not. By calling it *das Nichtige* he means that (1) it is the negation of God and has therefore no share in the Being of God, and (2) it is the negation of God's creation and has therefore no share in the being of the creature. Nevertheless, it *is,* and can therefore be said to possess only the being of nonbeing.

[205] See III, 3, 334–342 (295–302).

[206] III, 3, 350, 403 (308, 349 f.).

[207] III, 2, 274 ff. (229 ff.); IV, 1, 517 f. (465 f.).

embodied in Nietzsche, who, says Barth, was interested in that which was not himself only as a paradigm, symbol, or projection of himself.[208] So the devil says, in effect, that man is essentially without God and without his neighbor; he has nothing, nothing but himself, his " freedom," and, of course, nothingness, *das Nichtige*. And just as the devil can find room in the fact that I am not God and not my neighbor, so also he can find room in the fact that I *am not,* but am always becoming in freedom — in a movement toward the future. Not being myself is bad, so the devil says, and I must exercise my freedom to be myself. But this freedom to be myself is illusory, for the self is a gift of God and neighbor and cannot be won as a creature of my own so-called freedom, responsibility, and will to power. No longer free in a joyous " outward step " (*Tritt nach aussen*) man is now wrapped up in himself as such, laden with the burden of responsibility and subject to the vanity of nothingness.

Free for the impossible, to live not from God in freedom from the world, but to live apart from God, and subject to the vanity of life in the world, and to the bondage of *das Nichtige* — this is the dimension of the freedom from which one is set free by the revelation of Christ as God's eternal will.

Freedom from Pride and Sloth

In the world man presumes to have a freedom from God and neighbor in order to fulfill the meaning of his so-called freedom out of self and the world. However, in the world is also Jesus who has actually fulfilled man's freedom in its authentic dimensions as a freedom in and for the grace of God and the neighbor. Since the authentic freedom of man is actualized, the prideful, so-called freedom of man to live apart from grace and in self-responsibility is an impotent gesture; his so-called freedom has the power of impotence. Yet, it is precisely this powerless power that he claims. He will not accept the law of God as the law of grace, but rather as the law of self and duty.

[208] III, 2, 278 (232).

"We absolutely do not respect the law as the form of grace." [209]
The law that originally expresses the gift and actuality of life
in the grace of Christ now expresses the impotent potentiality
of life in man and his world as such. The law that promised
life now becomes death.[210]

To sum up: in the world, with the law of God no longer
conceived as an expression of God's grace, powerful and effective in Jesus, man is proud of his freedom and power, yet impotent, tired, and slothful in the efforts to realize the good.[211]
As we have seen, when man rejects God, he loses "the necessary
presupposition of all knowledge of the necessity, the worth, the
promise, and the claim of the other, the neighbor." [212] And
now, without the discipline of God or the neighbor, he falls
into disorder, loses himself in the world, where he suffers decay
and corruption. Given over to himself, he is lost to the varied
lusts of his own nature which contend with each other and so
divide, conquer, and render him powerless. The mind would
free itself of the body and forfeit its responsibility of government, whereas the body at the same time would free itself of

[209] II, 2, 830 (743).

[210] For a good, quick look at Barth's view of the impotent power of sin
and man under the law, see his discussion of Romans, ch. 7, in *A Shorter
Commentary*, pp. 74–87. Barth writes that "while the Law claims me for
God, sin insinuates that I ought to satisfy the Law's demands myself. . . .
It insinuates that I am too good for the grace offered me in the Law, that
I should refuse it and that instead of the faith demanded by the Law I
should present to God my own work" (p. 82). However, any one who lets
himself be so enticed and "presumes to fulfill the Law himself and desires
to ensure God's grace for himself by his own efforts, can only learn from
the Law (Rom. 7:14) that he is *carnal*, that he *cannot* hold his own as a
man before God, that he *cannot* carry out his intentions of becoming
righteous" (p. 84). The trouble is that the good he seeks is not in him
or the world. (P. 85.) He is what Barth calls a "queer saint" who, like a
saint, seeks to do the good, but in the strange manner that he rebels against
the good he seeks (p. 84).

[211] So Barth defines sin as the pride that rejects the actuality of God's
condescension in grace to man which would make the law a form of grace.
He also understands sin as the laziness which rejects the actuality of his
exaltation in Christ that would make his power potent. IV, 1, 395–573
(358–513); IV, 2, 423–564 (378–498).

[212] IV, 2, 473 (420).

the mind in order to pursue its own appetites. The mind is too tired to rule, and the body is too lazy to obey. Man becomes a vagabond, without direction and discipline, without order and unity. Just as man tries to cover the pride in which he is bound over to himself with the guise of a freedom-so-called — a commendable emancipation — and just as his proud separation of himself from his fellowman is heralded as the freedom of "objectivity," so also his own disintegration and impotence, depending on the direction it takes, is praised now as an exercise of "spiritual" freedom and then as the expression of the freedom of "nature." [213]

The driving power of man's impotence and laziness is anxiety. Taking life into his own hands, having decided to be *a se,* to exist in the freedom of independence and responsibility, man must care for himself. This care becomes immediately a paralyzing, fatiguing anxiety because the world in which he must find life and fulfill the law holds out only the promise of death. Understandably anxious, man rushes to fill the void in response to the lusts of his mind and body in the freedom of his reason or in the freedom of nature. Also, his anxiety for his own life and his own projects necessitates an "objectivity," a freedom from his neighbor that prevents his being distracted by the needs of his neighbor. And finally, certain of his own responsibility, he cannot hear or accept the message of God's gracious responsibility for him as revealed in Jesus.

This prideful freedom in which man becomes subject to the paralyzing fatigue of anxiety is the bondage from which Jesus in his humility as priest and in his victory as king once and for all sets men free.

Freedom from Falsehood

We have seen that when man rejects Jesus, he manifests a false freedom — an impossible freedom that binds man to nothingness and the vanity of the world, and within the world, a powerless freedom, a powerless power that binds him in service

[213] IV, 2, 517 (459).

to the law and his own lost self. And now, within his own self
and spirit, he exhibits another dimension of this false freedom
— a foolish freedom that binds him further to his own ignorance and damnation.[214] This phase of freedom-so-called is
established by the fact that the rejection of Jesus is also the
rejection of the faithful witness to the truth. As man rejects
Jesus in order to possess for himself Jesus' eternity and actuality, so now he rejects him in order to possess for himself Jesus'
truth. Whereas the previously discussed dimensions of the freedom of sin have a predominantly external aspect, an *extra nos*
reference to God and the world, this last dimension has a primarily inner aspect, a personal quality which is born of the
inner witness of Jesus' spirit with the spirit of the Christian.
Barth designates this particular phase of sin (*cum grano salis*)
" the Christian form of sin," since to lie about the truth requires having heard it as only the Christian has.[215] The lie is
that truth can be had without Jesus, and the freedom which
seeks to possess and express this truth so-called is what Barth
calls the "*Menschen Narrenfreiheit*," the freedom to be a
fool.[216]

Since this freedom-so-called is a response to the witness of
the truth it is not so much a freedom from the truth as it is a
freedom to circumvent and twist the truth. It is exercised as an
" evasion tactic." [217] The fact is that Jesus and the truth cannot
be separated, so that truth is in and from him and not in or of
us; it can be possessed, therefore, only through the sacrifice of
ourselves, only as we bear our cross.[218] Furthermore, the truth
is that *God* is in Jesus, so that to know Jesus as the truth is also
to obey. These two truths are the truth that man would ex-
change or avoid for the lie. The lie alleges that truth is in man
and not in Jesus and that it is to be mastered rather than
obeyed. Man is fool enough to regard his freedom as such to

214 Barth discusses this dimension of sin in IV, 3, 425–531 (386–478),
under the heading, " The Lie and Damnation of Man."
215 IV, 3, 432 (374).
216 IV, 3, 512 (449).
217 IV, 3, 500 (434).
218 IV, 3, 507–515 (440–447).

be true. " He even regards himself to be in the glorious position . . . of being able to conceive and create a God. . . .
And since he can conceive and create a God, how close, how
similar, yea, how identical, he must be to God! " [219] Rather
than sacrifice his own lie in obedience to the truth that is with
God in Jesus, he abstracts it, and expresses it in his own sovereign freedom.

However, while man cannot altogether deny the claim of
truth, he can get around it by making it harmless, by creatively
ordering it into a system.[220] These systems can be extremely
religious and moral, as when the truth of *Jesus* as the God-man
is exchanged for the system of theology that roots in the *principle* of God-manhood. Systematic truth can be dealt with and
controlled in the freedom of man.

However, this freedom from the truth through the lie that
man is true and that through his freedom truth comes to expression is, in reality, another form of the bondage of sin. With
the freedom of truth exchanged for the truth of freedom, with
truth abstracted from the grace of God in Christ, man's freedom is in reality lost, and he falls victim to the very schemes
and systems by which he would master truth and avoid its
claims. For instance, he becomes " absolutely dependent," a
mere expression of " being," or a " being toward death," or
what have you. He becomes the slave of his own creatures and
is thereby threatened with damnation. The reason for his
damnation is evident: " He will not let the truth of his salvation from guilt and slavery stand, but would rather change the
truth into its opposite because he wishes to live altogether from
and in the truth into which he would transform the truth." [221]
And in this his intention he wishes to be taken seriously. And
what is the meaning of the denial of salvation other than the

[219] IV, 3, 518 (449).
[220] " He constructs a theoretical and practical system of truth. He establishes truth parties. He defends frontiers of truth. He opens schools for
truth, and truth academies. He celebrates truth days and entire weeks of
truth. He organizes formidable field weapons of truth. He makes so much
of the business of truth that Jesus Christ by comparison is an amateur and
a bungler." IV, 3, 502 (436).
[221] IV, 3, 531 (462).

affirmation of damnation, and the denial of election other than the election of rejection? [222] Although he still has time, man can be damned, for God will not be mocked. If the salt has lost its savor, wherewith shall it be salted? If the Christian refuses the truth, how shall he again hear it?

This lie in which man would free himself from the truth is the bondage to damnation from which Jesus as Word and prophet is powerful to set the Christian free.

Freedom from Silence

Corresponding to the fourth dimension of freedom-for as freedom for the world through creative unity with the Spirit, we should speak of a final freedom-from — a freedom from the uncreative silence of a spirit subject to the stifling and confuting sounds of the world. Yet, without a creative word from man, this same world, for all its sound and fury, cannot deliver itself from its travail and into its destiny as the creation of God. As we looked to Berdyaev for the development of the final form of freedom-for, so also we shall look to him for a discussion of this final form of freedom-from — the freedom of man from silence and the freedom of the world from bondage.[223]

FREEDOM FOR FREEDOM

It should be apparent that since little can really be said about freedom-from that has not already been said about freedom-for, so also can little be said about freedom for freedom that has not been said already. The reason is that Barth makes no final separation between the speaker and the content of God's eternal will, between the savior and the actuality of salvation, between the witness and the event of hearing. He does not separate finally God's eternal word, its historical actualiza-

---

[222] IV, 3, 533 f. (463).

[223] This dimension of bondage is suggested by Barth's discussion of "The Christian in Distress" (*Bedgrängnis*). He refers to the fact that the witness of the Christian is for the world, the outer world, whose many voices threaten the voice of the Christian. See IV, 3, 704–710 (615–620).

tion, and the witness to this word and its actualization in man's hearing. Consequently, one cannot be free for Jesus (and so truly free) without at the same time being set free for this freedom by Jesus himself. We saw that there is a creaturely freedom of man, an original freedom-for, which is an eternal verity because of God's eternal election of Jesus and all men in him. We saw also that man exists in a bondage to an impossible freedom which has no ground in creation, and that man's original freedom, together with his deliverance from this false freedom-so-called, is actualized in Jesus. In Jesus, man is free for freedom. We saw further that man is free in faith to accept and to realize in his existence the freedom he actually and already has in Jesus. This freedom for his freedom in Christ is a freedom for which he is set free by the word and witness of the living Jesus.

This unity of freedom and liberation, in every one of its aspects, is the very essence of Barth's view of freedom; it gives to faith the quality of " freedom," so that it is always spontaneous and joyful, so that when *I* do *what Christ* gives me to do, there is no contradiction, but the occurrence of the original, the possible, the most joyful; there is freedom. Jesus is no threat to freedom, as a form that might jeopardize content or as an object that might deny the subject. To be free in, for, and through Jesus is to be free indeed. In a word, Jesus is both the goal and ground of freedom, subject and object, alpha and omega.

Before we turn from this discussion we need to give special attention to the last dimension of freedom as freedom for freedom, namely, the work of Jesus by which he sets the Christian free in faith for the freedom that he has actualized in himself and to which he witnesses in his word. This work of Jesus is that of his prophetic office, in which he speaks a decisive word about himself and shines a revealing light upon his achievement.[224] The revealing, prophetic work of Christ involves him,

[224] IV, 3, 49 (46). See "The Glory of the Mediator," IV, 3, 1–424 (1–367).

as it were, in another history, the history in which on the one
hand he brings to pass the knowledge of himself by the Christian believer and on the other hand he overcomes the willful
ignorance and lying alternatives in which the Christian inevitably exists. The witness of Jesus is effected through Scripture
and proclamation which are analogous to the earthly existence
of Jesus in whom the light was originally manifested in its past
once-for-allness. In the word of the church this original light
shines once again to become the decisive factor in Christian
existence. Barth insists, however, that it is Jesus himself and
not the Scripture or proclamation as such that makes this witness; it is not the memory of the church that brings Christ to
life but, rather, the living Christ himself.[225] Through the kerygma — the witness of the Scripture and the church — the resurrected and living Jesus himself sets man free for the freedom
of faith, for existence in the knowledge of Jesus.[226] " As he who

[225] " The existence of the holy scripture means that God's word, as it is
spoken once and for all in God's revelation in Jesus Christ and through the
Holy Spirit, is not only distant from the Church but also near in the witness of the prophets and apostles. It stands not only over against the
Church but it is also given to the Church. It is not only something that
remains strange but it has become both the task and the authority of the
Church itself. It has and holds in the form of the Holy Scripture its own
incomparable authority and freedom — as high above all human authority
and freedom as heaven is above earth — so it also establishes . . . in the
Church human, but nevertheless, legitimate and necessary authority." I, 2,
832 (743 f.) .

[226] The kerygma — Scripture and preaching — as the words of men
points beyond itself to the Word of God, and the Word of God speaks
through it. The study of Scripture must, therefore, be critical and historical. It must acknowledge fully the fact that the words of Scripture are human. At the same time it must recognize that as a matter of historical fact
these words point beyond themselves to a mystery, to Jesus, who can and
will speak for himself. The exegete who is " objective " without presupposition, and who is unwilling to presuppose the possibility of anything beyond man, his world and words, will necessarily be unhistorical, uncritical,
and incompetent as an exegete of Scripture. To hear the Bible one must
look to where it points; yet one cannot look except through the human
word. Historical study is critical, historical in the narrow sense; it is also
theological. Barth insists *mutatis mutandis* that the same holds for all human words. They all point beyond themselves to a mystery that can only
speak for itself. Consequently even in this realm there arises the possibility

is not in need of later remembrance in order still to live and to live again (even as the one who lived once before) , he has risen from the dead, appeared, and revealed himself to his own." [227] The knowledge of Jesus cannot be gained, therefore, as an answer to the hermeneutic question, for " the history of Jesus Christ occurred in its primary form as the history that surpasses all other histories " and there can be no preunderstanding of history generally which Biblical interpretation presupposes.[228] The actuality of this secondary occurrence has its possibility only in the original occurrence — Jesus himself; from the standpoint of the Christian the actuality of knowledge precedes and establishes its possibility. Since the encounter with Scripture is an encounter with the first word of all words, the word that is " in the beginning," Barth wins from it a hermeneutic principle for the understanding of all human words. This is the principle of actuality which means, as we have seen, that the possibility of hearing and understanding the *Sache* — that which is meant in the speech of another — roots in the sheer actuality or event (*Ereignis*) of that hearing.[229] It is important to note, therefore, that the analogue for the interpretation of Biblical hermeneutics is not the model of historical understanding but, rather, that of living conversation. The Bible is not a book *about* the *dead* past but, rather, the living, present voice *of* the *living* past. The Christian is together with the Bible not as he is together with Gibbon's *Decline and Fall* but as he is together with a living friend, namely, the resurrected and living Jesus.

---

of misunderstanding even though the words are heard. Only when one is open to that to which the words point, only when one does not master the words but is gripped by them is the word correctly exegeted. Thus, a proper hermeneutic does not seek to open Scripture, to master it by historical study or hermeneutical understanding, but through this study to be mastered by Jesus. Barth must take seriously the historical study of the Bible, but more seriously the history of Jesus' living prophecy. See I, 2, 503-523 (457-472) , " The Scripture as Witness of God's Revelation." See especially pp. 513-523 (464-472) .

[227] IV, 3, 256 (224) .

[228] *Ibid.*

[229] I, 2, 514 (464 f.) .

The fact that the word of God is not accessible outside of its actuality, that it is not dependent upon a hermeneutic, is what Barth points to when he speaks of the Word in its essence as "personal," "mystery," "free," and "subject." [230] That the word of God, who is Jesus Christ and who is first witnessed in the Scripture testimony of prophets and apostles, should be witnessed again in the preaching of the church is evidence of the freedom of Jesus Christ as prophet. The instrument and token of this freedom is the threefold form of the Word — Jesus, Scripture, and Proclamation. There is no way to extract or possess the essence of the word outside this threefold form, inasmuch as Jesus, who is God's word, speaks only through preaching and is present in preaching only through Scripture. The only reason preaching is not mere church words void of a divine content is "the fact that the Bible is read to us in Church, and that we are related to this fact." [231] When the Bible is not read and when it is not heard, there is nothing the church can do; without God's revealed Word it is at the mercy of God's hidden grace as it is manifest in the world's judgment and correction.

This circular relationship between the three forms of the word is the event of the Word's freedom in which the word remains a subject, not object. In order to speak correctly of this freedom and subjectivity of God in his word " we must ask not only who is the self-revealing God, but also *how* this happens and *what* is the result." [232] The answer to these questions and to the broad freedom of the possibility that undergirds the mystery of the word and its hearing so that it is not sheer magic is implicit in the revelation itself, namely, the Trinity of the incarnate God. By virtue of the unity of the Father and Son in the Holy Spirit, in an analogous fashion Scripture and church

---

[230] See I, 1, 141–143, 168–194 (155–158, 184–212). Note especially Barth's reference to Bultmann among others. I, 2, 754 ff. (673 ff.) .

[231] I, 1, 280 (304) .

[232] Claude Welch, *In This Name* (Charles Scribner's Sons, 1952), pp. 163 f.

are one in the unity of the Spirit which is Jesus, the living Word.[233]

It is important to recognize that although the Word of God — Jesus in his prophetic office — is free, he nevertheless makes use of the voice and words of men (i.e., his freedom creates freedom in the church). But, as Barth says many times over, God " is not bound to these; he does not hand himself over to them, so as to be conditioned by their faithfulness or unfaithfulness, perfection or imperfection, cleverness or foolishness," but rather, he shines his light in and in spite of these words.[234] He speaks through Scripture whose words are " the concrete bearer of the Church's government," the orignial foundation, limitation, and determination of human freedom.[235] And, as surely as the church's freedom is a freedom for Jesus, it is, as we have seen, a freedom for Scripture, a freedom to explicate Scripture in exegesis and to apply it in its own words as a proclamation.[236] The use of these human words witnesses to the *analogia fidei,* to the fact that by the grace of God which gives voice to his word and hearing to the church, the words of men (in Scripture and in church), the language of Canaan and the many languages of man in every age, become analogues of the word of God. Accordingly, Barth finds it necessary no longer to speak dialectically, with a " yes " and a " no," but undialectically, in the language of Scripture and in the language of a Scripture-controlled philosophy. To say no and yes to this language is to stand out of grace and faith. There is no higher language than that which is sanctioned, blessed by the incarnation; were such to exist it would, like the simple anthropomorphism of the Bible, speak only by virtue of grace and faith.[237]

[233] See I, 1, 307–310 (332–335), where Barth states the necessity of developing the doctrine of the Trinity in the context of his discussion of the Word of God.
[234] IV, 3, 257 (225).
[235] I, 2, 777, 781 (694, 697).
[236] I, 2, 796 (709 f.).
[237] See I, 1, 16–23, 239–261 (17–25, 260–283), especially 257 f. (279 f.). Also, note Balthasar's discussion of the development of Barth's theology

Barth designates the history of Jesus' prophecy through the word as the history of salvation, which, unlike the history of reconciliation (from Bethlehem to Easter) is incomplete and in process. It is also a history of conflict in which Jesus overcomes the ignorance and deceit of men and establishes true knowledge of his reconciliation. The fact that the process of salvation takes time means that it gives time to man — time for him, his faith, and his love. The light that shines when the living Christ speaks shines not into a void but upon the face of man, bringing him out of darkness into light and establishing him in his responsibility for the interpretation and proclamation of the message of Scripture.

Barth reminds us again, however, that while the history of prophecy is a history of man's response, it is also and first of all the history of God's sovereignty and freedom, so that the victory of the Word is always experienced by the Christian in its sheer actuality, and only then as a possibility or potentiality. The analogy is one of grace and faith and not one of being. This does not mean, however, that the Word is in contradiction to man. The Word goes out in battle not against man in his created nature, but against man in his alien existence as a lying, deceiving sinner. In his created nature, together with the created glory of all reality, man is a proper stage for the unfolding glory of God. What would the unity of God mean " if the relation between the *gloria Dei* and its *theatrum*, between reconciliation and creation, were merely one of mutual hostility "? [238] While the words and lights immanent in the world cannot contain the word of God, the word of God can take them up and set them on the way that is the life of Christian faith, in a life of service to the Light, the light of the living Jesus.[239] This is done, of course, in a preeminent way when Jesus makes use of Scripture and preaching.

under the headings " Wendung zur Analogie," and " Vollgestalt der Analogie," pp. 93–180.
[238] IV, 3, 172 (151).
[239] IV, 3, 174 (152 f.).

Once again we have been made aware of the unsystematic nature of Barth's theology. We have seen him insist that Christian knowledge is a testimony to the freedom and actuality of the Word. And yet he now insists, in his last volume, that the victory of the Word is contingent upon the freedom of man's response to the Word, that indeed man is free to refuse the Word and suffer damnation. Some unity is suggested by his distinction between the created nature and the sinful nature of man, so that while the Word owes no debt to the sinful nature of man to which it is wholly inimical, it does wait upon man's created nature, whose destiny is nothing but the hearing of that Word. But it is obvious that while this distinction perhaps clarifies, it does not satisfy, and the search for unity and understanding continues. Barth would warn us, however, that Jesus himself is the only point, albeit mysterious and inaccessible, at which these lines finally do come together; he alone is the unity we seek.

5

NICOLAS BERDYAEV: FREEDOM TO CREATE

WE FOUND THAT BULTMANN'S effort to understand man in terms
of an existentialist view of freedom cannot stand. Tillich is
right, therefore, to seek to give freedom and existence an ontological base. But the cost to freedom of this ontological foundation proved to be too dear. Barth begins not with an existentialist view of freedom, nor with an ontology, but rather, with
the God-man — Jesus, and it has been the thesis of this study
that the Barthian approach does make room for freedom as the
final and basic dimension of the human spirit. Berdyaev, whose
premises are also Christological, is right, then, when he makes
freedom and not existence or being the beginning point and
the ultimate category of his anthropology. And since he regarded himself as a philosopher rather than a theologian, it is
appropriate to begin this chapter anthropologically with an
investigation of Berdyaev's view of the freedom of man.

FREEDOM-FOR

In the case of Berdyaev, it is appropriate to begin even the
study of freedom-for with a consideration of freedom as such,
because in his thought freedom itself appears to be the ultimate human reality, and, in a sense, its own object. Freedom
even brought Berdyaev to Christ.[1] Freedom is before and be-

1 " Freedom has brought me to Christ and I know of no other path
leading to Him." (Nicolas Berdyaev, *Freedom and the Spirit*, tr. by Oliver
Fielding Clarke, p. x; Charles Scribner's Sons, 1935.)

yond good and evil. Freedom is the final mystery.[2] As this original and final mystery, freedom is the ground of being and not
the creature of being; it is rooted in nonbeing — *to mē on*, the
Ungrund, the primal abyss. Although this idea of the meontic
is a very debatable concept, let it be understood for the moment merely as a symbol for the ultimacy of freedom and its
priority over being.[3]

Freedom-as-Such

Since freedom is first, it can be revealed and understood only
symbolically in the terms and symbols of its own creatures, the
first of which is the human person itself.[4] Freedom is the depth
of personality, the very source and light of its being. When
Berdyaev speaks of " the Spirit " or man as " spiritual," he most
often means simply that the essence of existence is freedom.[5]
However, his personalism and spiritualism, his insistence on
" interiorization," is not to be confused with narcissism or
solipsism, for within the depths of the person, in the profound-
est subjectivity of freedom, the self meets that which is most
real or " objective." [6] The ultimate reality or meaning of the
spirit does not force itself from outside by necessity but, rather,
manifests itself from within, through freedom.[7] All that is objective in the sense that it comes from the outside, such as the

[2] Nicolas Berdyaev, *The Meaning of the Creative Act*, tr. by Donald A.
Lowrie (Harper & Brothers, 1954) , p. 145.

[3] Nicolas Berdyaev, *The Destiny of Man*, tr. by Natalie Duddington
(Harper Torchbooks, The Cloister Library, 1960) , pp. 25 ff. See also
Berdyaev's *Dream and Reality: An Essay in Autobiography*, tr. by Katha-
rine Lampert (The Macmillian Company, 1950) , p. 212.

[4] Nicolas Berdyaev, *Truth and Revelation*, tr. by R. M. French (Collier
Books, 1963) , p. 76. See also *Solitude and Society*, tr. by George Reavey
(Charles Scribner's Sons, 1938) , pp. 32, 159 ff. Also, *Dream and Reality*,
pp. 288 f., and *Slavery and Freedom*, tr. by R. M. French (Charles Scribner's
Sons, 1944) , p. 27.

[5] Nicolas Berdyaev, *Spirit and Reality*, tr. by George Reavey (London:
Geoffrey Bles, Ltd., The Centenary Press, 1939) , p. 26. See also *Freedom*,
pp. 117, 121.

[6] " In man is revealed absolute being." (*Meaning of the Creative Act*,
p. 60.) See Berdyaev on solipsism, *Dream and Reality*, pp. 36 f., 308.

[7] See *Meaning of the Creative Act*, pp. 146 ff., and *Freedom*, pp. 117–120.

natural order of necessity, the moral order of law, and cosmic order of being, is itself fundamentally and first of all already the creative expression of the free spirit. Freedom, therefore, is not to be confused with that slavish, so-called freedom of the will which is ever subject to an objective order whose options it is obliged to accept. True freedom is, rather, the creator of the moral order and of the " free will." [8]

Freedom is an ultimate reality, beyond and before good and evil, the meontic source of being itself. And freedom is the depth, the ultimate meaning of personality. Thus, while freedom can neither be deduced, inferred, or understood from anything extrinsic to it, nor be reduced finally to any other terms, it does bring something intrinsic with it which may be distinguished from freedom, as content is from form. It brings with it reality, truth, and meaning — a genuine content — and thereby a certain distinction within itself between freedom-assuch and freedom-in-truth. This distinction is the source of a possible tension. Freedom may willfully remain freedom as such, expressing itself without commitment to its appropriate content. Freedom as such, which Augustine designated the *libertas minor,* is " that initial and irrational liberty which is prior to good and evil, and determines their choice "; whereas true freedom — the *libertas major* — is " that intelligent freedom which is our final liberty in truth and goodness." [9] The *libertas minor* is the freedom of the old Adam, the " natural man," and is " purposeless and infantile, a mere desire to escape our swaddling clothes." On the other hand, the freedom of the new Adam — the " spiritual man " — is " a freedom which possesses a definite content; it is inward and positive, a desire to live for God and in God." [10]

At this point Berdyaev's thought is neither clear nor consistent, but can be understood in part as we recognize its limiting function. He wants to insist that truth is not extrinsic to

8 *Freedom,* p. 125.
9 *Ibid.,* p. 147.
10 *Meaning of the Creative Act,* pp. 147, 149.

freedom, that freedom is originally true — hence, the *libertas major*. Yet, recognizing the recalcitrance and sinfulness of freedom, he realizes that there is an antithesis between freedom and truth but will not allow that truth must therefore deny or overcome freedom. Even in sin there remains the *libertas minor*.[11] The redemption of the *libertas minor* and the question of the source of the *libertas major* will be themes of the third section on " Freedom for Freedom."

For now, we ask about the substance of true freedom, about freedom as freedom-for, as freedom for those realities through which it is symbolically manifested. Here the reader is struck by the richness and variety of the language Berdyaev employs, and the effort must be to see what pattern, if any, is apparent within this variety. We are asking where is true freedom going, what is it doing, and how does it behave?

Personality

The first symbol relative to freedom in its material dimension is the concept of personality. The goal of freedom is the realization of personality, or the ego. The ego, says Berdyaev, " becomes conscious of itself as the product of its own activity," and the activity or path along which the ego realizes itself is " the path of freedom." [12] The ego or personality in its axiological aspect is also designated by Berdyaev as the *Gestalt* of personality, which is the " unique . . . unrepeatable form " of personality " present as a whole in all the acts of personality." [13] As for character, it is the quality of the person in whom his *Gestalt* has found and continues to find expression.[14] " Genius " and the " image of God " also designate the goal of freedom. Genius is the image of God in man and designates man as a whole in his ability to " break through to the primary

[11] *Solitude*, p. 90; *Destiny of Man*, p. 55.
[12] *Solitude*, p. 88. He states that the Ego is " synonymous with freedom " (*ibid.*, p. 87).
[13] *Slavery*, p. 23.
[14] *Ibid.*, p. 47.

source of life " and to express himself in an activity that is
" truly original and not determined by social influences." [15]

Whether it be designated *Gestalt,* " geniality," or *imago Dei,*
personality, says Berdyaev, is " my whole thinking, my whole
willing, my whole feeling, my whole creative activity."[16] And
Berdyaev underlines the word " my," meaning that the pursuit
of personality is at the same time a particular and free expression of the self; personality is the *telos* of *my* freedom.

That act of the spirit in which freedom realizes personality,
in which one moves from himself to his true personality, is
" transcension " — which is not to be confused with objectification whereby man finds himself an object in a realm of heteronomous determination. To the contrary, in transcension " man
finds himself in the realm of freedom," and that destiny which
meets him in this outward movement has a personal character.[17] Man transcends himself when he is determined from his
own personal depths, in freedom, and not by externals and
some type of necessity.

History

The result of transcension is the incarnation of the spirit.
" Spirit is inward, and that special symbol is one of its attributes. . . . But this inwardness comes to be exteriorized." [18]
History is the record of the spirit's incarnation as it freely
leaves itself to exteriorize itself for others. Consequently, history is essentially a myth whose truth is not empirical but symbolic.[19] When history in its empirical aspects becomes reality

[15] *Destiny of Man,* p. 129. It should be noted that the concept of " genius " is important to Berdyaev. In the earlier work, *Meaning of the Creative Act,* pp. 170–190, genius tends to be a gift only of the elect and aristo-
cratic few, whereas in later writings (*Slavery,* pp. 57 f., and *Destiny of Man,*
pp. 57 f., 129 f.) it designates a fundamental dimension of the *imago dei*
which exists for all men.

[16] *Slavery,* p. 25.

[17] *Ibid.,* p. 30.

[18] *Spirit,* p. 49.

[19] *Meaning of the Creative Act,* p. 21. See also *Truth and Revelation,*
pp. 78 ff.

itself instead of a symbol of reality, then man is lost in objectivity and is subject to historical and worldly determination. History is symbol and myth as long as man remains free in his historical action, as long as history reveals the free spirit.

The revelation of the spirit in history takes place " for the sake of the world," for the sake of a communion with the world and others. Communion is neither mere communication nor the oppressive collectivity of society, for these are authoritarian, imposed, or achieved compulsorily from the outside. They know only the objective, do not reach the inner man in his solitude, and thus have little value as symbols of the spirit.[20] Communion, on the other hand, " does away with the objective . . . [and] can only take place between the Ego and the Thou, between one Ego and another." [21] The communion that comes in and through freedom as a result of the symbolism of history is what Berdyaev and the Russian tradition designate as *sobornost,* which " can never mean authority," but is always a predicate of freedom.[22] Thus, while in freedom man comes to himself, he also comes to himself in and through historical communion with others.

The Berdyaevian view of freedom and history cannot be understood on these anthropomorphic premises alone, as a quick perusal of Berdyaev's *Meaning of History* makes very clear. Human destiny, he writes, is both terrestrial and celestial. It " is not only an historical but also a metaphysical, not only a human but also a divine destiny; it is not only a human but also a divine drama." [23] History is predetermined by celestial history, just as man's personality is first of all " God's idea." [24] Personality, he states, " postulates the supra-personal: it could

[20] *Slavery,* p. 202; *Solitude,* p. 187; *The Realm of Spirit and the Realm of Caesar,* tr. by Donald A. Lowrie (London: Victor Gollancz, Ltd., 1952), pp. 116–125.

[21] *Solitude,* p. 185.

[22] *Realm of Spirit,* p. 123.

[23] Nicolas Berdyaev, *The Meaning of History,* tr. by George Reavey (London: Geoffrey Bles, Ltd., 1945), p. 41. See Oliver Fielding Clarke, *Introduction to Berdyaev* (London: Geoffrey Bles, Ltd., 1950), p. 103.

[24] *Meaning of History,* p. 44; *Destiny of Man,* p. 55; *Solitude,* p. 162.

not exist but for a Higher Power, a supra-personal content." [25] Therefore, " our function at every period, at every moment of our historical destiny, is to determine our relation to the problem of life and history in the terms and according to the criteria of eternity." [26] Freedom which is responsible to this eternal dimension is true freedom — " the supramundane freedom which liberates from the slavery of the world," the freedom whose goal is " the realization of the Kingdom of God." [27]

History occurs in time, and some clarification of what Berdyaev means when he speaks of history as the goal of freedom is gained by a consideration of his view of time. He speaks of three kinds of time — cosmic, historical, and existential. [28] Cosmic time is the time of nature — repetitive time in which there is no real creativity, no freedom, no humanity. It is " calculated by mathematics on the basis of movement around the sun, calendars and clocks are dependent upon it, and it is symbolized by the circle." [29] The second kind of time is the time of history, and it takes place in cosmic time. It is, like cosmic time, a time of causality and necessity, but also a time in which every event is unrepeatable. [30] Its symbol is the line, no point of which contains the others, no present moment of which can hold the past or grasp the future. Historical time is the objectification and fate of existential time by which time is separated from man and freedom. Existential time is the time of man, the time of which man is the subject. It is not mathematical or quantitative; its measure is subjective — " the intensity of experience." [31] It is the time in which the metahistorical

[25] *Solitude*, p. 162. " There is no human personality if there is no existence which stands higher than it, if there is no higher world to which it ought to rise." (*Slavery*, p. 37.)

[26] *Meaning of the Creative Act*, p. 196.

[27] *Truth and Revelation*, p. 31; Nicolas Berdyaev, *The Beginning and the End*, tr. by R. M. French (Harper Torchbooks, The Cloister Library, 1952), p. 32. See also *Meaning of the Creative Act*, pp. 144–150.

[28] *The Beginning*, p. 206.

[29] *Ibid.*

[30] *Ibid.*

[31] *Ibid.*

— man, truth, and freedom — shine through. This is the time of creation, the time in which history is made. History, therefore, created in existential time, falling in its own time toward cosmic time, must eventually be possessed by one or the other; it cannot remain neutral. In a later section we shall speak of man's freedom for microcosmic redemption, an aspect of which is the creative exercise of existential time in acts of memory and prophecy which claim historical time for man and for freedom, and so deliver it from the clutches and tyranny of objectified, cosmic time.[32]

Creativity

Before we seek to give more material content to personality, to the divine idea which is freedom's content, it is important to remember that this content of which we speak materializes only in freedom. This means that God does not project from heaven a divine blueprint — his idea for man — which man is then free to accept or reject; rather, the revelation of my personality is an eternal idea which it is freedom's task to realize. It is " not a revelation of God but something which he has kept secret. It is something which God does not reveal directly to man, but he looks to man to complete the revelation himself." [33] The essence and goal of freedom are inseparable from freedom itself. This unity of freedom and eternity is paradoxical, for on the one hand man " feels himself, as it were, possessed by a higher power, by a daemon, and yet at the same time has a sense of extraordinary freedom, of scope for the expression of his own will." [34] That is, God is freedom and acts only in freedom; he is spirit and acts only in spirit.

Obviously, the divine realm, the realm of truth and value, is not to be understood as an " objective realm " that manifests itself apart from and without the action of the free, human

---

[32] See also the discussion of time in connection with the freedom of God and eschatology. *Supra,* pp. 230 f.

[33] *Truth and Revelation,* p. 125.

[34] *The Beginning,* p. 178.

spirit. A category with which Berdyaev protests most effectively against this misconception is "creativeness," a notion that unites inseparably freedom and its material norm. For this reason no concept, other than freedom, is dearer to Berdyaev's heart than creativity. It conserves the reality not only of freedom, but also of the eternal dimension of which we have been speaking. "Eternity is eternal newness, eternal creative ecstasy, the dissolving of being, in divine freedom." [35] Creativeness is, then, the appearance of the eternal in time, metahistory in history, and which, from the standpoint of time and history, is ever new. And this newness comes not only from God's freedom but also from the unfathomable depths of man's freedom, so that "man's answer to God's call cannot entirely consist of elements that are given by and proceed from God. Something must come from man also, and that something is the very essence of creativeness, which brings forth new realities. It is, indeed, not 'something' but 'nothing' — in other words it is freedom, without which there can be no creative activity. . . . In every creative conception there is an element of primeval freedom, fathomless, undetermined by anything, not proceeding from God but ascending towards God." [36] There can be no inspiration without freedom. It can be seen then that creativeness — the expression of interacting divine and human freedom — is the same thing as the realization of personality (human freedom) and God's idea (divine freedom). From the standpoint of all that is — nature and history — the appearance of man in his creative acts is *ex nihilo*. The world is created not by God only, but also by man; it is a divine-human work. Thus, creative freedom is prior to being; it is the existence from which proceeds the essence of reality. "Everything leads us to the conclusion that being is not the ultimate depth, that there is a principle which precedes the emergence of being and that freedom is bound up with that principle. Freedom is not ontic but meonic." [37] As for being, it is "congealed freedom." [38] Be-

[35] *Ibid.*, p. 170.   [37] *The Beginning*, p. 111.
[36] *Destiny of Man*, p. 128.   [38] *Ibid.*

ing is the phenomenal world of Kantian thought; it is also the noumenal world of German idealism. It is the deceptive world of senses, and it is the abstract product and object of human thought. It is the "abstraction and hypostatization of attributes and qualities"; in fact, "being is a predicate only." [39] Being, as the created product of the spirit fatefully abstracted from spirit and freedom, is that from which freedom must ever seek to remain free. Kant saw that true metaphysics is a metaphysics of freedom, but he never prepared tools for such a metaphysics, and merely brought the older metaphysics of being to an end. Berdyaev would pick up where Kant left off, to build "a metaphysics of freedom . . . derived from Kant." [40] However, inasmuch as Kant never developed this metaphysics, Berdyaev would have to go beyond him. It was a mistake of German idealism to deny the thing-in-itself — freedom — and to move in a monistic direction. Berdyaev's thought is frankly dualistic, moving within the tension between freedom as the thing-in-itself and the phenomenal world of being. Creativeness, as it tends to fall off into being, is the encounter between these two realms.

Cosmic Redemption

We have seen that in transcension man creates his personality and at the same time historical communion with his fellow. However, man creates not only in relationship to his fellow-man, but also in relationship to the whole of reality. In this dimension, transcension or creativity effects a transfiguration, sanctification, and renewal of being. "Man must work for the illumination and spiritualization, not only of his own soul and body, but also of the soul and body of the whole universe. The spiritual must not be separated from the 'psychical' and natural; rather, it must illuminate it and spiritualize it." [41] The world of space and time is created to receive the spirit and to find its being and meaning as a symbol of the spirit. The cosmos is never fully adequate to its symbolic responsibility and

[39] *Ibid.*, p. 95.　　[40] *Ibid.*, p. 8.　　[41] *Freedom*, p. 27.

thus is ever needful of the activity of the spirit. But at the same time the spirit needs the world as the means of its symbolic expression. Creativeness then is not creation out of nothing, but out of the material which the world supplies.[42] Thus man's creative responsibility toward the world roots in the world's needs, but even more so in the fact that man belongs to eternity and is " called to assume a ruling position in the world." [43] In this his creative and redemptive role, man is " the sun," " the microcosm," " *the center of the world, bearing within himself the secret of the world, and rising above all things in the world.*" [44] The creative act is eschatological, bringing the eternity of the Kingdom of God to the world, and so transforming the world into a new heaven and a new earth.[45]

The outer world, the macrocosm, has three major aspects — history, nature, and society — and in each of these the redemptive creativity of man is expressed. In the realm of history man's creative memory and prophetic vision are the source of renewal and redemption. History in this context means both time past and time future. History as time past, although it is the past objectified record of imperfect, fallen humanity, is nevertheless the realm of truth and meaning; for, as we have seen, while history is the expression of man's free spirit, it is also the revelation of eternity.[46] Yet, there is in history also a principle inimical to freedom. " Time reveals an evil, deadly and destructive principle. For the death of the past hurried on by each consecutive instance and its plunge into the darkness of non-being, implied in every progress of time, are the very principles of death itself. The future is the murderer of every past instant." [47] This destructiveness is evil, and the spirit cannot allow it to stand. " Is it sufficient to say that the past has been? " Such a view " favors an interpretation of history and its

[42] *The Beginning*, p. 173.
[43] *Ibid.*, p. 172.
[44] *Meaning of the Creative Act*, p. 58. See also *Freedom*, pp. 200–202.
[45] *The Beginning*, pp. 232 f.
[46] *Meaning of History*, pp. 36–44.
[47] *Ibid.*, p. 70.

process of fulfillment which transforms everything into rapidly changing and ultimately spectral instants devoured by succeeding instances which all crumble away into the abyss of nonbeing of similar perishable instants." [48] Such a view also denies that the past is in any sense an eternal reality. However, by virtue of its eternal depth, the past may be part of the creaturely stuff out of which the creative person shapes his cosmos. Memory is the instrument of creativity which rescues the past; it is " the principle which conducts a constant battle against the mortal principle of time." [49] While it knows that the past has an eternal dimension, it also knows it to be an event of freedom, so that to understand the past and overcome its separation from the present, historical memory also must be an event of freedom, and must apprehend the past as part of its own existence. The inner soul of history emerges only as it is creatively transformed in the freedom of historical memory. To grasp the great epochs of history " we must inform them with our own spiritual destiny, for considered superficially, they are all inwardly dead to us." Consequently, it may be said that historical memory " is an inalienable part of the historical tradition." [50] Because history is made of eternity, it abides and is never merely past; because it is made also of man and freedom, it abides only as it passes through the creativity of freedom functioning in the " historical memory." The creative redemption of historical tradition in which the past is present as the greater part of consciousness is one phase of freedom's goal and personality's self-realization. It should be made clear that this creation is only partially *ex nihilo*. The future that man creatively writes is drawn from the past which is present to us through its participation in eternity. History comes from history.[51]

[48] *Ibid.*, p. 71.
[49] *Ibid.*, p. 73.
[50] *Ibid.*, p. 18.
[51] The past, which is the objectification of the Spirit, is good insofar as it provides the stuff from which man creates his cosmos; it is evil insofar as it resists creative repossession by the Spirit.

Man's creative renewal of time is not complete with historical memory; it also includes the prophetic spirit which delivers
man from the tyranny of time to come. For, " if the inner remembrance can enable man to apprehend the non-existent
past, the prophetic spirit should likewise be able to reveal the
non-existent future." [52] Prophecy is not to be confused with
scientific prevision which views both past and future objectively, as static and determined. Man is free to infuse the future
with the meaning of eternity that proceeds from his own
spirit.[53] Just as the historical memory rescues eternity from
time past, so the prophetic spirit gives it dominion over time
future.[54] The ghosts of the dead past and the unborn future
are made living realities through the creativity of human freedom, just as they lose their substance again by a failure of human creative freedom.[55] But again, this redemption of time
and history through freedom is also possible because time itself, despite its will to death, is situated in freedom and eternity.[56] Freedom is the creator of eternal and meaningful time.

A second major phase of freedom's creativity is the act of
knowledge by which the world of things and objects is orga-
nized and integrated. There are two factors in the act of knowledge. The first is its " creative factor, manifest in the free
agency of the existential subject . . . who is absolutely original." [57] The second factor is the Logos, which is divinely in-

[52] *Solitude,* p. 143.

[53] *Ibid.*

[54] " Just as it is possible to consider eternity in time, so it is to transcend
closed time and transpose it into eternity on the condition, of course, that
it evinces the eternal principle. Time therefore is not a finite circle into
which nothing eternal can penetrate, but one that can be extended to comprehend it. This is one aspect of the problem. The other assumes that time
itself is rooted in the depths of eternity. And thus what we call time in our
world historical process, in our world reality, which is a process in time,
is a sort of interior period, a sort of interior epoch in eternity itself."
(*Meaning of History,* p. 64.)

[55] *Ibid.,* p. 72.

[56] *Ibid.,* p. 69.

[57] *Solitude,* p. 75.

spired. " Thus knowledge is not merely the reflection of Being in the subject in the form of speculative knowledge, but also necessarily the creative reaction of the subject's illumined freedom to Being, as a result of which Being is modified." [58] Freedom constitutes knowledge in its creative aspect, and Logos constitutes its cosmic aspect. Together they constitute man as the microcosm.[59] While the cosmos also has its own reality, imprinting itself upon man as well as receiving the imprint of man upon itself,[60] man still remains the center who " gives life and spirit to nature through his creative freedom," or kills and fetters it " through his own servitude and his fall into material necessity." [61] The whole creation is " groaning in travail " as it awaits man's redemption to freedom and creative responsibility. Man as the microcosm is a mystical, spiritual truth, for viewed naturally he appears subject to nature and destined to revolve around the sun. But when he is understood spiritually, in the light of freedom, man " should be the sun of the world round which everything else revolves." [62] In the act of knowledge or " intellection " the universe is redeemed and its meaning restored and enhanced, for intellection both " discovers the meaning, the cosmos, underlying the meaningless " and " adds to the existing reality, which thereby assumes a greater significance." [63]

The activity of the knowing subject takes two forms. The first is objectification, " a process which helps the subject to orientate himself in a dark and degraded world " that otherwise forces the subject into submission.[64] Technology is the highest expression of such objectified knowledge. The second way in which the subject overcomes the world is by means of existential philosophy, " which dispenses with objectification." It approaches the world in the light of human existence and

[58] *Ibid.*
[59] *Meaning of the Creative Act*, p. 58.
[60] *Ibid.*, p. 63.
[61] *Ibid.*, p. 71.
[62] *Ibid.*, p. 77.
[63] *Solitude*, p. 71.
[64] *Ibid.*, p. 72.

"can illuminate the objective world wherein *meaning* is revealed, the meaning of human existence and of the universe as a part of the Divine Being." [65]

Berdyaev has stated that man is the sun, the truth for the world. But the world, the realm of being, is fallen away from man and so from its divine freedom. It has become subject to a necessity in which the elements of its hierarchy are estranged from each other, continue in strife and conflict, and are held together by external restraints. But while the world is not so fallen and so void of truth as to disintegrate, yet it is not so human as to exist in freedom. In this context of a fallen and objectified world, objectified knowledge is a necessary concession; it is "epistemological adjustment to the world for the sake of victory over the world." [66] By this concession man becomes once again the microcosmic center and subject in order thereupon to become the source of redeeming freedom. While objectifying knowledge does not overcome objectivity, it is nevertheless a victory of the spirit that does manage to encompass objectivity "in the form of technical supremacy." [67] It is also an expression of redemptive freedom to the degree that the material results of such knowledge are "social, intended for communication." [68] Science, because of its universality and generality is "the appropriate mode of communication in the spiritually disintegrated, objective, and social world." [69] However, technical mastery is not truth in freedom, nor is scientific communication communion in freedom. These technical victories of the free spirit merely establish a beachhead for the final victory of the free spirit in "existential knowledge."

Existential knowledge is knowledge in which man not only receives the world as object into himself, but goes out of himself to fill the world with himself. "The creative act of the personality enters the cosmic hierarchy, gives it deliverance

[65] *Ibid.*
[66] *The Beginning*, p. 45.
[67] *Solitude*, p. 77.
[68] *Ibid.*, p. 80.
[69] *Ibid.*

from the power of lower, materialized hierarchies." [70] The relation between man and the world becomes inner and personal, for only man, the microcosm, knows the macrocosm.
Man's spirit, says Berdyaev, " *claims an absolute supernatural
anthropocentricism; he knows himself to be the absolute center
— not of a given, closed planetary system, but of the whole of
being, of all planes of being, of all worlds.*" [71] This statement,
somewhat typical of the poetic flights which characterize *The
Meaning of the Creative Act,* means simply that man is prior to
the world, that whatever truth the world may possess, it remains
not only without freedom but without the fullness of truth if
man remain objective to it. Man is the creative, active center
from which the circumference is described, rather than the
passive point to which all radii are directed. To know existentially is not so much to receive the truth from the world as to
impart and to enclose the world within the truth. Existential
knowing does not save man in the world so much as save man
from the world and for the world.

When one knows existentially — affectively, inwardly, freely
from the heart — when his knowing is at the same time his
self-realization — then he finally overcomes alienation, objectification, and necessity. " What is near and dear to man does
not compel him." [72] The primary truth is spoken, as Buber has
shown, in the primary word " I-thou " in which the object becomes a " thou," a reality essential to my subjectivity and for
which my subjectivity and commitment are essential.[73]

The creative memory and creative prophecy rescue eternity
from time and time for eternity, but not completely. The

[70] *Meaning of the Creative Act,* p. 156. This type of knowledge is also
designated " intuitive " by Berdyaev. See *Solitude,* pp. 72 ff., and *The Beginning,* pp. 67–80.

[71] *Meaning of the Creative Act,* p. 78.

[72] *Ibid.,* p. 150.

[73] *Solitude,* pp. 106 ff. It should be noted also that since man is the microcosm, the " thou " is not limited to human beings. So Berdyaev writes:
" The company of animals, especially of those who have lived with me give
me very great delight, and I would like this companionship to continue
after death " (*Dream and Reality,* p. 28) .

eschaton is not only the creative victory of the moment, but also that which is coming at the end of time with the final advent of the Kingdom. Creative knowledge rescues the world from objective detachment and bondage to necessity for the sake of freedom and truth. Scientific knowledge achieves this victory only by concession, and the greater victory of existential knowledge is never complete and awaits " the end of this age."

Love

At this stage we may ask the question — the material question — about the quality of truth which man realizes through his creative freedom. Berdyaev states that creativity means " the individual creation of values." [74] He also says that " all creativity is love and all love is creative." [75] Love is the content or value of creativeness, and love is the unity of freedom and order. Thus the realization of the personality in freedom is the ordering of the self by the divine idea, the unifying of the self by its *Gestalt*. This is what it means to love oneself. The realization of the personality by its historical existence means the deliverance of time from its brokenness into past and present into its unity in eternity. The creative act of knowledge unifies the cosmos and in its existential form creates the unity of I and thou. The final and fullest expression of love finds its goal in " the union of souls, fellowship and brotherhood." [76] " Love unites organically and satisfies qualitatively. Love means the going out of this world from its heaviness, its fetters and its fractionization, into another world, a world of freedom and unity." [77] Love has therefore two elements. " There is a love which ascends and there is a love which descends, love which is *eros* and love which is *agape*." [78] There is a love which " satisfies qualitatively " and a love which " unites

[74] *Destiny of Man*, p. 132.
[75] *Ibid.*, p. 141.
[76] *Ibid.*, p. 187.
[77] *Meaning of the Creative Act*, p. 267.
[78] *Slavery*, p. 55.

organically." Insofar as love is the satisfaction and realization of the personality, it is *erōs;* insofar as the realization of the personality, is a love that unites, love is *agapē*.

FREEDOM-FROM

The Fall

Since freedom and truth are the original facts, there is in the beginning nothing over against man from which he must be free. The myth of paradise symbolizes this original wholeness, the unity of freedom and truth, although in this original state man is yet to have " the experience of thought and freedom." [79] But the freedom which can sin is there, and in the exercise of this option man falls. He elects a distance from the truth by stepping away from it into nonbeing and chaos, so that truth and nonbeing henceforth confront him as objects of conscious choice, as good and bad. The state of moral consciousness is the fallen state.

In this view, Berdyaev has a ready explanation of the fall — namely, meontic, uncreated freedom. Uncreated freedom is as eternal as God, so that the truth of God is no necessity for man. As an event of uncreated freedom the fall cannot be blamed on God; nor is it a kind of necessity rooted in the ontological structure of reality. No, the fall presupposes only the actuality of freedom; it is man's sin and his guilt, although it is at the same time his greatness, for of what other creature can it be said that he has freedom from God (and so also freedom for God)? Although the fall means a loss of freedom in the sense that man now suffers the obligation of moral decision, Berdyaev insists that freedom is original, that once upon a time it existed in pristine purity, and that the fall therefore is a kind of temporal and not an eternal reality. It is not the way *reality is;* it is what *man chooses*. Creative freedom is itself the ground and source of good and evil; the real issue of ethics is therefore beyond good and evil. Ultimately, man is not to be understood

[79] *Destiny of Man,* p. 39.

in terms of the moral consciousness, but the moral consciousness in terms of man (who can transcend this consciousness
only in myth).[80]

To this point the thought of Berdyaev seems dangerously
dualistic, and yet he would avoid that appearance. He insists, in supralapsarian fashion (as Barth does), that Christ
precedes Adam and that the fall is not only an unfolding and
glorification of man, but even more, an unfolding also of the
triune freedom of God. " The Fall of the first man, Adam,
had positive meaning and justification, as a moment in the
revelation of creativity, preparing for the appearance of the
Absolute Man." [81] The Absolute Man is the man in Christ, the
man who answers God in freedom; he is also the man in whom
God enters freely into the abyss of man's freedom and sin.
Insofar as God eternally or absolutely wills Christ as the unity
of God and man in freedom, he is, in a sense, *culpa felix* —
the one who wills the freedom with which man sins. The exercise of that freedom, even in sin, is therefore an unfolding of
the eternal purpose of God. " The fall of the first Adam was a
necessary cosmic moment." [82] Or again: " Toleration of evil
is part of God's providential plan." [83] Berdyaev's meaning is
that the freedom of the sinner, but not the sin, is necessary. It
is necessary because God wants man to be free for him, but
even more ultimately, because God wills to enter into that
freedom. Through participation in the freedom of man, God
is revealed as the Triune God who is divine not in his static
transcendence of man but rather in his living participation in
the freedom of man. By his emphasis on the Triunity of God,
Berdyaev also insists that God's freedom for and with man does
not exclude or annul man's freedom and that the freedom in
which man sins is a genuine freedom, not a mere divine mode
or an unfolding of a divine necessity. Man's freedom is not God

80 *Ibid.*, p. 40.
81 *Meaning of the Creative Act,* p. 148.
82 *Ibid.*, p. 149.
83 *Destiny of Man,* p. 41.

" only playing with himself," [84] and yet God takes freedom into himself, " descends into the abyss of freedom," so that we are not left with an insoluble and unredeemable dualism. The sin of man is therefore both a revelation of man and God; it is a moment in the revelation of the God-man, the Absolute, transcendental man, Jesus Christ. This is not to deny sin, but to affirm that more ultimate than sin is God and man, truth and freedom — the grace of Christ.[85] In sum, Berdyaev states that the notion of creation " has meaning and dignity only if the creation of the world be understood as the realization of the Divine Trinity . . . as a mystery of love and freedom." [86]

So, although the fall is included in the freedom of God it is not denied or excluded by that freedom, and the effects of the fall are real — namely, as we have seen, freedom's separation from God and entrance into the chaos of nonbeing, where it becomes conscious of being and nonbeing as good and evil and objects of so-called " free " choice. No longer free in the creation of the good, man is now bound by the consciousness of the good (and evil) . His freedom becomes his " obligation." This consciousness and obligation shut out both the orginal creative freedom and the original divine truth. Yet, once the conscious distinction between good and evil has arisen, it remains necessary; good must overcome evil. But on the other hand, the situation is tragic, for good cannot overcome evil; indeed, it exists by virtue of the evil it must overcome. Hope of redemption from evil lies in the fact that " the purpose of life is perpetual creativeness, and not obedience to laws and norms." [87] The good overcomes evil not when it is the object of free choice but the creative ground of freedom itself. " The fundamental question is to determine not the purpose, whether immanent or imposed on us from without, which our moral

---

[84] *Ibid.*, p. 24.

[85] In *Truth and Revelation*, Ch. VIII, Berdyaev rejects traditional doctrines of hell because they make sin and the freedom of sin ultimate and the freedom in truth of " Transcendental Man " penultimate.

[86] *Destiny of Man*, p. 29.

[87] *Ibid.*, p. 42.

life ought to subserve, but the source of the creative energy which is realized in our life." [88] Man, redemption, and creativity are beyond good and evil. For this reason Berdyaev insists that the fall is temporal; there was a time, a reality, prior to morality; otherwise, authentic man, the man of freedom and truth, could never appear.

As we have seen, the moral consciousness, once it has arisen, has a relative value. The distance from the truth taken by freedom justifies the efforts of the good to overcome the evil of this separation and distance. This necessity Berdyaev acknowledges in his discussion of the ethics of law.[89] Yet the distance is not one that the law of the good can overcome, but it is one that only freedom in the good can overcome. Redemption is the reunification, through the entry of Christ into freedom, of freedom and truth, in which the good becomes the source and not the object of freedom. The ethics of redemption are the ethics of renewal.[90] But given the unity of truth and freedom, then freedom has the freedom (not the obligation) of truth; it becomes a creator of truth. As creator man is the subject of the third form of ethics, the ethics of creativeness.[91]

Objectification

The fall, then, means that man separates the truth from himself, and in his sin looks for it objectively, outside — as a law unto his freedom — rather than inside as the source of freedom's creativity. The spirit or inner dimension of objectification has been characterized by Berdyaev as the "bourgeois spirit." This characterization of the spirit of sin reflects, of course, Berdyaev's experience of the Russian Revolution, but he regards it to be just as much an aspect of Communism as it is of capitalism. It is the spirit of bondage and slavery in which man understands himself not in the image of God, not as one born in the unity of truth and freedom which is the unity of Christ. In this spirit, man would rather understand himself

88 *Ibid.*, p. 44.
89 See *ibid.*, pp. 84–102.
90 *Ibid.*, pp. 103–125.
91 *Ibid.*, pp. 126–153.

as a son of Adam, born in splendid separation from the divine center, in a conflict between truth and freedom. So removed from Christ the Son, man is no longer a true person, the sun, the microcosm. No longer is he a free spirit and the source of the cosmic hierarchy and unity; rather, he is now the atom, solitary and lonely. With no center he can be no center; without depth he cannot provide depth. Without light he can shed no light; without being, he cannot be the creative source of being. " In everything he wants to appear and is powerless to be." [92] No longer believing in another supernatural world, he can believe only in this natural world. The resulting bourgeois spirit is a hollow concupiscence driven to constant and vain search for true depth in an outer world of mere appearances. Bewitched by the surface, it " dislikes miracles " and denies symbols; in effect, it forfeits the " tragic consciousness of guilt " which prohibits such identification of appearance and reality. In sum, the bourgeois spirit is " nothing but the rejection of Christ." [93]

It must be emphasized, however, that while the bourgeois spirit is unspiritual and objectifying, it is nevertheless an act of the spirit in the sense that it proceeds from the heart of man and becomes a spirit in which man exists. Freely, man surrenders his freedom to objects which then become the center. The tragedy of sin is that sin is at once the expression and the oppression of freedom, an event that testifies both to the glory and the ignominy of man and freedom.

Monism

Philosophically stated, objectification of the bourgeois spirit is a monism in which the unity that embraces the duality of subject and object is overcome and replaced by the imperialism or objectivity of the subject or the object. The individual

[92] Nicolas Berdyaev, *The Bourgeois Mind, and Other Essays,* ed. by Donald Attwater, tr. by Countess Bennigsen (Sheed & Ward, Inc., 1934), p. 23.
[93] *Ibid.,* pp. 20, 25.

person no longer exists in his own hypostasis, but becomes a mere expression of either an objectified and transcendent subject or object. For example, freedom and love, which are originally correlated and essential to each other, are now separate, with each objectified and making imperious claims upon the other. True freedom, freedom in love, now becomes freedom-as-such, arbitrariness. Such " freedom without Christ the Liberator, is the freedom of the Old Adam, freedom without love." It is diabolic freedom, purely formal freedom, freedom without Logos, without Christ.[94] For all its efforts to save itself, this freedom, " without content and void," is actually a freedom " to desire emptiness, to turn away towards nonbeing." Freedom-from without first being freedom-for is finally no freedom at all.[95] This kind of freedom is the freedom of individualism which does not say, " I want this," but rather, " I want what I want." [96] But since it has claimed to be all in all, subject and content, it also tolerates not even " I," and the person who would find life in such freedom dies and is " reborn in necessity," subject to " a slavish psychology, a psychology which has lost its freedom, a psychology of the age of childhood." [97] The man who is possessed by the will to power or abstract freedom " is in the grasp of fate and becomes the man of destiny." [98] Nietzsche, in resistance to all objectification, asserted his freedom absolutely, only to find himself in an ironic bondage to the objectified freedom of superman. When man is separated from the divine-human center, he cannot affirm himself, except as he affirms some " objective " support that is finally intolerant of the personal spirit.[99] The principles of truth and love will not be denied and assert themselves

---

[94] *Meaning of the Creative Act*, p. 152. See Ch. VI, pp. 144–179, *passim*, and *Freedom*, pp. 117–157, for a discussion of the relationship of love and freedom.

[95] *Meaning of the Creative Act*, p. 147.

[96] *Ibid.*, p. 153.

[97] *Ibid.*, pp. 147, 153.

[98] *Slavery*, p. 63.

[99] *The Beginning*, pp. 32 f.

destructively against freedom, either, as in Nietzche's case, by an ironical return of the principle of superman upon freedom, or by setting themselves in direct opposition to freedom in the form of law and necessity, as expressed, for instance, in the transcendental ego of idealism.

Before we pursue further this question of sin (from which man is to be set free) , it is important to bear in mind that the relationship between truth and freedom which we have referred to above is not one of polarity, such that each has legitimate claims vis-à-vis the other; in this relationship freedom has the priority. Freedom is not denied by the grace that brings truth from God, nor is there any truth in the cosmos that is not first an expression of freedom. The reconciliation of truth and freedom is not a synthesis born of some common ground, but it is rather the repossession of truth for freedom, yet in such a way that freedom is itself truthful. This unity in freedom is the unique gift of Christ.[100]

We have seen that not only is freedom originally united with love, truth, and meaning, but that it is also an inner reality that at the same time expresses itself *outwardly* and *symbolically* in the concrete events of history. " Man is an incarnate spirit." [101] This latter unity also roots in Christ, who is both inward and outward, spirit and flesh. When the center in this God-man is surrendered, then the unity of flesh and spirit is also surrendered, and the inner contends with the outer, and outer with the inner.[102] Because of this duality, idealism and materialism, for example, stand mutually opposed, neither tolerating the other or its own true ground in the incarnate spirit of man. Without foundation in the unity of the God-

100 The priority of freedom is the reason why Berdyaev insists that ethics must go beyond the ethics of redemption in which truth and freedom are brought together, to the ethics of creativity in which freedom itself becomes the source of truth.

101 *Spirit and Reality*, p. 57.

102 " Berdyaev will have nothing to do with the theory that knowledge is completely determined by the object . . . nor with the opposite theory of idealists that the world is constructed by the subject." (Clarke, *Introduction to Berdyaev*, p. 85.)

man, the spirit of man is betrayed in its incarnation; it finds itself not incarnated but objectified. The objects it creates as symbols of the spirit impose themselves upon the spirit from the outside as if they were things-in-themselves, as if they were reality rather than symbol. Internal expression is exchanged for external impression, and it is no longer what proceeds from the mouth but what enters it that matters.

Just as the fleshly symbols of man are objectified and no longer belong to man, but are extrinsic, objective, so also the symbols of the spirit, the ideas of man, are no longer his. They become objective and transcendent, and the free person belongs to them, rather than they to him. So the inner contends against the outer and outer against inner, in and through man, yet without him. Man, the subject of a creative unity, finds himself the object of a destructive conflict.

We have also seen that the spirit incarnates itself for the sake of true community, or *sobornost*. But, as a result of the fall from the God-man, in whom God and man exist for one another in true *sobornost*, the unity of personality and community is broken, and the person and the other stand in the tension of the free individual versus the collective society, each begetting its antithesis because of its monistic and objectifying pretensions.[103] Societies are formed by individuals to protect themselves against individuals, and individualism is a reaction to the oppressiveness of society. The sacrifice of the conflict is the free spirit of man which knows itself only in the creation of *sobornost*.

Man as free spirit, man as incarnate spirit, man as spirit in community, is man in history. The symbols with which man expresses himself unto the end of community are living symbols; they constitute in their connectedness a myth, a running symbol of the spirit of man. But with the fall, history is severed from its origin in the spirit; it is objectified, and stands off from man as the past or the future — neither of which tolerates " my " spirit, the inner reality that dwells in the pres-

[103] See *Slavery*, pp. 130 ff., and *Solitude*, pp. 180 ff.

ent moment. History is no longer a spiritual heritage or promise; it is now an external fate, the reality and existence of necessity.[104] It may be comprehended as a materialistic or an idealistic necessity, in terms of spirit or flesh, along Marxian or Hegelian lines, but it is in each instance " objective " and the spiritual dimension is reduced to a link in the relentless evolution.

The result of the creative expression of the free spirit in the events of history and in the reality of *sobornost* is also the microcosmic shaping and redeeming of the cosmos, the realm of nature. Accordingly, the world belongs to man, as the light belongs to the sun. But when man falls from his center, from the God who in his incarnation claimed the world for man, then the world also falls away from its center and is objectified, and is thus ever escaping the dominion and liberation of the spirit. Man may conquer the world with knowledge, only to be overcome by the " law " of nature. He may direct it to spiritual ends by his technique and machinery, only to find himself in the service of technology and the machine. Culture becomes civilization, and the creator becomes the victim of his creature.[105] Certainly, the elucidation of nature in knowledge and its control in technology are at one level efforts of the free, loving spirit to liberate the cosmos by infusing it with light and to order it by turning its power and oppressiveness into liberating tools of the human spirit. Thus no one would really want to turn back the clock and return to the past in retreat from contemporary objectification. The objectified world of yesteryear, with its plethora of hostile spirits, is not preferable to the tyranny of the machine, which has liberated man from

104 " Man creates history and packs it with his own creative power. Yet history treats man with indifference and cruelty; there is a real demonism in history." (Nicolas Berdyaev, *The Divine and the Human*, tr. by R. M. French, pp. 178 ff.; London: Geoffrey Bles, Ltd., 1949.)

105 *Realm of Spirit*, pp. 46–50. See also *Meaning of History*, pp. 133–160. It is a recurring theme of Berdyaev's thought that the Renaissance liberated man from nature and organic existence only to turn him over to the tyranny of forms and finally to the machine.

the toilsome burden of nature. The production-line tractor is preferable to the handmade plow, even though the production line itself is as oppressive as the spirits of old. No, the problem remains; it is past as well as present, and the solution does not lie in a romantic retreat to uncivilized nature or to yesterday's culture. It appears then that the history of *this* world is the history of objectivication, of man in contradiction to his own subjectivity — that divine, transcendental self which is hidden in Christ.

This bondage has its expression also in religion. For Berdyaev, love is not only man's outreach to his true self and to the world; it is also the outreach of religion toward God. In this realm man's bondage reaches its ultimate because it is directed against the ultimate. By these chains man is kept from responding to God. God, who is Triune, two in one, is now one and one, with nothing between. He, too, is divided and denied. As the God of freedom, he is removed to remote, arbitrary transcendence. He is the God of " transcendent egoism," the God whom Feuerbach properly identified as the result of man's self-objectification.[106] Or he is the God of slavish immanence, the God who is a slave to the causal necessity of the world's processes, which are now apotheosized as providence and grace. Of course these two errors frequently combine in the most implausible of combinations, as ironic shadows of their original unity. So, on the one hand, God is affirmed as a transcendent egoist, to whom all the attributes of the most irrational of human egoisms is attributed.[107] He is the vindictive judge, exacting eye for eye, tooth for tooth, according to his caprice damning some to hell, saving others with a grim humor that heaps coals upon the heads of the damned. On the other hand, he is this most predictable God of providence, whose ways are as dependable, unmerciful, and with as little regard for humanity as are the ways of nature. This type of sinful religion binds man to a God whose egoism denies love

106 *Truth and Revelation*, p. 118. See also pp. 100 ff.
107 *Ibid.*, pp. 55 f., 114 f.

and whose law obliterates freedom. He is a God who has not come to save, but to destroy.[108]

It remains to be said again that the sin of objectification is a sin of the spirit; in it the spirit is both affirmed and denied. The spirit must create its objects if there are to be objects to which the spirit bows the knee. The tragedy of sin is not the tragedy of destiny or fate; it is a tragedy of freedom, a tragedy within the spirit itself; historic fate and its tragic implications are but one symptom of the tragedy of freedom. So sin is not so much the death of the spirit as it is its sickness and disease. It is a perversion, distortion, but not a dissolution of the spirit. Thus even individualism and collectivism in their mutual exclusiveness achieve a sick minimum of true community, and in religion, the opposition between transcendence and immanence in objectified thinking are weak echoes of triunity and God-manhood. The world cannot overcome spirit any more than it can restore it. Spirit is a gift of God, of God-manhood, of Christ. Indeed, in Christ, who lives eternally as the God-man, man abides as the eternal man-God. " If you are a Christian there can be no End but Christ." [109] But even more basically — if you are a man, there can be no end but Christ.

FREEDOM FOR FREEDOM

What is the ground and source of true freedom? What is its origin, and wherein lies the possibility of its victory over slavery and sin? These questions are difficult, for Berdyaev has stated that freedom is uncreated and original, a " well of unmeasurable depth," " the final mystery." Instead of having an origin or source, freedom is itself the origin and source both of man and the whole realm of being. However, we have also seen that man is a slave, that his freedom is problematic, so

---

[108] If this " forensic " type of Christianity is thought out to the end, " then the coming of Christ the Redeemer will not be for the betterment and salvation of men but it will make things worse and even intensify the ruin " (*Truth and Revelation*, p. 121). See also *Slavery*, pp. 82 ff.; *The Divine and the Human*, Ch. I, pp. 1–21.

[109] See Fielding Clarke's summary of Berdyaev's position, p. 119.

that the question of the source of authentic freedom must be raised. The answer can appear only in symbol and in the realm of the spirit, however, since freedom is prior to being, prior to man himself, and cannot be grasped directly.[110] Berdyaev acknowledges that existentialists are correct, then, when they deny that truth and freedom are objective aspects of the realm of being, but insists they are wrong when they deny at the same time the spirit and the language of myth and symbol.[111]

The Meon

Berdyaev's thinking rests upon two myths, both of which point to realities which immanently transcend man.[112] The first of these, for which Berdyaev is most well known and of which we have already spoken, is the myth of the *meon,* or the *Ungrund.*[113] Berdyaev refers to this symbol primarily in his earlier writings and in various circumstances — when he states that freedom is prior to being,[114] as he develops the concept of the divine life,[115] or when he is exercised by the problem of theodicy.[116] The *Ungrund* is the divine nothing — *to mē on* —

---

[110] *Freedom,* p. 52.

[111] " The existentialists of the new formation may say that my philosophical viewpoint presupposes the myth of God, the myth of the Spirit — let them call that a myth; this disturbs me not at all. This is the most universal and integral of all myths. What is most important is the myth concerning the existence of truth, without which it is difficult to talk about the truth of anything, not only about Truth, but also about truths." (*Realm of Spirit,* pp. 26 f.)

[112] " Immanent transcendence " means that there is a reality other than man, distinct from him, but which is not to be separated from him epistemologically. Man knows the transcendent only as he is and knows himself.

[113] Berdyaev's understanding of the *Ungrund* is derived from Jakob Böhme and Meister Eckhart; see *Destiny of Man,* p. 25. Böhme and Eckhart's influence is mediated by a Russian tradition that looks back to the rise of Freemasonry in Russia in the eighteenth century, as noted by V. V. Zenkovsky, *A History of Russian Philosophy,* 2 vols., tr. by George L. Kline (Columbia University Press, 1953) , I, 97.

[114] *The Beginning,* pp. 104 ff., and *Meaning of the Creative Act,* pp. 129 f.

[115] *Destiny of Man,* pp. 29 f., *Meaning of the Creative Act,* pp. 144 ff.

[116] *Dream and Reality,* pp. 178 f.; *The Divine and the Human,* pp. 90 f.; *Destiny of Man,* p. 25; *Freedom,* p. 165.

the eternal source of freedom. Of this, God himself is born
and from it he creates. According to this concept, freedom, as it
exists in the creation, is not created by God nor is it determined
by God; rather, it is part of the nothing out of which God
created.

By calling this thinking symbolic and mythological Berdyaev
disallows rational inferences which violate the myth. The only
way this myth can be transcended is in terms of another, and in
fact Berdyaev does posit another myth, but before we turn to
it let us examine more closely the function of the myth of the
meontic in his thought. In the first place it resolves for him
the theodicy question. "Throughout my religious development," says Berdyaev, "I have been much exercised by the
problem of theodicy. . . . I have said on many occasions that
the only serious argument in favor of atheism is the difficulty
of reconciling an almighty and benevolent Deity with the evil
and suffering in the world and in human existence. All theological doctrines which deal with this problem appeared to
me as intolerable rationalizations. Theodicy reaches down to
the mystery of freedom, which is not susceptible of any rationalizations. . . . The issues involved in this problem have
led me to the recognition of uncreated and uncaused freedom,
which is tantamount to the recognition of an irreducible mystery, admitting of intuitive description but not of definition." [117]

On the other hand, in his autobiography, Berdyaev maintains that meontic or uncreated freedom "is a limiting notion,
describing symbolically a reality which does not lend itself to
logical definition." [118] The meontic puts limits to the ontic; so
to say that human freedom is meontic is to say that it is prior to
and not contained within the realm of being. It means "that
man can be free only if his freedom is not determined by anything that is not himself; and that he is a subject only if he is
not a 'thing' fitted in or subordinated, in a causal or any

[117] *Dream and Reality*, p. 117.
[118] *Ibid.*, p. 288.

other way, to other things." [119] Insofar as freedom cannot thus be explained by anything else, it is "groundless," proceeding from the "*Ungrund*," explained by no being — *to mē on*.

The myth of the *Ungrund* also serves as a limit against rationalistic views of God which deny the notion of the divine life and freedom. The acceptance by Berdyaev of such "a dark and irrational premise" enables him to grasp and speak of "the mystery of the possible existence of movement in the inmost depths of the divine life." He is especially concerned to make possible an understanding of "the tragic destiny for the divine life," namely, "the passion of God Himself and His Son." [120] Only a strange, mysterious, and suprarational concept of freedom can enable us to comprehend the alienation of God from himself in the cross of Jesus.

Finally, the myth of the meontic is protection from an antihumanistic monism. Berdyaev does not believe that his or any authentic Christian experience is accounted for by an understanding of freedom which, by reducing all freedom to the divine, has God answering to himself in the experience of faith.[121] Meontic freedom guarantees the freedom implicit in faith, protecting against unchristian monisms and determinisms.

In our first section, on freedom's goal, we have seen that man is a unity of the divine and the human, truth and freedom. In answer to the question, Whence this unity? Berdyaev replies, in the first place and in part, with this vision of the *Ungrund*. According to this notion, freedom is groundless, without origin; it is the ultimate mystery; it is the beginning. This is the first myth. However, it fails to answer one decisive question, namely, How is this freedom to be united with truth, especially when it finds itself, as we have seen it, in bondage to sin?

[119] *Ibid.*
[120] *Meaning of History*, p. 55.
[121] *Freedom*, pp. 126 f.; *Truth and Revelation*, p. 48; *Dream and Reality*, p. 288.

Incarnation

In answer, Berdyaev goes on to state that whatever may be said for the *Ungrund*, " *the final, ultimate freedom, the daring of freedom and the burden of freedom is the virtue of religious maturity.*" [122] The existence of God is " man's charter of liberty." [123] " There is no freedom or Spirit without God, as its original source." [124] The very fact of man and his spirit is an " indication " if not a proof of God, and the primary source of Berdyaev's confidence in man's charter in God is the second myth, the myth of the incarnation.[125] " The restoration of man to his former dignity could be accomplished only by the appearance of the absolute Son of God, in the Incarnation." [126] " *Man's infinite spirit claims an absolute supernatural anthropocentrism.*" [127]

As a Christian *philosopher,* Berdyaev is concerned from the

[122] *Meaning of the Creative Act,* p. 158.

[123] *Realm of Spirit,* p. 41. " Freedom is possible only if, besides the realm of Caesar, there exists the realm of Spirit, that is, the Kingdom of God." (*Ibid.,* p. 42.)

[124] *Ibid.,* p. 32.

[125] Lampert exaggerates Berdyaev's view of the *Ungrund,* stating that it " renders man capable of confronting God in absolute independence " (Evgueny Lampert, *Nicolas Berdyaev and the New Middle Ages,* p. 53; London: James Clarke & Co., Ltd., n.d.) He goes on to state that the *Ungrund* has " disastrous implications " for Christology.

Clarke responds to Lampert, pointing out that a basic intuition like that of the *Ungrund* is no conclusion; it is a premise and cannot therefore be " unwarranted " as Seaver contends (*Nicholas Berdyaev: An Introduction to His Thought,* p. 87; Harper & Brothers, 1950) . Clarke in turn fails to observe the conflict between the two premises — the *Ungrund* and Christ, and that the former is not warranted by the latter. Zenkovsky comments to the point when he says of Berdyaev's conception of personal freedom that it " actually divides rather than unites men; and, since personality is ' prior ' to being and is not born from the ' womb of being,' an element of pluralism is present here. We found another ' screen ' for pluralism in the doctrine that freedom is ' not ontal but meonic.' " He concludes that Berdyaev's personalism " thus becomes a self-enclosure, which shuns all contact with the world " (*A History of Russian Philosophy,* II, 778 f.) . Zenkovsky fails thus to note that a Christology of God-manhood does preserve both unity and freedom.

[126] *Meaning of the Creative Act,* p. 73.

[127] *Ibid.,* p. 76.

beginning to the end of his thinking with man, with man in his freedom, and he insists that man's spirit and freedom cannot be derived from anything in the cosmos, even being-itself. Freedom is meontic. Berdyaev's philosophical faith is the firm faith that man is the ultimate reality and concern. As a *Christian* philosopher he is convinced that the other side of the ultimacy of man is the eternal reality of God. While freedom is not ontic, it is indeed theological, and while the world cannot give it, God does give it through the incarnation.

In many instances, Berdyaev combines the two myths, *Ungrund* and incarnation, so that true freedom is seen to root in that spiritual experience in which the divine, incarnate Logos encounters the meontic freedom of man.[128] Thus, revelation is the gracious elucidation and redemption of freedom; at the same time it is the creative appropriation of grace by freedom. This is what Berdyaev means by his famous confession: " Freedom has brought me to Christ and I know of no other path leading to him." [129] He also states: " Freedom in the acceptance of Truth cannot be won from Truth itself, for it is prior to it." Man has not only " freedom in God," but also " freedom in relation to God." [130] To put it all very simply — revelation is the encounter between the divine logos and uncreated freedom, between divine matter and human form.

However, Berdyaev himself does not let us rest here. The question of sin complicates the picture. The freedom with which man meets grace is freedom that is used to sinning; it is the problem, not the solution. This is the so-called freedom of the sons of Adam, who have lost their " royal freedom " and have " plunged into lower spheres of necessity " and have been deprived of their " place in nature, and placed . . . in slavish dependence on the lower spheres of the hierarchy of nature." [131] It is freedom which has become fate, fast bound to

[128] See Clarke's discussion, *Introduction to Berdyaev*, pp. 79–91.
[129] *Freedom*, p. x.
[130] *Ibid.*, p. 127.
[131] *Meaning of the Creative Act*, p. 71.

the laws of its own creatures; from the beginning it is a poisonous and destructive influence. This freedom — meontic freedom as such — which we have seen Berdyaev designate as the minor freedom, is hardly a fit subject for revelation. The problem is, How can freedom's evil be overcome save in its destruction? " The importance of human freedom and the superhuman nature of grace create an insoluble paradox." [132] The answer, says Berdyaev, " is contained in the mystery of Christ the God-Man. . . . Only in Christ the God-Man does the paradox of the relation between the Creator and the creature find its solution. That is the essence of Christianity." [133] From this point of view the real reconciliation between man and God does not take place " existentially " between man as such and God as such, between Logos and meontic freedom, but rather, eternally in the unity of the Trinity as disclosed in Jesus, in the " reconciliation " between God the Father and God the Son in the unity of the Holy Spirit. " The freedom of the Son is that in which and by which the free response to God is effected. It is the source of the freedom of the whole human race. . . . The freedom of the Son of God has its source in itself and in Him. . . . But the whole generation of Adam is in the Son of God." [134]

The subject of revelation is first of all Jesus and only secondarily every man who is included in him. The human subject of revelation is not " empirical man," but " transcendental man," whose existence is the condition upon which the possibility of religious and spiritual experience depends.[135] The freedom which receives revelation is a freedom which from eternity participates in revelation, and this is the freedom of Jesus Christ, the eternal Son.[136]

[132] *Destiny of Man,* p. 35.
[133] *Ibid.* See also *Freedom,* p. 135.
[134] *Ibid.,* p. 137.
[135] *Truth and Revelation,* pp. 16 ff.
[136] Seaver describes the coincidence of freedom and revelation in ethical terms. " How can I know Him as Redeemer unless and until I follow him as example? And how can I follow him as example if he is not wholly kin to me? " (Seaver, *op. cit.,* p. 16.)

This mythological thinking which begins not with man but with Christ — transcendental man — makes necessary another critique of the transcendental, the critique of revelation which goes beyond the critiques of the pure and practical reason to bring into view as far as possible " transcendental man " (instead of transcendental reason), since " earthly man always limits revelation and frequently distorts it." [137] The critique of revelation must first demonstrate that any truth that is not received in freedom is not authentic. In Dostoevsky's legend of the Grand Inquisitor, the Inquisitor represents the Antichrist, who would have truth without freedom, who would suffer the loss of man for the sake of truth. Christ, however, is the original unity of truth and freedom, whose truth is manifest only in freedom. Secondly, the critique of revelation will therefore show that the freedom which receives revelation is the freedom of a new spiritual, transcendental, and divine humanity.[138] " If Christ is not only God but also man (which is what the dogma of the two natures teaches us) then in redemption not only the divine nature played its part but also the human nature, that is, the heavenly spiritual nature of mankind." [139] The original subject of revelation is the man in Christ, " transcendental man," the " Adam Kadman " of which the *Kabbala* speaks. As Paul wrote, " Your life is hid with God in Christ."

[137] *Truth and Revelation*, p. 19. The condition of spiritual knowledge is not reason, nor does spiritual epistemology require a critique of reason. Rather, the condition of spiritual knowledge is not transcendental reason but transcendental man, who comes into view through a " critique of the Spirit." The beginnings of such a critique are set forth in *Truth and Revelation* (see pp. 7–9) .

[138] Schultze rightly observes that the spiritual humanity presupposed by revelation is a churchly humanity. " *So führt ihn nicht die Wissenschaft sondern die kirchliche Erfahrung, die eine Art geistig Lebens bildet, hin zu Christus.*" (Bernhard Schultze, *Russische Denker*, p. 362; Wien: Verlag Herder, 1950.)

[139] *Freedom*, p. 177.

Incarnation as Symbol

An analysis of Berdyaev's conception of the incarnation must focus on his understanding of it as a symbol. A symbol in Berdyaev's usage is both distinguishable and yet inseparable from the reality it symbolizes. I would say that it has both material and formal aspects, each of which is distinguishable from and yet necessary to the other. The reality symbolized by the incarnation is the eternal reality of man in the unity of freedom and truth. That this reality is *symbolically* united with the incarnation is evident in the fact that mere knowledge of the historical Jesus does not disclose the truth; and yet, there is a *unity*, inasmuch as only through the historical Jesus is the truth revealed.[140] The relation between the symbol and the reality of the incarnation has an analogy in the relationship between the inner and the outer aspects of the human spirit which is created in the image of Christ. Thus, while the spirit of man cannot be identified with the body, it does not follow that the spirit can be separated from the body, or that there is a natural hostility between them. Chiding against any separation between the incarnate Jesus and eternal truth, Berdyaev appeals to Dostoevsky, who, he says, " has a moving word about how, if truth were on the one side and Christ on the other, it would be better to refuse truth and to go with Christ." [141] The best evidence, however, of Berdyaev's doctrine of the incarnation is the conclusion he draws from it — on the one side the humanity of God and on the other side the divinity of man. *" In Christian revelation the truth about man's divine nature is really only the reverse side of the medal of the truth about Christ's human nature."* [142]

The incarnation is a symbol, and must be a symbol, because it " shows us that the meaning of one world is to be found in another, and that this meaning is revealed to us in the lat-

140 *Truth and Revelation*, p. 60; *Freedom*, pp. 89–93.
141 *Meaning of the Creative Act*, p. 44.
142 *Ibid.*, p. 81.

ter." [143] And it not only shows us the relationship between the
two worlds, but is itself the effective bridge between them.[144]
Christ is the original bridge, and through him man also becomes a bridge, a symbol of eternity, just as the world, through
man's participation in it, becomes a symbol of man and of
eternity. The unity between Jesus and what he symbolizes is
thus dialectical. From one point of view Jesus reveals the
eternal unity of God and man, and from the other he is that
unity. He is both the symbol and the reality, form and content. He is a distinguished symbol that points to the other
world by pointing to himself and a central symbol in which all
other worldly events may become symbolic.[145] The incarnation
is therefore what may be called an "absolute symbol." [146]
Without such a symbol, man either becomes a symbol of the
outer, absolutized world (realism) or the world becomes a symbol of man's inner, absolutized spirit (idealism), but in either
case that which presumes to be the center and source of symbolic meaning is itself symbolic of nothing and void of meaning. Berdyaev confesses his faith in the absoluteness of Christ
when he states that "if God does not exist, neither does man,
nor do I exist myself." Essential for him is the fact of Jesus' resurrection, and not the mere theory.[147] The absoluteness of Jesus
is further indicated by Berdyaev's respect for the concept of
dogma. Dogmas, he says, "possess absolute and indefectible
truth." They speak of "ontological realities, original life itself
and original existence." [148] And these ontological, indefectible

[143] *Freedom,* p. 52. "Christ's humanity is the symbol of which the divinity is the meaning." (Seaver, p. 59.)

[144] *Freedom,* p. 43.

[145] "There must be a center from which revelation emanates and we
are Christians in virtue of our belief in such a center." (*Truth and Revelation,* p. 46.)

[146] Dogmas are such symbols, and they convey truths of "absolute importance" (*Freedom,* p. 76).

[147] *Ibid.*

[148] *Ibid.,* p. 77. It is interesting here to observe that in Berdyaev's definition myths symbolize original *life,* original existence, whereas in the
case of Tillich they are symbols of ultimate *being* and the structures of
being which are prior to life and existence. Barth makes a point similar to

truths are bound up with historical facts, such as the existence and resurrection of Jesus. The language of doctrine with which one defines or understands the facts is not by any means settled, but dogmas do set final limits.[149] But because dogmas are symbols, they are not stultifying and "can be given a deeper significance and can be thrown into relief by a new form of gnosis." They can find their symbolic expression in "new dogmatic formulas." [150]

Revelation

The discussion so far has concentrated on the reality of Jesus as the incarnation, showing that while he is symbolic, he is, nevertheless, the reality of that which he symbolizes, and, in this sense, an absolute symbol. Our attention now turns briefly to the symbolic dimension as such, to the epistemological question of how the reality is conveyed and appropriated. There are two aspects to the answer — first, the event of revelation through the symbol, and, second, its appropriation through the mystical experience. Needless to say, these are two aspects of a unified experience.

The way in which the truth is revealed through Jesus as a symbol is finally a mystery, but a mystery that can be approached negatively. Berdyaev would thus show how the truth could not be revealed except through this symbol. Only a concrete, particular, once-upon-a-time, once-for-all human event could effectively claim man for eternity and at the same moment impart freedom.[151] Without commitment to a con-

---

Berdyaev's when he designates Biblical myths as *Saga*. Tillich suggests that symbols are concrete in concession to the concreteness of historical and fallen existence, whereas Berdyaev claims they are concrete because of the ultimacy of life, freedom, and concrete existence.

149 *Freedom*, p. 78.

150 *Ibid.*, p. 81.

151 Solovyov presses a like point: "A universal organism expressing the absolute content of the divine principle is preeminently a unique individual being. That individual being or the realized expression of the absolute living God is Christ" (*A Solovyov Anthology*, arranged by S. L. Frank, tr. by Natalie Duddington, p. 37; Charles Scribner's Sons, 1950).

crete symbol the reason of man is invariably bound by the general reality, by the laws and structures of being. But a concrete symbol, which springs uniquely and surprisingly onto time's pages without causal connection to past or future, engages the spirit by disengaging it from the world and causality and by setting it free to create and renew the world. It enables man to abandon " concepts in favor of symbols and myths." [152] When concreteness is not violated and does not become bound to conceptual structures, then reason remains creative and free.

However, a concrete symbol would lead only to chaos and despair if it were merely concrete and not also a symbol, a symbol of eternity. Simply any story — a novel or biography as such — will not do. Only a sacred story, the story of a man whose story is also the story of God — the story of Jesus — can truly liberate and liberate for truth. Such is the symbol of the incarnation, a symbol that delivers the spirit both from slavery to the world and for the freedom of the divine world. Just how the incarnation is both symbol and reality, how it both hides and discloses its word and substance, cannot finally be understood. Revelation is not so much " understood " as it is mystically experienced. Certainly the truth of the symbol can be gained neither through objectifying, historical investigation, nor as a subjective projection of faith. The fact is that as symbol the incarnation is a worldly event that sets man free from the world and his own false, empirical self, in order to reveal to him a truth from beyond the world.

Before we consider the mystical appropriation of revelation the cause of clarity will be served if we acknowledge again the dialectical and circular nature of the discussion. We have seen that the content of revelation is the unity of Logos and freedom, of God and man, in the eternal Christ — " transcendental man." But, at the same time, the form or symbol in which this content is revealed is itself the incarnation, Jesus of Nazareth. Through the God-man — Jesus — our eternal God-manhood is revealed, and in this same God-man our eternal God-manhood is created. Jesus is both the form and the content of the revela-

[152] *Freedom*, p. 74.

tion, both reality and symbol. We have seen a similar dialectic in Barth, for whom Jesus is both the eternal, preexistent, elected Son of God and also the actual, historical event and fulfillment of that election. Only the mystical experience of faith and revelation can begin to understand this mystery.

Mysticism

Mysticism, then, is the way to "understand" and receive revelation. It is neither objective nor subjective. It is opposed to naïve realism that identifies symbol with revelation and to idealism that identifies the subject of revelation with revelation. Both views in effect deny revelation. Mysticism, on the other hand, "teaches that the depths of man are more than human, that in them there lurks a mysterious contact with God and with the world." [153] It appears to be simply a designation for an experience that transcends the subject-object cleavage, an experience of God that is at the same time an expression of the self and freedom. It is an experience whose presupposition is neither theoretical nor practical reason, but rather, "transcendental man" who is neither God as such nor man as such, but the God-man, man in Christ. This means that Christ who comes *to* man at the same time "enters the human heart and *changes* the whole nature of man." [154] It is the experience of immanent transcendence in which God does not confront man as one who is "out there," separated and alien, as the objective facts of nature are, but rather from within, as a human deity, as a God who is at home with man. Berdyaev's mysticism and immanentalism are very natural and necessary implications of his Christology. God is so much with man that man at the depths is with God; why should man look "out there," beyond, above, as it were; he looks within, not to find the self, but the ground of the self, God in his humanity.

Yet this mystical experience is a response to revelation. God's manhood and man's deity have their roots in Jesus Christ, and are revealed to mystical experience through the mediation of

153 *Meaning of the Creative Act*, p. 296.
154 *Freedom*, p. 254. (Italics are mine.)

the central symbols of the faith. Berdyaev is aware of the dangers of the mysticism of identity, in which man loses himself in deity. On the other side, he eschews objective thinking which interprets God, grace, and revelation after the model of nature, objective to and outside man. He refers to the experience of Paul on the Damascus road as an illustration of authentic mysticism. This was truly a subjective experience, but it was just as truly an experience of transcendence which was not to be separated from its embodiment in historical symbols. Man's encounter with God at the depths of his spirit is, religiously speaking, mystical.[155]

Revelation occurs in the spiritual or mystical depths. To the extent that Berdyaev tends to engage in the work of theology he is involved in a critique of revelation that would provide revelation with its proper subject — spiritual rather than empirical man. His procedure is to eliminate from the language of religion such objective categories as the relationship of cause and effect and notions of necessity. Berdyaev attacks especially the doctrines of grace, predestination, providence, and hell. An intelligible critique of these doctrines must proceed not directly from the mystical experience but from its symbolic witness which is summed up in the dogma of the incarnation and the notion of God-manhood. Grace, then, is not to be viewed after the analogy of nature, as an alien imposition that is hostile to man and freedom. Quite the contrary, it is the grace of the God who is human, whose divinity is the source of humanity, whose humanity is the source of divinity. Grace is not a force without, but a spirit within.[156] Traditional theories of predestination, following the models suggested by feudal serfdom and later forms of social organization rather than that of the divine *sobornost,* view the relationship of God to man as the arbitrary mechanical manipulation of the desti-

---

[155] *Ibid.,* p. 239. See also *Meaning of the Creative Act,* pp. 296 ff.

[156] See Schultze's discussion of faith, Christ, and church in Berdyaev. He objects that Berdyaev's inwardizing and mysticism jeopardize the authority of Jesus and church. (*Russische Denker,* pp. 374, 378 f.)

nies of man. The traditional doctrine of providence is no better. " It makes God appear always as an autocratic monarch,
making use of every part of the world, of every individuality,
for the establishment of the common world order, for the ad-
ministration of the whole to the glory of God. This is held to
be a justification of every injustice, every evil, every sorrow, of
the parts of the world." [157]

Berdyaev is most offended by the idea of hell, which is guilty
of objectification and the turning of a spiritual reality into an
objective place. Furthermore, it is blasphemous, attributing to
God, as the vindictive judge of all who oppose him, the most
demonical aspects of human nature. In sum: it is " reckoning
without Christ." " One of the voices that speaks in my soul tells
me that all are doomed to hell, because all more or less doom
themselves to it. But this is reckoning without Christ. And the
other voice in me says that all must be saved, that man's freedom must be enlightened from within, without any violence
done to it — and that comes through Christ and is salvation."[158] The critique of revelation as suggested by these particular critiques is summed up by Berdyaev as a break with
forensic Christianity,[159] the type of religion in which " human
cruelty has been alienated into the sphere of the transcendent
and ascribed to God." [160] In this religion God is self-seeking
and self-vindicating. At the heart of Berdyaev's objections to
such egoistic religion is that it denies man in the affirmation
of God; it denies the freedom of man in asserting the freedom
of God. It conceives revelation as an objective, natural, and
necessary process in which man and his freedom have no part.
Whereas true religion, the religion of God-manhood and
" transcendent altruism," insists that every appearance of God
is also an appearance of man. Every act of the freedom of God
is at the same time the liberation and invocation of man. This
is why Berdyaev insists that " revelation takes my freedom for
granted, my act of choice, my faith in something which is still

[157] *Slavery*, pp. 88 f.
[158] *Destiny of Man*, p. 278.
[159] *Truth and Revelation*, p. 114.
[160] *Ibid.*

invisible and which uses no force upon me." [161] Accordingly,
" there is no conflict between grace and freedom: grace is only
transfigured freedom." [162] The spiritualization of revelation
means simply that it must be received from the depths, in freedom. Yet, paradoxically, that freedom itself with which man in
the mystical experience receives revelation is its gift.

THE FREEDOM OF GOD

Berdyaev's Christology, while and as it speaks of man's
eternal deity and his historical deification, also speaks of God,
of his eternal manhood and historical incarnation. Because
God is who he is, Christ is, and man is, and this, the last phase
of our discussion, might well come first, as in the case of Barth.
I began, however, with a discussion of the freedom of man because this is Berdyaev's interest and because I believe Berdyaev's Christology provides a proper base for such a beginning.

Since Berdyaev's anthropology is implicity so radically theological (or Christological), this concluding discussion of the
freedom of God serves in large measure to summarize, explicate, and underline what has gone before. Specifically, Berdyaev's Christological view of God leads him to affirm three
mystical truths about God (mystical insofar as they are symbolic accounts of the spiritual experience of God). These
three truths are: (1) the humanity of God, (2) the Triune
life of God, and (3) the kingly freedom of God.

Humanity of God

In Berdyaev's estimation, the mystics alone have grasped the
truth of the humanity of God. The substance of their understanding, and Berdyaev's also, is that God *is not* and *cannot be*
without man. Eckhart has said that " before the creature existed God was not God." Angelus Silesius agrees when he confesses: " I know that without me God could not endure for a
moment. . . . I am as great as God, and He is as little as

---

[161] *Ibid.*, p. 48.   [162] *Realm of Spirit*, p. 44.

me." [163] Interpreting these remarks, Berdyaev warns against
a metaphysical or theological misunderstanding which fails to
appreciate that such language is symbolic, mythological, and
should not be misconstrued by objective thinking to read as
though man were thus lost to God or God to man. The unity
is, says Berdyaev, that " of the infinite love between God and
man " so that " the loving subject cannot exist a moment without the loved object." [164]

This line of thought, of course, is rooted in the incarnation
just as it is also the " explanation " of the incarnation. God belongs to man, is " human " because he first belongs to Christ.
" God is not a person except in Christ." [165] Christ, and in him
all men, is eternally with God. " The Divine Son and Man is
born in heaven and on earth, in time and in eternity, above
and below." [166] Since Christ belongs to God from eternity, it is
an error of all abstract monotheisms to separate either God
from Christ or man from Christ. The beginning of theology
and anthropology is Christology. " Christianity is the religion
of the divine Trinity and God-humanity. . . . The second
Face of Divinity is manifested as the human face." [167] As the
original object of God's yearning and love, Christ is the first
Son, but insofar as in Christ's response is included the response
of us all, we too are creatures and sons from eternity. And
since man is the microcosm, the sun, the free and creative
center of the universe, the universe itself is in Christ from the
beginning. Christ is in God, man is in Christ, and the cosmos
is in man; all things are in God.[168] Christ first, but through
him, man and then the world. " Oh, certainly man is not God,
he is the son of God, but not in the unique sense that Christ

[163] *Freedom*, p. 194. The theme of the humanity of God runs throughout Berdyaev's writings. See *The Divine and the Human*, p. 22; *Truth and
Revelation*, pp. 53–57. 123 ff.; *Meaning of the Creative Act*, pp. 320 f., and
Dream and Reality, p. 301.
[164] *Freedom*, p. 195.
[165] " *Gott ist keine Person nur als in Christo.*" From Jakob Böhme,
cited in *Meaning of the Creative Act*, pp. 78 f.
[166] From Böhme, cited in *ibid.*, p. 79.
[167] *Freedom*, p. 216.
[168] *Ibid.*, p. 198.

is the Son of God; but man is a participant in the mystery of
the nature of the Holy Trinity and is a mediator between
God and the cosmos [just as Christ is the mediator between
man and God]." [169] Those who think of God as the absolute are
guilty of " the transference to God, and to the relation of God
to the world and to man, of conceptions derived from the slavish social relations which obtain among human beings, the
relation of master and slave." [170] One might charge Berdyaev
with anthropomorphism in his concern to view God in relationship to man rather than as the transcendent absolute. To
this, Berdyaev replies that anthropocentrism is not to be
avoided. God does place man at the pinnacle. It is to man that
revelation comes; it is in man that the Son is incarnate. The
question is not whether we shall speak anthropologically but
whether or not our anthropology is correct — whether our
symbols shall be drawn from the divine transcendental man,
Jesus Christ, or the realm of objectivity where the truly human
hardly appears.

The Triune Life

Our thinking is thus directed to the second aspect of the
divine nature — the interior life of God, or what Berdyaev
calls the " theogonic process." Once it is seen that God's heart
is open to man in Christ it follows not only that man may, but
that man " must think not only about himself and his own
salvation and well being; he must also think of God and His
interior life." [171] Holy Scripture, insofar as it presents us with
Christ, " presents us with a psychology of the Divine and speaks
to us of the affective and emotional life of God." [172] Why, asks
Berdyaev, are those who object to the idea of God's nostalgia,
his passion, his inner life and tragedy, precisely those who talk
of his " wrath "? " Why," he asks, " is it less humiliating to ad-

[169] *Meaning of the Creative Act*, p. 79.
[170] *Truth and Revelation*, p. 8.
[171] *Freedom*, p. 211.
[172] *Ibid.*, p. 210.

mit the existence of the feeling of offense in God than to admit divine languor?" [173] Thinking, which denies the divine
life, which stresses the impassible gulf between God and man,
and which conceives him as the Absolute, confesses in effect
the inhumanity of God.[174] It makes the divine life and tragedy
impossible and inconceivable, and renders the incarnation
meaningless.

For God to live for another, as he does in Jesus, he must
be a living God. For God to suffer for another he must be
free to suffer. For God to become man he must be eternally
human. Berdyaev is particularly concerned to avoid a Docetism
that denies to God any real participation in the sufferings of
Jesus. He would show that the divine life means that God has
so radical a freedom for another that he can lose himself in that
other, as in the tragic loss of his Son. As we have already seen,
Berdyaev introduces the idea of meontic freedom to underline
his case for the divine life and freedom. It is this fact of such
" a dark and irrational premise " that " implies the possibility of tragic destiny for the divine life." [175] He would argue
that such a notion is demanded by the incarnation itself.

Yet Berdyaev also roots this divine life and freedom in another symbol — the symbol of Triunity. " The perception of
God as a Trinity is the perception of the inner, esoteric movement within God." [176] God's life is a restless quest, wherein as
Father he eternally seeks the Son and as the Son he eternally
seeks the Father. Thus the Father is born, or comes to be, as
he finds the Son, and so also the Son is begotten in his search
for and finding of the Father. Within the divine nature there
is a genuine community, a true freedom of relationship between Father and Son in the unity of the Spirit.[177] Each is
contingent upon the loving freedom of the other, and in this

[173] *Ibid.*, p. 211.
[174] *The Divine and the Human*, p. 115.
[175] *Meaning of History*, p. 55.
[176] *Freedom*, p. 192.
[177] " The loving Subject and the loved Object find the fullness of their
life in the kingdom of love which is the Third Person." (*Freedom*, p. 199.)

contingency, free to suffer loss in each other. It is this eternal capacity of God for freedom and love that makes possible the incarnation and a relationship with man which respects human freedom. Indeed, this freedom in God is the source and meaning of freedom as such; freedom is expected of man just as God expects it of himself. " To understand the interior relationship between God and man as a drama of freely-given love is to lay bare the sources of history." [178] Berdyaev does not mean that God's eternal nature needs man and history, but rather that out of the overflow of the Father's love he reaches out through the Son for the freedom of man, so that man might share in the love and freedom of the Trinity.[179] We are reminded again of Berdyaev's words: " The second face of Divinity is manifested as the human face, and by this very fact man finds himself at the centre of being." [180] The coming of God to himself in the Son is also his coming to man. Herein, says Berdyaev, is the " primal drama and mystery of Christianity . . . the genesis of God in man and man in God." [181] This divine life is the authentic basis of humanism. Man is as important to God as is his Son, Jesus.

We are now able to understand Berdyaev's objections to the so-called " exoteric " view of creation which is " obliged to maintain the cruel idea that God created the world capriciously, without necessity, and entirely unmoved from within." Creation, according to such a view, " is without significance, not divine, and for the most part condemned to perish." [182] Christologically understood, creation is necessary to God, because in his Triune nature he has a commitment to man for the sake of which he must create. To the extent that Christ and man are objects of God's love and longing, in his divine heart as it were, so also is creation. It is not " exoteric " but

[178] *Meaning of History*, p. 53.
[179] " Through Christ, man becomes a participant in the nature of the Holy Trinity." (*Meaning of the Creative Act*, p. 79.)
[180] *Freedom*, p. 206.
[181] *Meaning of History*, p. 56.
[182] *Freedom*, p. 190.

"esoteric." Esoteric thinking, which is "symbolic theology," gives rise to "an esoteric conception of the mystery of creation" as the interior life of the Divine. The mystery is "the need which God feels for His other self, of one who loves and is beloved." [183]

Although this line of thinking suggests it, Berdyaev rejects the notion of the identity of God and man. He develops the ground for his rejection by insisting, paradoxically, that the eternal process of which we have been speaking is not a sign of a deficiency which God makes up in the time process; for the divine need is satisfied in eternity. "The fact that God longs for His other self, for the free response to His love, shows not that there is any insufficiency or absence of fullness in the Divine Being, but precisely the superabundance of His plenitude and perfection." [184] The divine life is complete; it is "a mystery which is accomplished in eternity." [185] However, "it is revealed to us in spiritual experience, for everything that takes place above has its reflection below. Similarly the process of divine birth which transpires in heaven takes place also in us, in the very depths of our being." [186]

Berdyaev's Christological doctrine of God is offered in defense of man, and he therefore is careful to insist upon a view of God compatible to man and to freedom. His reasoning is circular, however, for his only confirmation of man and freedom is his Christology. In any event, his theology is concerned to affirm a God who is not inimical to man, and that means a God who is free and respects freedom, who indeed grounds it. In my judgment he has done this in terms of his Christology and his understanding of God as Triune. The notion of Triunity, because of the distinction it makes between the Persons of the Godhead, grounds freedom. But the concept of *unity* in separation protects the idea of divine freedom from the danger of identification with the freedom of man, a danger that the meontic concept suffers. Nevertheless, just as he invokes

183 *Ibid.*, p. 191.
184 *Ibid.*

185 *Ibid.*, p. 193.
186 *Ibid.*, pp. 193 f.

the myth of meontic freedom to undergird the freedom of man, so also he employs it to deepen the notion of God's freedom and life. Since we have noted the use of the meontic concept earlier, we need here only observe again that the use of it in this context is mystifying. Berdyaev has confessed to the fact that the symbols of Christianity are just that, symbols or myths which cannot be explained but which are offered in explanation of existence of man and freedom. As far as I understand his Christianity, Berdyaev accounts well for man and his freedom. Now, however, he feels constrained to account for his accounts, to " apprehend the mystery " of God's existence, to " explain " the capacity of God for passion and tragedy. In this effort to get to the bottom, his spirit is the same as that of the rationalist who will not accept God for an answer. Furthermore, Berdyaev's efforts to mythologize his myth find him with fundamental contradictions which admit of no resolution. He offers no third myth. The Christological myth is the myth of redemption, of freedom and *love*. The myth of the *Ungrund* abstracts freedom from love. Although it will be discussed in the next and final section on God's freedom, it is relevant at this point to mention Berdyaev's optimism, his eschatological confidence, which is hardly explainable if " in the nature of God, deeper than Him, lies a sort of primal dark abyss." [187] Since this abyss, from which proceeds human sin, is deeper than God and the source of God's own existence in freedom, it is an eternal threat to redemption. Fortunately, Berdyaev delivers us, I feel, from this problem. His intentions and and interests are adequately maintained by the symbols of incarnation and Triunity. If we accept seriously his designation of the *Ungrund* as a limiting notion, we can understand Berdyaev to mean simply that no theory of being can account for man and freedom, least of all for the freedom and tragic possibilities of the divine life. Ontically speaking, freedom, whether in man or God, is meontic. But, if taken too seriously, Berdyaev's doctrine of meontic freedom becomes ontic, albeit

[187] *Meaning of History*, p. 55.

in a negative way. It would be a wonderful Trojan victory for objectified being, if it forced Berdyaev, while rejecting it, to reject love and Logos, the final hope of man. Is not Berdyaev right when he says that the notion of divine, Triune life constitutes the primal mystery? " The mystery of Christianity is the mystery of unity in duality finding its solution in trinity-in-unity." [188] The primal mystery needs no explanation; it cannot tolerate it. I can understand Berdyaev's *Ungrund* only when it is demythologized by the primal mystery of Triunity and understood as a limiting concept — antiontic, in defense of mythological, Christological thought. These criticisms of Berdyaev's meontic idea are crucial to the interpretation which this analysis is making. I am convinced that the meontic is not an intrinsic aspect of Berdyaev's thought, that it is a secondary myth or symbol which finds its real meaning in the Christian interpretation of the crucified and risen Christ.[189]

Whatever one may conclude, it is clearly the intention of Berdyaev's understanding of God to say that God finds himself in man so that man finds himself only in God. God is the source of man's existence and freedom, for God himself exists in freedom. Through Christ, man is moved to the pinnacle to share in the internal life of deity, to share in the nature of the Trinity. His life is " hid with God in Christ." He is free in time because he is free in eternity.

Kingly Freedom

In conclusion, we need to underline a point we have already made, namely, that for all Berdyaev's emphasis on the distinction and separation of the Persons in the Trinity, he also

[188] *Freedom*, p. 199.
[189] Note that in *The Realm of Spirit*, pp. 42–48, the dynamic nature of God is defended upon Christological grounds without the concept of the *Ungrund*. This is Berdyaev's last work. *Truth and Revelation*, a posthumous publication, also in defense of the dynamism and humanism of God, resists appeal to the meontic, especially Chs. VI–IX, pp. 90–154. *Freedom and the Spirit* argues largely on Christological grounds, as in Ch. VI, pp. 189–238.

stresses the unity of the three Persons. While he is constrained
to speak convincingly of the divine life and suffering, he is also
free to speak of the divine power and sovereignty through
which God remains one and sovereign even in the midst of his
separation, suffering, and tragedy. While it is proper to insist
on the divine restlessness, as Berdyaev has, it is also necessary
for him to take note of the divine rest to which the notion of
the divine life may not be opposed.[190] Saint Simon the Theologian witnesses to the coincidence of life and rest in God
when he invokes God: " Come Thou, Who remainest unmoved
yet Who ever moveth and dost direct Thyself toward us." [191]
God lives, but he lives as one God and king, even though he be
so in and through the tragedy and suffering of the separation
of the Persons in the Godhead. His threeness is a threeness in
unity; his Trinity is also his Kingdom. " The Kingdom of Love
in freedom is the Kingdom of the Trinity." [192]

This final mystery of unity in freedom in which God is free
to be God and king and yet suffer the tragedy of life and separation is the ground of Berdyaev's hope and eschatological
confidence. We have already seen that out of an overflow of
his love, not out of inner necessity, God has given to his Son
the face of humanity. As a consequence, the freedom of God
to maintain unity in separation with his Son is also the freedom of God to maintain unity with man, even with a man who
is distinct and separate from God in the reality of his own
freedom. On this ground Berdyaev insists that Christianity is
essentially Messianic and eschatological. " The eschatological
interpretation of Christianity is alone its deep and true interpretation." [193]

The Messianic hope is a hope for the coming of Christ, and
with the coming of Christ also the coming of man and the
world in and through men — the new heaven and the new
earth. " Only in the second coming of Christ, in the form of
Christ, the Coming One, will the perfection of man appear

[190] *Freedom*, p. 191.   [192] *Ibid.*, p. 139.
[191] *Ibid.*, p. 193.   [193] *The Beginning*, pp. 202 f.

in its fullness." [194] And this will mean "not merely the destruction of the world, and judgment," but "also the illumination and transformation of the world . . . the entry upon a new aeon." [195] This will be a new aeon in the sense that it will not be a moment in history, but a time beyond history, the day of resurrection. The Second Advent does not deny history, but takes it up and transforms it. The end cannot be an end in history because of the objectification that occurs in time and history. Historical time objectifies the past and denies its present reality. It "mercilessly crowds out what was." [196] A fulfillment in time would of necessity exclude the past, and Berdyaev insists that "we cannot simply cast aside the history of thousands of years." [197] The secular idea of progress — which is an historicizing and objectifying of Christian Messianism — denies to time past the privilege of fulfillment. But past time is objectifying also in that it takes time away from man who is the original source of time and history. In historical time, man falls into the realm of causality and necessity and becomes an object of, rather than a creator of, time. In a sense, historical time has fallen from its original nature as existential time — the time of man that expresses his metahistorical freedom and spirit. The coming of the Messiah deobjectivizes history and time and gives it back to man as the vessel and symbol of his creative and free spirit. The end "is the transformation of the world, and man creatively and actively takes part in it. It is the new heaven and the new earth." [198] And man, who is the center of this new world, exists in unity with his fellowman through the *soborny* born of the God-man Christ. "My destiny cannot be isolated; it is linked with the destiny of history, with the destiny of the world and of mankind. The fate of the world and of all humanity is my fate also, and *vice versa*, their fate cannot be decided without me." [199] Should there be a hell, then it is for all men; if for you, then for me also.

[194] *Ibid.*, p. 251. [196] *Ibid.*, p. 162. [198] *Ibid.*, p. 237.
[195] *Ibid.* [197] *Ibid.*, p. 208. [199] *Ibid.*, p. 235.

Such is the substance of Berdyaev's confidence and hope, born of the freedom and unity of the Triune God, who is free to *be God,* and yet *with* men. He refuses to be oppressed by the realm of historical, objectified time; he has no " desire to ascribe a sacred character to this necessity." [200] As impressive and oppressive as time is, Berdyaev confesses to the sovereignty and freedom of God and therewith to the sovereignty and freedom of man: " I know that this necessity is illusory and I believe that it can be conquered and that the power through which such a victory is possible, is called God — God the Liberator. But my faith in victory is eschatological and my religion is prophetic." [201]

Because Berdyaev's thought is notoriously unsystematic, any attempt at a systematic presentation — such as I have undertaken — is necessarily rather highly interpretive and, in Berdyaev's language, " creative." Such a statement is for the same reason also open to criticism for being one-sided, arbitrary, and, perhaps, erroneous. The literature on Berdyaev suggests, however, that there are two basic interpretive routes: Berdyaev can be understood primarily in philosophical terms — in terms of his existentialism and its antithesis of " objectification." [202] Or he can be understood in Christological terms — in terms of the unity of God and man through the God-man, Christ. [203]

From the first perspective Berdyaev's thought appears to be subjectivistic and solipsistic. His " apotheosis " [204] of human

[200] *Ibid.,* p. 253.

[201] *Ibid.*

[202] See Bernhard Schultze, *Russische Denker,* pp. 361–379; Matthew Spinka, *Nicolas Berdyaev: Captive of Freedom* (The Westminster Press, 1950), who begins his study of Berdyaev's thought with a chapter on his existentialism (pp. 93–112); Roman Rossler, *Das Weltbild Nicolai Berdjajews* (Göttingen: Vandenhoeck & Ruprecht, 1956), p. 85, who finds the idea of objectification the dominant motif of Berdyaev's middle and late period; V. V. Zenkovsky, *A History of Russian Philosophy,* II, 760–780, who reduces Berdyaev's thought to romanticism.

[203] See Fielding Clarke, *Introduction to Berdyaev;* Evgueny Lampert, *Nicolas Berdyaev and the New Middle Ages;* Michel Alexander Vallon, *An Apostle of Freedom: The Life and Teachings of Nicolas Berdyaev* (Philosophical Library, Inc., 1960).

[204] Zenkovsky, II, 769.

creativity swallows up and denies any significance to the objective world which, for Berdyaev, has fallen into the hopeless nonbeing of " objectification." Although generally appreciative, the Catholic commentator Bernhard Schultze finds that with this subjectivism and denigration of the objective world Berdyaev arrives at an inadequate understanding of the church which denies the proper authority of the visible and " objective " church.[205] Zenkovsky says that these two basic motifs — freedom and objectification — taken together mean a solipsistic subjectivism that makes of man an idol and object of worship. " Leontyev's charge of anthropolatry — i.e., the setting up of man as an object of worship — applies to no Russian philosopher more than Berdyaev." [206] Man in his creative freedom is all; the outside, objectified world is nothing.[207] Yet, says Zenkovsky, Berdyaev's view has the ironic effect of voiding the concept of creativity of any real meaning, since the objective world immediately casts the created product into the limbo of objectification and nonbeing.[208] He concludes that Berdyaev's thought is not really free; it is the prisoner of his passions. " The brilliant and striking quality of Berdyaev's writing, which sometimes casts a genuine spell over the reader, grows dim when one analyzes his ideas; this brilliance contrasts sadly with the fact that his theoretical constructions are tangential to the dialectic of Russian philosophy." [209]

This line of criticism is sound if Berdyaev's thought be understood in terms of the dialectic of freedom and objectification, or, in other words, as a dialectic of subject and object. But if we take the second approach which Berdyaev himself authorizes when he states that true anthropology is Christology, then I think the weight of this criticism is obviated. We have seen Berdyaev reject existentialism as such for its lack of myth

[205] Schultze, pp. 372, 379.
[206] Zenkovsky, II, 767.
[207] *Ibid.*, pp. 765, 769.
[208] Zenkovsky fails to note Berdyaev's repeated insistence on the power of freedom to redeem and renew the objectified world. Berdyaev has this confidence through Christ.
[204] Zenkovsky, II, 769.

— namely, the Christological myth. On these Christological grounds Lampert rejects the charge that Berdyaev's thought is solipsistic. Berdyaev, he states, is " preeminently concerned with existence as *correlation*, with life as the vital relatedness of man to God (God-manhood) and of man to man (community, *Sobornost*) ." [210] In sum: " Christ the God-man is the vital pivot of his thought." [211] Clarke contends that " what gives Berdyaev's thought its inner consistency is that it is rooted in . . . the experience of Christ." [212] Christology delivers Berdyaev from a hopeless dichotomy of subject and object, and while the world does objectify and bring the fall, freedom in Christ has the presence and the promise of creative, redemptive renewal of the world. Christology also gives consistency to Berdyaev's thought, so long as this consistency be understood as the " inner " consistency suggested by Clarke. I would say that Berdyaev's thought *contains* a consistent stream, but not that his thought as a whole *is* consistent. Vallon is carried away with his own rapture when he states that Berdyaev's "philosophy is all of one piece." [213] A Christological reading therefore justifies a systematizing attempt, but it does not eliminate all problems and inconsistencies. My statement has attempted to identify and delineate the aspects of this fundamentally consistent Christological anthropology. In the concluding chapter I hope to show that it is a relevant anthropology and that it provides the stuff of a more consistent and systematically adequate statement, especially when brought into dialogue with the thought of Barth's *Church Dogmatics*. For the moment I am willing to stand with Lampert when he says that " Berdyaev's thought is a signpost on the way to true inwardness, to a creative return of man's spirit to the divine-human sources of being." [214]

210 Lampert, p. 94.
211 Lampert, p. 36. See also Vallon, p. 293, where he rejects on grounds of Berdyaev's Christology a subjectivistic interpretation of Berdyaev's thought.
212 Clarke, p. 175.
213 Vallon, p. 312.
214 Lampert, p. 83.

6

A THEOLOGY OF FREEDOM

In this concluding chapter, in the section entitled " A Christian View of Freedom," I summarize the preceding chapters and delineate the view of freedom that has emerged from this study. In the section entitled " Toward a Theology of Freedom " consideration is given to the question of the sources of and the possibilities for a further development of a theology of freedom. Finally, under the heading " A Theology of Freedom " I indicate some of the aspects of such a theology.

A Christian View of Freedom

In order to review and set forth the substance of the preceding chapters, I raise again the four questions: *For* what is man free? *From* what is man free? *How* is he set free for freedom? And, finally, in what sense is *God* free?

Freedom-for

Rudolf Bultmann's view of Christian freedom is reduced in the direction of an existentialist understanding of history, according to which history is fundamentally the responsibility of the existing individual, an expression of his own free decision in the present moment, instead of an extrinsic fate forced upon him. History is not in any essential way the source of man; rather, man is the source of history. " Freedom " signifies the possibility and responsibility of man for history; it is basically an ethical category.

Such a view of freedom is based upon the acceptance of death as the basic dimension of existence. In the acceptance of death man acknowledges that he is dead to the world and that the world is dead to him. He cannot gain his life from the world but must accept, insofar as he transcends death by taking it into himself, the responsibility for creating his own life out of the dying stuff of the world. Freedom is the obligation and burden in which the reality of the present and the hope of the future depend. Freedom is the responsibility to create and write history.

This freedom cannot be given by Jesus of Nazareth, inasmuch as he belongs to the past. It can be given, however, by a present word — the preaching of the church — so long as it contains no objective or worldly content that might limit freedom's horizon and responsibility. For the Christian, this word is the word of Jesus as the crucified Christ, which is nothing more or less than the word that death is divine and the future is man's destiny. It declares that man's responsibility to create history is his freedom, and with this declaration it bestows freedom itself.

Bultmann's view has the merit of making man, or existence itself, the focus of the gospel. This certainly is in keeping with the Bible, which, whatever else it may say, is concerned with man — his redemption and his freedom. It is correct in establishing man in his responsibility for his world, rather than giving to the world the responsibility for man. It would seem, therefore, inappropriate to wish to gainsay this understanding of freedom as the responsibility for the future and as a call to historical existence. However, Bultmann's view fails at two fundamental points: first, it does not give an account of the Christian attachment to Jesus of Nazareth; second, it does not account for the depth or source of human freedom. Let us examine these two points briefly by way of further review.

As regards the first criticism, there is no doubt that the word in which God acts to announce the divinity of death is a word which Jesus both was and spoke. It is, however, impossible to understand what the word has to do with Jesus as a concrete person of the past, except that, as a matter of fact, it had. Nor is it possible to understand why the church so obviously felt that it was just because Jesus was who he was, the man of Nazareth, crucified under Pilate, that his word was the eschatological, life-giving word of God. This failure to relate to Jesus is fatal. On Bultmann's ground it is hard to understand why Jesus and his followers did not remain in the fold of John the Baptist, whose message was essentially the same (prophetic) message of Jesus, except to the extent that Jesus' message perhaps attached to himself and was more hopeful than John's. A Christian theology that fails to seek to understand the unity of Jesus and the Christ fails altogether.

The first criticism is at the point of Bultmann's understanding of the second Person of the Trinity, whereas the second speaks to the inadequacy of his understanding of the first Person. I would suggest that Bultmann's theology is fundamentally a theology of the Spirit. The word, which comes alive by the work of the Spirit in preaching, does not in any understandable way proceed from the incarnate Son, nor does it apparently presuppose a prevenient, creative grace of the Father. We have seen an ambiguity in Bultmann concerning this last limitation, but by and large the only reality presupposed by the word and the Spirit is man himself. In his response to the word man draws upon no created ground; his existence is *ex nihilo*. Also, the Spirit presupposes no reconciling event in which the reorientation it demands is in a sense already realized; rather, that reorientation is achieved by man himself in the decision of faith. Out of his own reconciling decision man has life in the spirit, i.e., in the future.

The effect of this view of freedom in which freedom is understood exclusively in terms of an existentialist view of history is, ironically, the loss of freedom. Without roots in the creative and reconciling work of God the demand of history lays upon man an intolerable burden and responsibility. The future does not bring man into his own, but denies him all that he is, dragging him forward, rather than graciously receiving him. Existence demands an essence that man neither possesses nor can create. As Berdyaev remarked, the existentialists are right when they say that freedom is not objective, but they are wrong when they deny myth. Man cannot respond to the Spirit; he has no freedom without the myths of creation and reconciliation. The Spirit as such, the third Person of the Trinity as such, means law and not gospel, bondage and not liberation.

Tillich correctly calls attention to the limitations of existentialist theology when he observes that it replaces being-itself by nonbeing, by demanding of existence what it can give only when it becomes transparent to and rooted in the depths of being-itself. So, Tillich would establish existence in its creative ground and restore to theology the first Person of the Trinity. Freedom, he says, can be maintained only as an element in an underlying structure of being. Yet, we observed that this effort to ground freedom in being tends to deny the reality it would ground. J. Heywood Thomas raises a serious doubt as to whether the quest for an unambiguous reality — ultimate reality as such — is meaningful and suggests that when the philosopher looks carefully at reality as such and " tears it from its context and asks himself ' Now what is reality? ' he has successfully manoeuvred himself into an impossible position." [1] And in the context of this discussion, Tillich tears reality from its context in finite freedom (the only kind that man, finite creature that he is, can possess) by his quest for an abstract being or reality as such.

According to the main line of Tillich's thinking freedom is ultimately nothing more than a freedom of choice. Of course, the ultimate choice is not a choice of one among many possibilities, but rather the choice of being-itself on the one hand and the arbitrariness of finite existence subject to the limitations of nonbeing on the other. The price of freedom's founda-

---

[1] J. Heywood Thomas, *Paul Tillich: An Appraisal*, p. 41.

tion is its own surrender. If Bultmann surrenders man to the oppressive demand of the future and burdens him with the responsibility for the world unborn, Tillich tends to free him altogether from the burden of responsibility for the future by surrendering him to the dependable undergirding of being's dialectical self-realization. Of course, being does pass through " freedom," whose glory it is to admit to this passage, to stay out of its way, and so to surrender itself to its destiny.

In Trinitarian terms, Tillich's theology tends to be a theology of the first Person, of an eternal ground that allows only a transparent and passing present and a future which brings to expression that which already and eternally is. Bultmann's theology is a theology of the Spirit, which admits to nothing that is, allowing to the past and the present only that value they have for the future. Tillich and Bultman would free man from the world, from the present moment, and from the determination of the empirical — one by enslaving him to the future and the other by rendering him transparent to the eternal ground.

Tillich fails the Christian in his effort at self-understanding at the same points as does Rudolf Bultmann. First, he too is unable to explain the attachment of the Christian either to Jesus or to Paul's faith that it is Jesus Christ who sets us free. Tillich's " symbol " is no more essentially related to Jesus than is Bultmann's eschatological " moment "; both theologians point only to the fact of this attachment and neither can arrive at this point where precisely the faith begins. Whereas Bultmann does not speak of the depth and source of freedom, Tillich does indeed speak of such depth, even though he is unable to speak of the depth and source of *freedom*. I do not see that Tillich's ontology is a solution to the problems in Bultmann's conception.

When we turn to Karl Barth, we are led in an altogether different direction. Barth begins not with existence as such, neither with its divine depths nor with its spiritual horizons. Theology's ground is not God as such, or the Spirit as such, but God in Jesus Christ and the Spirit that proceeds from him.

Berdyaev also roots theology in the incarnation and in an understanding of the divine Triunity.

On these grounds the event of faith in Jesus is an event of freedom because it is formally and materially first. Man is not primarily or basically historical in the sense of being a maker of history, nor is he ontological in the sense of being the bearer and channel of being and reality. Viewed from the perspective of existence or reality as such man is irreducible; he is himself; he is free. As Berdyaev would say, man in his freedom is me-ontic, proceeding from nothing. Viewed theologically, man's freedom is from God and for God, and therein and therefore true freedom.

With this emphasis on the eternal election of Jesus Christ, Barth speaks broadly to the ontologist's objection to Bultmann. The presupposition of the call of God in Christ is not the *ex-nihilo* existence of man, but rather his eternal election in Jesus Christ; his calling presupposes the eternal covenant of God with man in Jesus and the world as the appropriate outer ground for this call. Faith presupposes nothing more or less than man himself in covenant with God, and this presupposition provides no ground for independent ontological analysis. On the other hand there is an ontological depth which means that the gospel call comes not as law but as gospel, as the call to the original, genuine and only possibility of man. Man's freedom is not a burden but a privilege, not a " must " but a " may."

Jesus is not only the expression of God's eternal word but also its actualization; he is the word made flesh and as such the event of covenant fulfillment. The meaning and intent of God's eternal will is its actualization in history. Barth here agrees in measure with Bultmann, the difference being that the history which God's eternal word first intends is the history of Jesus himself. It is his obedience that fulfills the covenant; it is he, in his obedient dying, who is open to the future. Faith in Christ does not presuppose a universal existential or ontic possibility but the possibility and actuality of Jesus. In sum, freedom conceived Christologically presupposes the reality of God's eternal will as its ontological ground and possibility and Jesus of Nazareth as its ontic or existential fulfillment.

Since the freedom of faith is also freedom for the already actualized freedom of man in Jesus, faith in Jesus cannot make any claim for itself. It repudiates sin and freedom so-called, not in exercise of its own positive freedom but in the name of the freedom and righteousness of Jesus Christ which it receives from him as a gift and a privilege. The freedom that faith has in itself as such is only a secondary freedom — a freedom that lives from the primary freedom of Jesus himself.

As the eternal word, Jesus is the ground of freedom that sustains Christian freedom from the reduction and surrender to the ontic depths of reality that it suffers in Tillich's theology. As the word made flesh Jesus is the event of freedom that delivers the Christian from the inhuman task of creating history *ex nihilo,* a task to which it is assigned by Bultmann. But, as we have seen, Barth goes on to say that this eternal and historical word which is Jesus and is in Jesus is also *word* to man — a call to man, or as Berdyaev would say, it is a symbol. This calling of Christ through his word demands immediately a hearer and an appropriate response from man in his own finite existence. Jesus as *word* calls forth faith as such, the event of man's acknowledgment, trust, and obedience. In this aspect, faith is in itself an event of creative and positive significance. As regards freedom, this dimension of faith establishes the freedom of Christ as also *my* freedom, as an event here and now of my decision and deed. This dimension of freedom is "existential" or "historical" in Bultmann's sense of the word and means an actual transformation of man's existence. Implicit in this dimension of freedom is the so-called freedom to deny the word, to lie about it, and so to suffer its judgment and damnation.

Finally, we remember that God speaks not only an eternal word, a word made flesh in and a living word witnessed by his Son, but also a creative word of the Spirit, in and with man, which gives to the man of faith a redemptive word for the world. Barth had stated that faith as a response to Jesus' word and witness, insofar as it is a creative expression of man, brings us to the threshold of anthropology. We are to the threshold only because the word in this context is a witness to *Jesus.* We move fully into anthropology when we leave Christology proper and turn to a pneumatology in which the Spirit is understood in its own hypostasis as a creative presence which gives to man his full place and provides him with a creative word to the world.[2] In his *Church Dogmatics,* Barth has not moved to this locus of theological concern, except implicitly. Berdyaev, however, operates primarily in this realm, as we might expect of an Orthodox Christian whose tradition, by its repudiation of the *filioque,* has allowed the work of the Spirit to come to more complete theological expression. By virtue of the gift of the Spirit, man is not only a creature of the grace of Christ, but also a source of creative grace for the whole cosmos. He becomes the microcosm, the sun, in whose spiritual vision the world finds its own being and meaning. Freedom-for becomes, in this respect, a freedom for the world. It is only because of Christ (a point more emphatically made and better articulated by Barth than Berdyaev) that man is free from the world in order to be free in his creativity for it. Thus Berdyaev insists that freedom is not historical in the existentialist or

[2] Not infrequently this implication of Barth's theology becomes explicit in the *Church Dogmatics,* as in the passage cited by Harvey Cox where he quotes Barth as saying, " We cannot say and demand and expect too much or too great things from man " (*The Secular City: Secularization and Urbanization in Theological Perspective,* p. 83; The Macmillan Company, 1965). Cox manifestly misunderstands Barth, however, when he claims that the " triumph of Barth's theology is a God who doesn't need man; therefore He can let man live. . . . As the last stages of myth and ontology disappear, which they do in Barth's theology, man's freedom to master and shape, to create and explore now reaches out to the ends of the earth and beyond " (p. 82). Cox is dead wrong. According to Barth, man is free to create because God is for and with him in Jesus. Were this not the case, we would have to ask Cox where it is that man receives the power and vision of creativity. In sum, Cox fails to see that anthropology comes at the end of Barth's dogmatics, as a logic of theology and Christology (ontology and myth, if you will). It does not really appear that Cox has read Barth.

Bultmannian sense, although history is freedom's symbolic expression. Also, freedom is not ontological in the Tillichian sense; rather, it is *meontic,* the nonbeing whence being flows. In a word, freedom is a mystical and spiritual gift of God-humanity.

In this respect it is indeed correct to speak of a "religionless" Christianity or a "secular meaning" of the gospel, understanding of course not that religion or freedom has secular meaning or may be reduced to secular terms, but the opposite, that the secular has meaning in religion and freedom, and must be understood as symbolic expressions of the spirit and itself be reduced in that direction.

In summary so far, we have seen that the Christian is free — free for God in Jesus, and in Jesus free for the world. Let it be noted again that this understanding of freedom does include the dimension of depth to which Tillich points, insofar as Jesus is the eternal word of God, or, as Berdyaev says, the transcendental God-man. Also, freedom for Jesus is freedom for the word, for the message of the church, as Bultmann stresses. But both Barth and Berdyaev would remind Tillich and Bultmann that *Jesus* is the depth and the word. A personal metaphor is in order here: in a living experience of love one finds a depth of meaning and a pattern of obedient existence, but above all one finds another — a person, with a name, who mystically transcends both the meaning in and the pattern of the relationship and the experience of love, who cannot be reduced to either of these dimensions, and who can finally be expressed and invoked only in the symbol of the personal name.[3] In the case of that love affair called Christian faith,

[3] Cox apparently misunderstands or has misrepresented the Biblical understanding in his statement that "when we use the word *God* in the biblical sense, we are not speaking about but 'naming.' . . . To name is to point, to confess, to locate something in terms of our history" (p. 242). This is true only at a secondary level of Biblical experience, because before man names God, God names himself or reveals his name, as when he gave his name to Moses who otherwise could not name God, or as when he "bestowed upon Jesus the name that is above every name." God commanded man to name the creatures, but hardly the Creator. This misunderstanding

that irreducible symbol, the name above every name, is the name of Jesus. Furthermore, we have seen that corresponding to the irreducibility of the name is freedom as the irreducible element of the relationship. Freedom for Jesus is freedom, and ultimately nothing else.

Freedom indeed contains no *thing* else, but it does contain some *one* else — the fellowman. From the beginning, Jesus is the brother of all men; the man who is free in and for Jesus is therefore free for and with others — and not merely in the sense of having his neighbor as an ontic option as if he were but one possibility within the broad horizon of the future. Gogarten is right in his criticism of Bultmann that freedom is not being-toward-death but being-toward-the-neighbor. In the language of Berdyaev, freedom is *sobornost* (which is like saying that love is also relationship). Nor is love of the neighbor a finite and qualified expression of an ultimate concern for being-itself. No, love for the neighbor is just that — love for the neighbor, and it is an event of freedom, as is the love for God in Christ, because it is original and appropriate, because it is eternal with God, an event actualized in Jesus, a truth revealed by his word, and a present reality created by his spirit.

Man is free — free for God, free in God for the world, and free with and for his neighbor. In sum, he is free for Jesus.

We should finally note that the positions of Barth and Berdyaev do answer to the criticisms made of Bultmann and Tillich. In the first place, as the discussion above makes evident, they do not divorce freedom from Jesus, either in its ground or direction, and to this extent fulfill the responsibility of theology to understand its faith in Jesus. Secondly, they are Trinitarian, combining faith in Jesus the second Person with faith in the Father's eternal grace and election as the ontological ground and the Spirit's witness and presence through the Word as the existential reality.

---

leads to a more fundamental error, as when Cox understands Moses rather than God as the one charged with " the work of liberating the captives " (p. 268) .

Freedom-from

Turning now to the second question, we ask from what is the Christian free? Originally and essentially he is free from nothing. When Barth says that the covenant is the eternal ground of creation he means that more basic than man's relationship to the world is his freedom for God in Jesus. Berdyaev means the same when he says that freedom is meontic, prior to the ontic, prior to anything. Freedom, therefore, is original. It is just because it is not free *from* in order to be free *for* that it is so unqualifiedly free, so spontaneous and so complete. Quite obviously this talk is, as Berdyaev would say, " mystical," as it must be because all our language and symbols are drawn from the ontic which is itself but an expression of freedom. The model of a personal relationship will once more help to clarify this point; I have in mind again the human experience of love. While it is true, secondarily, that the freedom one enjoys in love is a freedom from the claim of others, it in no wise needs such freedom *from* in order to be free *for* the loved one. As a matter of fact, once love becomes conscious of those from whom it is free, then it is at best ambiguous, and the purity of the unity which is its essence is qualified. Freedom, then, is initially, essentially, and finally a freedom-for that is free from nothing (and so everything). Nothing here is simply *ouk on,* which has not even the being of not-being. Bultmann and Tillich, on the other hand, both base freedom on a negative. Bultmann's view of freedom is essentially a freedom from the nothingness of the tangible and the past, and, as we have seen, Tillich's freedom for being is essentially a freedom from a finitude that participates in non-being. The consequence of these negative conditions is that they exercise at least a negative control. So, in Bultmann's understanding, the future appears to have only the content of that which the past is not, and thus man's past is the negative measure of his future possibilities. Tillich, on the other hand, not altogether unlike Hegel, insists that the life and self-realization of being depend on its becoming free from nonbeing and finitude. But freedom for Jesus contains no alternative. It is the peculiarity of the concrete and personal, the radically historical and once-for-all, that it can be defined in its essence by nothing else, either positively or negatively. The future is the negation of the past, as is the infinite the negation of the finite. Such statements may be more than tautological to some, but certainly there is no meaning at all to say, for example, of a person named John that he is not Bob, or not Jane, or not " Rover," etc., *ad infinitum*. What is it that is not Jesus? Empirically, ontically, everything is not Jesus, which is to say, nothing is not Jesus. Freedom for Jesus is freedom for Jesus, nothing more and nothing less.

However, freedom is freedom-from — in a secondary yet necessary way. Sin has entered, and freedom for Jesus is also freedom from sin. According to both Barth and Berdyaev, sin is groundless. We have seen Berdyaev attempt to express this groundlessness by rooting it in the un-grounded (*Ungrund*), in the concept of an uncreated freedom. We concluded, however, that these notions are best understood as limiting concepts which say nothing more than that sin roots in no necessity of man's essential selfhood and that it cannot be derived from the ontological structure of reality. Tillich, on the other hand, seems to give it an ontological base by his identification of the actualization of freedom with the fall in such a way that finite existence and freedom depend on nonbeing and sin. Bultmann, who generally avoids ontological analysis, simply identifies sin with actuality. So, for both Bultmann and Tillich freedom is essentially freedom-from — freedom from the visible actualities of the past or freedom from the finite, concrete particularities of selfhood. Tillich moves " down " from the surface to the depth, whereas Bultmann moves " out " from the past and visible to the invisible future.

Both theologians by rejecting the notion that the fall is in any sense historical or temporal and interpreting it rather psycho-ontologically (Tillich) or etho-historically (Bultmann) understand it to symbolize a split within man's existence — an antithesis within himself or his world rather than a " fall " of existence from relationship to God. The result is that freedom-from, as we have seen, involves essentially a freedom from the self, or at least from a dimension of the self, whether it be its past or its finitude. So salvation, the condition of being actually free-for, means the loss of this " negative " dimension of the self in the transparency of absolute faith or in the surrender of the past for the future. The last word for man and the main symbol of Christianity (for both Tillich and Bultmann) is the cross, whereas the resurrection is but a symbol for the fact that the cross is the *last* — ontological or eschatological — word.

Since Tillich's system provides an ontological depth, a ground that sustains the self in its loss, the element of grace and freedom is maintained; that is, the cross is not primarily a symbol of an ethical obligation but of an ultimate permission. Tillich's view of freedom-from is of a *freedom* of the self from the self. Bultmann's freedom-from is essentially an obligation, a responsibility of the *self*, a view that has the merit of seeking to preserve the self up to the threshold of its passage into the future, but at the expense of grace and true freedom. Bultmann's idea of freedom-from is a freedom of the *self* from the self. To reiterate, ultimately the logic of Tillich's view is a freedom that has *no* human subject, and of Bultmann's a freedom that has *only* a human subject. Tillich sees the sinner's salvation in the end of the sinner; Bultmann sees it in a rationalization of the sinner. Tillich is at home with Hegel, and Bultmann with Fichte.[4]

The alternative to these views is implicit in my criticism. That from which man is free is not in man, nor in his world. Man is free, not as he is free from himself or the world but as he is free from his whole self and his relationship to the world. The fall is not a split within existence, and it is not therefore an aspect of existence; it is not a line between depth and sur-

[4] Carl Michalson, *The Hinge*, p. 92.

face or between past and future, but a point and place in " the past " where man in depth and on the surface, in his past and in his possibilities, said he would be free from God, free from God's covenant purpose, and also free from his neighbor and his responsibility for the world. The fall is neither a possibility nor a characteristic of his finite existence in the world, but rather his existence in the world has the character of the fall. Now fallen from God, man's essential freedom-for is without a genuine, " spatially " transcendent object and must direct itself toward a contiguous object and so exclude at the same time the neighboring alternatives that it stigmatizes as nonbeing. Thus it chooses the future at the expense of the past, or the infinite " depth " at the expense of a finite " surface." True freedom-from, as both Barth and Berdyaev show, is a freedom from all dimensions of the self and the world, so that no dimension of reality has even this negative principality and power.

The model of love is again helpful: if one falls out of love, suffers the loss of depth and meaning and the pattern of loving obedience, and is left only with a surface " fallen " (or should we say " estranged "?) from the depths and a present without a future, do we conclude that salvation demands a freedom from the surface so as to be free for the hidden depth of meaning, or that the past must be sacrificed for the possibilities of the future? Barth showed that it is the devil, " *das Nichtige,*" which gives the created and good negativities of life a demonic depth and directs freedom to attack these rather than the devil himself. Consequently, man finds himself attacking a dimension of life as such rather than life in its denial of God. Can these self-destructive efforts to rationalize the violation of the relationship of love either justify the faithlessness of the lover or heal the broken heart of the betrayed? No, because freedom for God, like the freedom for the one who loves, is not a freedom which divides and denies but rather a freedom which unites and affirms. That from which love is free is any imperious claim of a form without a content, of a meaning or a future without the loved one, just as Jesus would free the Christian from the claim of a depth in which he is not present or a future where he does not dwell. Man is set free in Jesus from himself in his false relation to himself and the world in order to be one with himself and his world in a freedom for God in Jesus.

When man is free from a self-understanding based on a negative relationship to immanent, contiguous realities so as to be free for the transcendent relationship with God in Jesus, then he is at one with himself and his world. He discovers his depth and his future and is free for the responsibility of creatively expressing these in the world. He is now in a position to articulate and express the depths of this relationship in a type of Tillichian philosophy which demonstrates how the love of God in Jesus makes sense of the world, providing it with ground and meaning. Or, he may move in a Bultmannian direction to show how one indeed has a new existence in the love of Jesus and how this love provides man with a future which transcends all the possibilities he might otherwise possess. But thanks be to God, it is a future which preserves the past, so that he who is now also will be in the future. And while Jesus does provide a radical and infinite depth of meaning (as Tillich insists), this meaning is for the *person* in all his finitude and existential limitation; the eternal is *his* eternity, it is eternal *life*. Berdyaev especially demonstrates how true philosophy is not the necessary condition for understanding Christianity, but how Christianity is the condition for a meaningful philosophy. It is not the critique of reason or an analysis of man's possibilities that sets limits and provides categories for the knowledge of God, but a critique of the spirit and an understanding of the new man in Christ that provide the condition for true philosophy. Karl Barth's theology is not the end of philosophy. True, theology is queen, but she is not without a consort and royal offspring.

In the introduction I called attention to the tendency of Christian theology from its beginning to synthesize the New

Testament Christian view of freedom with the Hellenistic, to regard freedom not only as the renewal of the self by a restoration of the relationship to God and grace (New Testament view) but also as a return to the original and " natural " self (Hellenistic). Obviously it is the judgment of this study that Bultmann and Tillich are guilty of this confusion and have confused faith as the understanding of God with " self-understanding."

Freedom for Freedom

Christ has set us free for freedom, says Paul. Freedom in both of its aspects as freedom-for and freedom-from is restored to man by the convincing reiteration of the love of God in Jesus Christ. We touched upon the gift of freedom in the review of " Freedom-for," where we were reminded that freedom-for is freedom for Jesus as a living word and symbol. To set in sharper relief the position I am taking, I would consider the alternatives proposed by Bultmann and Tillich. Freedom, according to Bultmann, is indeed a gift, a gift of the word of God. But since the freedom given is altogether a type of existence, the saving word must be demythologized so as to speak *to man* without at the same time saying anything to him — except, by implication, the man himself whom it addresses. This is the word that was spoken by Jesus, a word that was Jesus to the extent that on his cross he became nothing, giving up his reality and actuality for the future. This word, however, is not bound to the past but is spoken again and again in the church and in the mystery of grace is heard as the word of God whereby it becomes a possibility of the existence of the Christian — a possibility symbolized by the resurrection. The word is life-giving because it has no content, because its substance is its form as address which demands that the hearer give it content by his existence and free decision in the moment.

Tillich also teaches that freedom is a gift of the word of God. But he does not demythologize; quite the contrary, he mythologizes, so that the word has content and says something to the believer. We might say that Tillich's viewpoint is wholly mythical or symbolic, meaning that the word of God is altogether transcended by its depth and meaning; it is altogether content and its form is accidental. Since this is the case, the word may take many forms; it may be a historical fact, a present word, a myth or a liturgy; it may be one, it may be many. The universe is sacramental, and all its dimensions are potentially symbolic of its divine depths. It happens that for the Christian the word finds ultimate expression in Jesus as the Christ, whose cross demonstrates that the form (Jesus in his finite selfhood) is accidental and must in sacrifice become transparent to the depth — the ground of being. So, rather strangely, while the cross for Bultmann makes form the substance, for Tillich it establishes form as accident. Accordingly, the reception of the word as Tillich conceives its establishes a different kind of freedom. If for Bultmann form demands existence (form) instead of granting essence, for Tillich the depth symbolized by the form " grasps " the believer at the price of his finitude. In terms of freedom, it gives man " the courage to be," whereas for Bultmann it opens man to the future. For Tillich, the faith in which freedom roots is an ecstasy, a possibility that is beyond the limits of finitude; for Bultmann, faith is obedience, an exercise by the will of the possibilities of existence. In both cases, however, the " freedom " of faith is a gift — a gift of the word of God which for the Christian has its highest expression in the crucified Jesus. The difference is, as we have already observed, a difference in Trinitarian thinking; Tillich conceives the word as essentially the word of the God who eternally is — God as Father, whereas Bultmann understands it as essentially the word of the eternally existing God — God as Spirit.

But the Word which bestows true freedom is neither of God the Father nor of God the Spirit; it is, rather, the word of God — Father, Son, and Holy Spirit, the word of *Jesus* and not the word of Jesus *as* — as the Christ transparent to his depth, or as the Christ eschatologically present. This word has depth,

but it is not depth; it addresses man, but it is not mere address.
It is one thing — Jesus of Nazareth — in whom God the Father
is present in depth, God the Son in fact, and from whom God
the Spirit moves as word. The unity and the totality is in the
man Jesus — the Father is his and the Spirit is his. We cannot
reduce this word; it is one word — the name of " Jesus," the
name that is above every name. This word, though it has three
forms, is one: it is an eternal word, an incarnate word, and a
spiritual word. It is the word of God's love — the love which
is eternal, which has in fact appeared, and which wills to be
actualized again and again in the lives of the faithful. The possibility of combining these strange and apparently incompatible aspects in one word is possible only when the word is understood first of all as personal rather than as ontological or
eschatological. And for the personal the only adequate symbol is the personal name. Our experience of the reality of another person, while it can be designated ultimately by no word
but the personal name, may reveal, *mutatis mutandis,* three
dimensions not unlike those in which the word of God appears.
Above all else, another person is a *fact* in time and place which
also contains for us depths of meaning and confronts us, explicitly and otherwise, with a word that calls forth a new existence. That the person as fact is essential to our experience
is witnessed by the inadequacy of and radical difference in the
experience of the relationship when the other is dead and
gone and when the name no longer symbolizes a fact but only
a memory (though it still contains some meaning and evokes
a form of existence). A widow as a widow actually retains
meaning in the name of her husband, and while her husband
did live, he would not really have lived as her husband, nor
would she have really known who he was, had his name not
transcended the mere fact of his existence to disclose his hidden depth and meaning and if the fact had not meant for her
a pattern of faithful responsibility. But even here a wife can
give no name for the meaning she finds nor for the future
toward which she exists but the name of her husband, who did

in fact exist and would not be known to her except for the fact of his existence. A personal word is a word that points to a fact which is meaningful and existential, but which is not reducible to any of its elements: it is not an ontological word — a mere symbol transparent to its depth, for at its depth it itself appears. It is not an existential or *geschichtliches* word, a call to decision for the future, for it is itself the very substance of the future. It is not a factual or a commonsense *historisches* word, for as mere fact it is without meaning and makes no difference for my existence. Yet there is no word without the fact, no word which does not speak of the facts.

The word which is Jesus bestows a different kind of freedom, as we have seen. Such freedom is not a self-transcending ecstasy or a willful act of obedience. It is, rather, that " trust " in which *I* find *myself* by living out of *myself* toward another, in which *I* decide for myself as a being toward another and not against myself in whole or in part. For such faith the New Testament picture of Jesus has an absolute, symbolic value. The picture is symbolic just as the empirical data of a *man's* experience of another person is symbolic of his real self. At the same time it is an absolute symbol for which there is no adequate substitute, just as no other evidence mediates the reality of another person quite like his own physical presence.

Faith is also mystical, inasmuch as it knows its object in a manner for which it can give no good account, except in its own terms. It knows, as does one in personal relationships, that in its true existence and depth the reality of its object transcends the experienced meaning, the consequent life, or the acknowledged facts. There is no a priori critique of reason that establishes its epistemological possibility. It is, in this sense, mystical. If there is one word for the possibility of faith, one word that represents its subjective condition, it is " freedom."

The Freedom of God

Our last question concerns the freedom of God. What is the meaning of God relative to the freedom of man as we have viewed it? Again, my point of view, based upon Barth and Berdyaev, may be seen in comparison to both Bultmann and Tillich. As Schubert Ogden so well points out, the freedom of God according to Bultmann is essentially God's transcendence — his freedom from man.[5] The picture comes to mind of a young man in love with a tantalizing beauty whose apparent reality seems to fade into a fantasy of the future in that very moment when he seeks to touch and hold her. His life becomes a constant search, an ever unfulfilled movement toward the future and the reality of his dream. His existence would indeed be a "vanity of vanities" were it not for a sudden "eschatological" moment of revelation when he discovers the true grace of his beloved — that her freedom from him is actually her freedom for him, for thereby she breaks the shackles that bind him to the limits of his complacent and lifeless *Dasein* and gives him authentic existence in a life of movement toward the future. She loves him because in her freedom from him she gives him his own true existence. So Bultmann views God as one who in a moment reveals just enough of himself that man becomes aware of his divine absence, who is present in Jesus at the moment of his departure on the cross in order to disclose that he loves here and now just because he is no longer present. This moment of revelation is "eschatological" in that it transcends time and space, else it would not be a word of the hidden and transcendent God of the future but a word of the manifest and immanent God of the past. Such a word is the word spoken in the church by and about the crucified One, who as the dying one is not so much a fact of the past as he is a possibility of every present moment.

In Bultmann, God is free for man by keeping himself from man. The freedom of God and the freedom of man are negative concepts, void of content; each is free for the other because and

[5] Schubert Ogden, in Bultmann, *Existence and Faith*, p. 17. Harvey Cox, in *The Secular City*, vainly seeks to distinguish his view of God from Bultmann's, but he could hardly be more Bultmannian than when he speaks of God as the one who "meets us in the wholly other," (p. 262) or as the "transcendent" that "comes from beyond the self" (p. 260).

as he is free from the other. This means, as we have seen, that Christian freedom becomes abstract freedom as such. Tillich, on the other hand, understands God to give man freedom by his continuous freedom for man. God, as the very ground of man's being, is so radically and so thoroughly for man that man's *freedom* seems in jeopardy. God is so committed to man because his own life and history are at stake; thus it is also difficult to understand in what sense God is really *free* for man. At least the elements of grace and contingency are lacking in his view of the divine freedom, and God and man are in no significant way finally distinguished from each other. In this tendency Tillich's theology reveals an inadequate doctrine of the incarnation, in which he confuses history as such with Jesus. Traditionally, the incarnation teaches that God's need for another is met by his living for Jesus. Without a vision of the actuality of the incarnation in Jesus this need of God for another must now find itself in humanity as such, and since this is a necessity of the divine nature, neither man nor God appears free from or free for this " necessity." According to Tillich, being, and not freedom, is the common denominator between God and man.

These criticisms of Bultmann and Tillich point toward a more adequate doctrine of the freedom of God. Following both Barth and Berdyaev, we have seen that God's freedom is not a corollary of the existence of man as such but of the man Jesus Christ. Thinking about God, as well as thinking about man, must be Christological, and on this base, Trinitarian. Tillich's theology tends toward a Trinitarianism, but without a good Christological-*incarnational* base, so that the Triune nature of God unfolds and realizes itself in history and man rather than in Jesus, with the consequences we have noted. (Just as Bultmann's theology tends to be incarnational but without a good Christological-*Trinitarian* base.) A true *Trinitarian-*Christological conception of the freedom of God will insist with Tillich, first and foremost, that in Jesus, God is free *for* man and that man may therefore be free *for* God, but it will also agree with Bultmann that God is transcendent and *free* of man and that therefore and at the same time man has room to be *free*. Both emphases can be made on the Christological ground that because God has been heard, obeyed by, and so glorified in the response of Jesus, and in him by and in all men, he is free to be *for* man in the Holy Spirit without fear of losing himself in the contingent event of man's decision. Accordingly, man is also given freedom *for* and with God. We can thus agree with Tillich that freedom has content and destiny. At the same time the Christian knows that only the man Jesus has fulfilled the law and exhausted the meaning of freedom, so while the Christian is truly free for and with God there remains, nevertheless, in God a personal and unsearchable depth that draws freedom in openness toward the future (as Bultmann so rightly stresses) .

Just as Christology permits us to speak of a freedom of God *for* man and a freedom of man *for* God that has both substance and possibility, being and future, so it guarantees that God is *free* for man and that man is *free* for God. If the realization that in Jesus, God's freedom *for* man meets the obedient response of man's freedom *for* God inhibits the exaggerated theological transcendentalism and anthropological existentialism of Bultmann, so also the understanding that in the one man, Jesus, God's *freedom* for man meets man's *freedom* for God saves theology from either a pantheistic or panentheistic monism. The incarnation is the effective expression of God's freedom, his freedom to overcome opposition to his gracious, covenanting purpose, for in Jesus, God does in fact live for another and for all; in Jesus, God's life is complete and his glory revealed. Therefore, his coming to every man in the Spirit is a coming not in a necessity born of the emptiness of his being, but in a freedom flowing from the fullness of his being in Jesus. Therefore, man as such is not a necessity of the divine nature, and when the Christian answers to the claim of God in Jesus, he answers in a true freedom, in a spontaneity that roots in the fact of his being in God in Christ, and not in the freedom of one whose finite being exists to be overcome by the becoming of being-itself. Man's freedom for God is not just another word for God's freedom to become himself.

The sum and substance of this discussion of God's freedom is that God is free because he is one with Jesus. There is only one, and one name, which guarantees the freedom of God — the freedom to be God and yet be God with man. This is the name *Jesus*.

We have seen that God is free, not only in his relationship to man, but also in his power to make this relationship known in revelation. For Bultmann, this freedom of revelation is expressed in the word-event, in the proclamation of the word of the crucified one as the eschatological Christ. Tillich sees revelation as occurring in the event of Jesus as a sacrament of the New Being. For Bultmann, the freedom of God in his revealing act may be reduced to historical (eschatological) terms, and for Tillich, to ontological terms. In either case, freedom is lost by this reduction, and God becomes subject, as does man, to a measure of control, insofar as either an existentialist or an ontological hermeneutic becomes a necessary condition for revelation. By giving the revealer and the revealed another name — the reality of the New Being or the eschatological future — the freedom of revelation is jeopardized. Only as the revelation is the revelation of Jesus is it truly an expression of divine freedom and grace. Only one name gives access to the mystery of the relationship between God and man — the name that is above every name, the name of Jesus.

TOWARD A THEOLOGY OF FREEDOM

This study has attempted to assess contemporary theology by asking the material question: How does it understand Christian freedom? The first four chapters contrasted the theologies of Bultmann and Tillich on the one hand and Barth and Berdyaev on the other, showing that Bultmann and Tillich tended to reduce " freedom " and " Christ " to other more " basic " terms. Let us look at the results of this reductionism.

Reductionism

What I designate "reductionism" may be seen at several points. In the first place, Tillich and Bultmann find no significance in the expression "freedom for God." Both would reduce (demythologize or ontologize) this expression, Bultmann in the direction of existence, Tillich in the direction of being. Furthermore, it is characteristic of their approach to insist that the notion of " Jesus " as the source or content of freedom must also be radically reduced. Not Jesus, says Bultmann, but the proclamation concerning him; not Jesus, says Tillich, but his being as the reality of the New Being.

Moreover, in each of these cases we found that the concept of Christian "freedom" was capable of a reduction which brought into question its meaning as "freedom," or at least jeopardized that aspect in which freedom is a spontaneous and creative expression of the personal, concrete individual. Thus, in Bultmann, freedom is freedom from all that is, all concreteness and particularity, in order to be open for " the future." In Tillich, freedom is transparency to the ground of being.

In sum, apart from Barth and Berdyaev, these theologies find better designations for God than the name " Jesus "; they know a name or names above that name, and they also know that it is more than " freedom " for which the Christ has set us free. My thesis is that when these symbols — Jesus and freedom — are no longer ultimate, the corollary follows that neither God nor concrete, personal manhood is a meaningful concept. In this way, Tillich, and especially Bultmann and his followers, could claim (and in most cases they do) to operate under the rubric of Bonhoeffer's "religionless Christianity." " To be a Christian," says Bonhoeffer, " does not mean to be religious in a particular way . . . but to be a man. It is not some religious act which makes a Christian what he is, but participation in the suffering of God in the life of the world." [6] It is one of the signs

---

[6] Dietrich Bonhoeffer, *Letters and Papers from Prison* (Fontana Books, William Collins Sons & Company, Ltd., 1964), p. 123.

of the imagination and creativity of modern theology that it appears to know just what these last words of Bonhoeffer mean. Although Bonhoeffer himself pointed equivocally to Barth's theology as a start in the right direction and rejected Bultmann's approach because of its " typical liberal reduction process " (wherein the " mythological " elements of Christianity are dropped and Christianity is reduced to its " essence ") ,[7] it is nevertheless generally held today that nonmythological theologies such as Bultmann's and those of certain of the post-Bultmannians are the true bearers of the Bonhoeffer legacy. If it were Bonhoeffer's meaning that religious language must not be language about God or man (God-manhood) but about " being," " existence," " conscience," or " Word-event," or other such " worldly " realities, then the case can be made for this claim.

Much of the logic of the mood of present and prevailing theology is expressed in van Buren's *The Secular Meaning of the Gospel,* where he points out that " the solution proposed by existentialist theologians consists of eliminating all ' objectification ' of God in thought and word, but since Bultmann also objects to using the word ' God ' simply as a symbol for

---

[7] *Ibid.,* p. 110. Of course Bonhoeffer did not mean at all such a " translation " or reduction into worldly terms. He agreed with Barth that the gospel could not be reduced. His objection to Barth was that while Barth recognized the religionlessness of modern man and made therefore no attempt to build upon it, he was satisfied simply to talk in church to church people, and failed to address himself to the religionless world. This is Barth's so-called " positivism " (see Bonhoeffer, p. 109) . In a sense, my treatment of Barth in conjunction with Berdyaev and Russian Orthodoxy is designed to suggest a Barthian answer to Bonhoeffer's objection, to say on the basis of Barth's theology that the Christian man is in the world as a man — a creative man, to use Berdyaev's language. The Christian speaks in the world, insofar as he speaks theoretically, not as a theologian but, because of his theology, as a profound philosopher — much as Berdyaev spoke. In effect, the answer to Bonhoeffer lies not in a reduction of the secular to the sacred or the sacred to the secular, but in a proper rendering unto God his due so as to render unto the world its due. Is not this the direction in which Bonhoeffer himself pointed when he said that to be a Christian is not " to be religious in a particular way . . . but to be a man "?

human experience, the word ' God ' appears to refer to nothing at all." [8] Religionless Christianity appears to be Godless Christianity, and van Buren properly complains that " we do not understand . . . by what logic Bultmann and Ebeling continue to use the word ' God ' as though it had a quite specific reference." [9] Van Buren's objections root, however, not so much in the bad logic of Bultmann as in the alleged meaninglessness of " God " to secular, empirically oriented man.[10] This is a problem which Bultmann tacitly recognizes but which van Buren would explicate by a " linguistic analysis of religious assertions." He shows, in effect, that if we are to talk to a secular society in a meaningful way, then our language must be subject to empirical verification. This requires that religious language cease to make cognitive claims and understand itself instead as a " blik." A " blik " is a " fundamental attitude " or basic presupposition not achieved by empirical inquiry but upon which everything we do depends.[11] Van Buren rejects the cognitive approach because it " would contradict our point of departure " and " mark off a certain area of experience as ' religious,' " and would lead " Christians into the trap of the reductionist tendency of nineteenth-century theology, where they are tempted to fight a defensive action against all other knowledge." [12] He is forced to agree with Braithwaite that theism is wrong, that the language of faith has a meaning to be explored by linguistic analysis, and that the word " God " must be abandoned.[13] To say that the language of faith is meaningful means that it submits to a type of verification — namely, insofar as it indicates or leads to a commitment, to a way of life. " The view I put forward," says Braithwaite, " is that the intention of a Christian to follow a Christian way of life is not only the criterion for the sincerity of his beliefs in

[8] Paul van Buren, *The Secular Meaning of the Gospel*, p. 83.
[9] *Ibid.*
[10] *Ibid.*, pp. 83 f.
[11] *Ibid.*, p. 85.
[12] *Ibid.*, p. 99.
[13] *Ibid.*, pp. 99 f.

the assertions of Christianity; it is the criterion for the meaningfulness of his assertions." [14] Although van Buren objects to
nineteenth-century reductionism, one is hard put for a better
description of his own procedure. He cites with approbation
these linguistic philosophers who " say that theology may not
be independent of ethics." He adds that " Christologically
speaking, these interpretations imply holding to the humanity
of Christ, to the man Jesus of Nazareth, and letting the issue
of his divinity fall where it may." [15] Evidently, van Buren regards the ethical demand for love as natural and self-evident,
so that anyone can readily recognize the claim of Jesus.

I have cited van Buren because he does demonstrate the
logic of the reductionism of which so much of contemporary
theology is guilty, guilty perhaps out of its own anxiety to
communicate and interpret the gospel to an empirically-
minded world. Van Buren makes it clear that we can speak
intelligibly so long as we do not speak about God. What he
does speak about is quite akin to Fuchs's and Ebeling's " word-
event," as, for example, when van Buren says that " the word
' resurrection ' (like the words ' duty,' ' love,' and ' God ') di-

---

[14] R. B. Braithwaite, *An Empiricist's View of Religious Belief* (Cambridge: Cambridge University Press, 1955) , pp. 15 f. Cited by van Buren,
p. 94.

[15] Van Buren, p. 102. It is one of the mysteries of a certain form of recent American Protestant theology, described by William Hamilton in his
article, " The Death of God Theology," that it would avoid myth, symbol,
and even references to God, and yet somehow or other hold Jesus to be
normative for faith. Hamilton tells us that he and his group really " do
not know, do not adore, do not possess, do not believe in God " (p. 34) .
Yet, he can state approvingly that " the Christian without God for van
Buren [one of the group] is Jesus' man " (p. 35) . This type of Protestantism which " affirms both the death of God and the death of all forms of
theism " (p. 38) is nevertheless religious because it insists on " holding
fast to Jesus Christ " (p. 41) . Such talk is either idolatrous, gobbledegook,
or both. What in the world does the word " Christ " mean in such a context? Is it not clear that to hold fast to Jesus as Christ is religious and not
blasphemous only when Jesus stands in an unique relationship to *God?*
See William Hamilton, " The Death of God Theology," *The Christian
Scholar*, XLVIII (1965) .

rects us to the sort of situation in which a discernment fundamental to our whole conception of life and a response of commitment may take place." [16] The gospel history or word is not
that in which we look for a meaning like some "ghost in the
machine"; rather, "logically, to find 'meaning in history' is
to have a 'blik': an intention to behave in a certain way." [17]
That is tantamount to saying that the gospel story is a word
that gives rise to a word or concept with which to live. [18]

Just a brief comment regarding the results of van Buren's
approach. Now that Jesus can no longer speak to us of God,
he must speak of a verifiable way of life. Admitting to the
skepticism of historical criticism, van Buren feels free to characterize Jesus' way of life as the way of freedom, and he cites
impressive testimony and argues convincingly. He reduces all
Jesus' sayings in this direction, and Easter comes to mean that
after the death of Jesus it somehow happened that the disciples
"apparently found themselves caught up in something like
the freedom of Jesus himself, having become men who were
free to face even death without fear." [19] As impressive as van
Buren's enterprise is, it will not succeed. Freedom is not empirical. Jesus had told his disciples that they should fulfill the
law, that their righteousness should exceed that of the scribes
and Pharisees; none of the empirical evidence prevents us from
regarding Jesus as absolutely under law. Paul knew that sac-
rificial acceptance of death is not necessarily a token of love
and freedom. "If I deliver my body to be burned, but have
not love, I gain nothing." Just as freedom cannot be reduced
to its empirical symbols, so it cannot be disclosed by them.
Freedom is a spiritual reality, a gift of the meeting between
God and man, and van Buren can speak convincingly about it

---

[16] Van Buren, p. 89. Similarly, Ebeling understands "word" as that
which "brings something to understanding" (*The New Hermeneutic*,
Vol. II of *New Frontiers in Theology*, ed. by James M. Robinson and
John B. Cobb, Jr., p. 93; Harper & Row, Publishers, Inc., 1964).

[17] *Ibid.*, pp. 112 f.

[18] *Ibid.*, pp. 113 ff.

[19] *Ibid.*, p. 128.

only with a debt to a language which his empirical approach regards as meaningless. Not only is he hard put to speak about freedom (which " somehow " arose in the disciples after Jesus' death) but his approach only by the stretch of the wildest imagination can be suspected of giving an account of what Christians have traditionally intended with their language. Thus we learn, for example, that " the meaning of intercessory prayer is its use: it begins in reflection upon the situation in the light of the Christian perspective and leads to appropriate action." [20] We should expect that faith as a " blik " has no missionary concern, and that is the case. " If man is slowly learning to stand on his own feet and to help his neighbor without the ' God hypothesis,' the Christian should rejoice." The meaning of the missionary claim for the Christian is that he is free to view the whole world as within his perspective or " blik." [21]

Possibly van Buren has written with tongue in cheek to suggest what Christianity is like when its meanings are subject to the canons of empirical verification. Perhaps he is exemplifying a reductionism *ad absurdum* which leads one to look for another way of speaking about Christianity or to surrender it altogether. As it now stands Christianity is for van Buren simply " one fella's blik," and hardly worth fighting for, let alone dying for.

Barth and Berdyaev are, of course, at odds with the position of van Buren (despite his efforts to base his theology on Barth), for both of these theologians insist on the irreducibility of religious language. They maintain the meaningfulness of symbols such as " God," " Jesus," " freedom," etc. But then the question arises whether such language can have any currency in the modern world. In a partial answer to this question I would suggest that there are two dubious axioms of much modern theology which necessitate a negative answer and demand the reductionism we have witnessed in van Buren. The first of these is that Christianity is a " historical " religion. The

[20] *Ibid.,* p. 189.   [21] *Ibid.,* p. 191.

entire hermeneutic discussion presupposes this axiom. Thus
van Buren states that "the language of Christian faith has always had to do with a particular man who lived and died in
Palestine." He then states that "this observation is often expressed by saying that Christianity is a 'historical religion.'" [22]
Yet, is it so obvious that Christianity is a history-based faith?
If it is granted for a moment that Jesus really lives, as the New
Testament seems to claim, then the language of religion should
not be understood on the model of history, but rather in terms
of personal relationships. Would it not be more correct to say
that Christianity is personal religion? The Bible would then be
not a bit of the past made present in the act of translation or
interpretation but, rather, a bit of the past addressing itself
directly to the present. We have already seen Barth and Berdyaev, Barth especially, refuse to raise the hermeneutic question and so reject the notion that the translation of the Bible
is largely an achievement of tradition and interpretation.

Polanyi's Philosophy of Freedom

The second rubric has to do with the possibilities of secular
man's self-understanding. The axiom here is the so-called "scientific world view" which, says van Buren, defines meaning in
terms of verifiability. This positivistic theory (of doubtful
philosophic worth) regards science as a convenient functional
relation between observed data, a relationship that can be
empirically verified. Michael Polanyi has for some time had the
temerity to challenge this concept of science (held largely by
philosophers of science) and to demonstrate rather conclusively
that it is not an adequate description of what science is about,
at least at its most creative level. He would describe scientific
discovery as "a passionate pursuit of a *hidden* meaning, guided
by intensely personal intimations of this yet unexperienced
reality." Aware of the dangers of this position, he insists nevertheless that the "hazards of such efforts are its essence; discovery is defined as an advancement of knowledge that cannot

[22] *Ibid.*, p. 109.

be achieved by any, however diligent, application of explicit modes of inference." [23] While it is far beyond the scope of this study to develop Polanyi's theory of "personal knowledge," it is apparent from what we have said that he has a concept of man's relationship to the empirical world that resembles what we have seen in Berdyaev's microcosmic conception, except that Polanyi's works have the distinctive merit of explicating precisely the way in which the empirical, scientific world of observable data is first of all the creature of human freedom. He states that " even if we admit that an exact knowledge of the universe is our supreme mental possession it would still follow that man's most distinguished act of thought consists in *producing* such knowledge." [24] His meaning is more evident when he states that " the participation of the knower in shaping his knowledge, which had hitherto been tolerated as a flaw . . . is now recognized as the true guide and master of our cognitive powers." [25] Man, in passionate commitment to a heuristic vision that is intuitive and not empirical, spiritual and not rational, is the creative source of the empirical and rational, both in the realm of history and nature.

If Polanyi is correct, and he appears to be, then the realm of science thrives, as does the world of the religious, on the nonempirical and nonverifiable. A Godless religion must be responsible for itself; it appears not to be demanded by modern scientific methodology, nor by the alleged " historical " nature of revelation. The ultimate axiom behind such religionless theologies is simply the spirit of modern " secularism," man's wish to be without God, rather than his fear as a modern that he cannot be with God.

There is, therefore, nothing intrinsic to the Biblical revelation or the situation of modern man that demands the reductionism of so much of modern theology. The Bible, as a wit-

23 Michael Polanyi, *Science, Faith and Society* (The University of Chicago Press, 1946), pp. 69 f.
24 Michael Polanyi, *The Study of Man* (The University of Chicago Press, 1959), p. 18.
25 *Ibid.,* p. 26.

ness of personal revelation, need not be reduced to historical language and hence be subject to the mercy of hermeneutics. And modern man, as one who shapes his world by an inward, spiritual vision, need not reduce the spiritual and personal either to nature or to an empirically manifest way of life. We need not be guilty of the kind of reductionism with which Polanyi charges modern science, " which sternly professes that ultimately all things in the world — including the achievements of man from the Homeric poems to the *Critique of Pure Reason* — will somehow be explained in terms of physics and chemistry," which assumes " *that the path to reality lies invariably in representing higher things in terms of their baser particulars.*" [26] So we need not reduce God to the " depth," to the " future " he offers us, nor the way of life resulting from a " blik." We do not need to reduce man in his freedom to expressions of being, or subjects of conscience, or whatever.

Russian Thought

In these concluding remarks I have suggested certain unacceptable alternatives to Barth and Berdyaev, beyond those of Tillich and Bultmann. At the same time I have indicated a resource for the further development and articulation of this theology of freedom — namely, the philosophy of Michael Polanyi, which might well be understood as a philosophy of freedom. And finally, I would mention the possibility for Protestantism of a developing dialogue with Christian Orthodoxy, especially Russian Orthodoxy. We have already seen how Berdyaev is a help in articulating implications of Barth's theology of freedom, and contrary to much popular opinion, Berdyaev is not an eccentric or unorthodox Russian thinker, but rather brings to expression a line of development that can be traced back fairly directly to the eighteenth century, and in a general way to the very roots of Russian religious thought. V. V. Zenkovsky identifies three roots of modern Russian thought — Eastern Christianity, the Russian struggle for free-

[26] *Ibid.*, p. 64. (Italics are mine.)

dom, and eighteenth-century Western thought as introduced by
Peter the Great.[27] The first two are the more basic, so that the
advent of Western thought in the eighteenth century only gives
new form and impetus to certain dimensions of the dialectic
already present in the tradition. The earliest roots are the
sacred and the profane — Eastern Christianity and Russian
freedom. The results are indicated by Nicholas Zernov's comments on the uniqueness of the Russian tradition. He points
out that from the beginning (since the Christianizing of Russia
in the tenth century) "the use of the vernacular left an in-
delible mark upon the Russian religious outlook." [28] This mark
is the mark of freedom, the mark of the secular and humane,
which was united with the sacred and holy as form with content. Along with this unity of the sacred and the secular, of
God and freedom, was the absence of the classical tradition
(until the eighteenth century). The result is the peculiar Russian piety described by Zernov: "The Russians were extremely
ritualistic, but singularly unclerical; they assigned great importance to holiness, but had little notion of ecclesiastical subordination. They were conservative yet allowed considerable
freedom of interpretation; they were strictly orthodox, but understood this term rather as stressing devotion to the beauty
and glory of worship than in the sense of correct doctrine." [29]
Certainly this is descriptive of Berdyaev, who is unclerical and
free in interpretation, yet orthodox to the point of insisting on
the infallibility of creed and councils.

This characteristic and indigenous piety results in a built-in
dialectic in Russian thought — the dialectic of the sacred and
the secular. There was from the beginning in Russian religion
a secular meaning of the gospel. Secularism was not, as in the
West, an imposition of Renaissance and Enlightenment, but
rather a requirement of the gospel. The symbol of this gospel
requirement is the God-man, Jesus Christ — both God and

27 Zenkovsky, *A History of Russian Philosophy*, I, 2.
28 Nicholas Zernov, *The Russian Religious Renaissance of the Twentieth Century* (Harper & Row, Publishers, Inc., 1963), p. 37.
29 *Ibid.*

man, sacred and profane. Berdyaev's concept of the humanity of God, of the God who demands freedom and the secularity of religion, is as old as Russia. But the dialectic is not easy to maintain, and the history of Russia, politically and philosophically, can be understood in terms of this difficulty. The danger is twofold — a secularization of the sacred and an apotheosizing of the secular. Thus Zernov can point to the strange phenomenon among the secular intelligentsia of the nineteenth century — namely, of a moral, Messianic atheism such as comes to expression, of course, in Marxism.[30] On the other side, one can also point to the religious nationalism of Orthodoxy, in which the Messianic hope is secularized as in the Slavophile vision of Holy Russia.

Although interrupted by the Westernizing efforts of Peter the Great which tended to depolarize the concept of God-manhood and its related themes, this indigenous and original mainstream of Russian thought prevailed, and a continuous line can be traced from the eighteenth century to the twentieth. Zenkovsky describes this line succinctly: " Beginning with Skovoroda, through the ' senior slavophiles,' and Vladimir Solovyov, up to our day [referring to the religiophilosophical movement of which both Zenkovsky and Berdyaev were members], the problem of the relation of reason and faith, of free investigation and ecclesiastical tradition, has occupied Russian minds." [31] The problem of this tradition is the problem of revelation and reason, God and man, faith and freedom. And to the list of those who stood in this tradition we could add other names familiar to the English reader, such as S. L. Frank (1877–1950) and Sergĭeĭ Bulgakov (1871–1944).[32]

[30] " Paradoxically the extreme conservatives among the Russians, the Old Believers, were psychologically and temperamentally the nearest to the nihilists of the extreme left." (*Ibid.*, p. 32.)

[31] Zenkovsky, II, 922.

[32] See S. Sergĭeĭ Bulgakov, *The Wisdom of God: A Brief Summary of Sophiology* (London: William & Norgate, Ltd., 1937) and S. L. Frank, *God with Us: Three Meditations*, tr. by Natalie Duddington (Yale University Press, 1946). See also Zernov, Appendix, pp. 331 ff., for a very helpful bibliography.

This brief look at the Russian tradition serves to make two points: first, that Berdyaev does indeed represent a mainstream in Russian religious thought, and, second, that this tradition deals from its beginning with the problem that presses modern Protestant theology, the problem of secularism, or the problem of freedom. We should thus add a third point, that the body of modern Protestantism cannot grow up to its full stature without ecumenical dialogue, and perhaps none could be more fruitful than the dialogue with this indigenous Russian tradition which, because of its integrity vis-à-vis Western classical tradition (despite its encounter with it), might well breathe life into what appears more and more to be a moribund Protestant theology.

The thesis of this study has been that " freedom " is an irreducible dimension of the Christian experience because the man Jesus is irreducible, because " Jesus " is the last word — the name above every name. We have seen this point made by Barth, and to a lesser extent by Berdyaev. But here especially is a contact point with Orthodoxy as such. Timothy Ware calls attention, for example, to the tremendous importance in Orthodox piety of the so-called " Jesus Prayer " — " Lord Jesus Christ, Son of God, have mercy on me a sinner." Ware comments: " Those brought up in the tradition of the Jesus Prayer are never allowed for a moment to forget the Incarnate Jesus. . . . Orthodox believe that the power of God is present in the name of Jesus, so that the invocation of this Divine Name acts as an effective sign of God's action, ' as a sort of sacrament.' " [33]

These final remarks obviously reach beyond the immediate concerns of this study, but hopefully they do indicate some of the possible implications of a theology of freedom — how it might be articulated through the help of Polanyi's epistemology and how it might lead to an ecumenical enrichment at least of Protestant theology. Karl Barth, with his Christology and

[33] Timothy Ware, *The Orthodox Church* (Penguin Books, Inc., 1963), pp. 312 f.

with his understanding of freedom, appears to be a beginning point for the development of such a theology.

A Theology of Freedom

We have designated three possible sources of a theology of freedom — Protestantism as in Karl Barth, philosophy and science as in Michael Polanyi, and the theological philosophy of the Russian tradition represented by Nicholas Berdyaev. Finally, let us consider in summary and conclusion the shape of the theology that would draw upon these sources.

First, it would be a nonsystematic theology. That is to say, the logical dimensions of this theology are constantly in the service of the divine, the " theotic " element. For this reason, Barth prefers the designation of " church dogmatics." And our analysis has made it surprisingly clear how Barth's *Church Dogmatics* steadfastly refuses to become logically one and coherent, how it combines, as it were, many theologies, and how in the last analysis it reduces all theological truth and unity to the truth and unity of Jesus' own person. It may be said that with many thousands of words Barth's grand theological enterprise has the effect of undercutting the theological enterprise as such — at least to the extent that it resists any formal logical coherence and will not be reduced to any material principle.

In a similar fashion we might note that Russian thought has not produced a systematic theology. Berdyaev rejected objectifying, rationalistic theology in favor of " apophatic " thought about God. Yet it must be said that Russian thought does not eschew a proper " theology," for it insists that all true philosophy is first of all Christology, that it roots in the historical event of the incarnation and that creeds and councils as witnesses of that event are therefore infallible. Barth and Russian thought are theocentric, if not theological; they would talk first of all about God, but not systematically, rationalistically, or theologically. In a word, such theology as regards its form is radically obedient and reverent, yet just as radically free and creative.

Secondly, this theology, while it is not systematic or theological, is Christological, inasmuch as it acknowledges the Lordship of Jesus, who possesses that "name above every name." And a Christological theology may also be designated "personalogic," to the extent that the only analogy for the knowledge of the person Jesus is the experience of personal knowledge. Personal knowledge is not to be confused with the historical knowledge of past and dead persons in order perhaps to know about ourselves; rather, it is the knowledge of living persons. To speak of Christologic as "personalogic" is therefore to presuppose the resurrection and the living presence of Jesus of Nazareth.

The language of personal, Christologic theology which presupposes the resurrection and living presence of the person Jesus of Nazareth functions differently from the language of theoretical or even practical reason. Basically, it operates in respect of the mystery that finally segregates persons, so that no linguistic or logical bridge between them is conceivable. The most fundamental word in this language is, therefore, the personal name. This language will also respect the fact that the union between persons takes place in freedom and mystery instead of being and existence. The language that speaks in and of such knowledge and encounter is highly symbolic; it points but does not arrive; it invokes but does not bind; it echoes but does not call; it imitates but does not authenticate. Barth's theology echoes what he hears in Christ, but the echoes clash and distort, forcing a repeated return to the word in the beginning. This distortion is vividly apparent in the case of Barth because of his classical heritage and the rationalistic tone of this thought which is continually interrupted and broken by the demands of its source and origin, Jesus Christ. Berdyaev's thought roots in a nonclassical tradition (although he does employ classical Western thought) and tends therefore to avoid the appearance of brokenness and failure, presenting instead an image of mysticism and nonrationality. The ecumenical approach to the personal-Christological theology proposed here will seek to appreciate the fact that while Christianity has survived in both forms, its future is best served by the effort of each tradition to hear and learn from the other. The substance of this second point, then, is that just as the form of theology is freedom, so also is its content.

In its third dimension this theology is what Berdyaev termed "meontic." That is, it does not acknowledge the ultimacy of the philosophical category of being. Insofar as philosophy is concerned with "being," this Christian thought is free and uncommitted philosophically. We have seen Barth "use" philosophy — existentialism, Hegelianism, Kantianism, etc. — but only a very dogmatic reading of Barth could ever contend that Barth's thought is bound to one of these schools. In a similar vein he steadfastly refuses to raise the hermeneutic question or to develop a so-called natural theology. It is, I think, just as difficult to reduce Berdyaev philosophically. Certainly he has a debt to Kant, but also to Hegel, Nietzsche, Kierkegaard, Bergson, etc. In sum, the hero of a meontic theology or philosophy is not being as such but, rather, the being of the philosopher. The gift of Christ is not being, but man; not philosophy, but the philosopher; not fate, but freedom.

It is but a short step to the final point — that the nonontic philosophy that results from a Christocentric theology is in its positive aspect an anthropological philosophy, a personal philosophy. It is at this point that the thought of Michael Polanyi is especially relevant. We have seen Barth, however, point in this direction by his constant identification of salvation with the freedom of man, as reflected, for instance, in his references to the "humanity of God." Berdyaev expressly states that true philosophy is anthropology, that man is the microcosm, the sun, and the source of the world's being and meaning. In sum, man is a creator, a creator born of God, who by God's grace is called to deliver the world from its groaning and travail. Berdyaev in the tradition of Russian thought has been espe-

cially concerned with the deliverance of society from its slavery
into its being in freedom and love. Polanyi sees the creative
role of man in the liberation and creation of the world of
nature.

By pointing out that a theology of freedom moves from
Christology to anthropology it is made evident that such a
theology has secular meaning — not meaning to the secular,
but the meaning of salvation and life *for* the secular. The
world groans in its travail, awaiting its deliverance through
the redemption of man — a redemption of which man has a
foretaste and so also a deliverance of which the cosmos has a
presentiment.